POLITICAL
CHANGE AND CONTINUITY

LIBRARY OF POLITICS AND SOCIETY
General Editor   Michael Hurst

PUBLISHED
Church Embattled: Religious Controversy in Mid-Victorian England
by M. A. Crowther
The Origins of Franco's Spain by Richard A. H. Robinson
The Politics of Government Growth by William C. Lubenow
The Peelites and the Party System 1846–52 by J. B. Conacher
Unionists Divided: Free Trade to Tariff Reform, 1903–10 by Richard
Rempel

IN PREPARATION
Court and Country in Portugal, 1680–1750 by John Villiers
The Countess of Huntingdon's Connexion by Alan Harding
The Pastoral Profession: the Theory and Practice of the Parish
Ministry in the Mid-Victorian Church of England by Brian Heeney

ASSOCIATED VOLUMES
Quisling by Paul M. Hayes
Key Treaties of the Great Powers 1814–1914   selected and edited by
Michael Hurst

POLITICAL CHANGE AND CONTINUITY

1760-1885:

A Buckinghamshire Study

Richard W. Davis

DAVID & CHARLES   NEWTON ABBOT
ARCHON BOOKS 1972

FOR ELISABETH

This edition first published in 1972 in Great Britain by
David & Charles (Publishers) Limited Newton Abbot Devon
and in the United States by Archon Books Hamden Connecticut

ISBN 0 7153 5724 7 (*Great Britain*)
ISBN 0 208 01307 5 (*United States*)

Set in eleven on twelve point Imprint
and printed in Great Britain
by Compton Press

Contents

Introduction

THE OLD landmarks in the political history of nineteenth-century England seem to be disappearing. The Reform Act of 1832, seen by the so-called 'Whig' historians[1] as giving the middle classes an important voice in politics and thus breaking the monopoly of the landed classes and commencing a gradual but almost inevitable process of democratization, is no longer viewed by most historians as a major break in English political life. Kitson Clark, for example, tells us that more than three decades after the first Reform Act, on the eve of the second, 'the prejudices, ways of thought and limitations of the old proprietary classes still lay heavy on politics, as it seems also to have been normally members of those classes whose hands still held most of the winning cards.' Their strongest suit lay in the fact that 'within the framework of the nineteenth-century party politics and under the skin of nineteenth-century life many eighteenth-century or near eighteenth-century practices and relationships were still effective.'[2]

Whig historians saw the nineteenth century as one of fairly steady progress, from reform bill to reform bill, for the causes of liberty and democracy. Recent historians emphasize the tenacity of traditional influences and the continuing dominance of the landed classes. Where Whig historians stressed change, recent work stresses continuity.

The continuing political dominance of the landed classes primarily derived, it is argued, from the fact that the electoral system continued to be weighted heavily in favour of places that were bastions of artistocratic and gentry strength. According to D. C. Moore, the first Reform Act did not constitute a blow to the political power of the landed classes, because after 1832 they were able to settle back 'to half a century during which their control was

absolute in the majority of remaining small boroughs, and . . .
English county divisions. . . .'[3]

Though they might not all state their case quite so forcefully,
most recent historians would be in general agreement with this
pronouncement. The control of the county constituencies by the
aristocracy and gentry has come to be accepted as almost axio-
matic.[4] As for the boroughs, Professor Gash reckons that after
1832 rather more than eighty members in England and Wales
continued to be returned by a patron or a family. If to these are
added most of the 159 members for English and Welsh counties,
we come close to half their total of 500 members. And, of course,
this takes no account of what it is suggested were a not inconsiderable number of boroughs where the interest was contested by
a few influential men, or shared by several.[5] After 1867 Professor
Hanham estimates only about half as many members, rather more
than forty, as being returned for proprietary or family boroughs.
But there were twenty-five additional county members, and, again,
a number of boroughs where dominating influence is supposed to
have been exercised by a few.[6]

In other words, what recent historians contend is that in a
majority of constituencies there existed what is often called, using
Bagehot's term, a 'deferential' electorate. It would probably be
more precise to say that in most constituencies most of the
electors responded to some sort of influence (influence which could
range from moral to brutal, and the response to which would probably not correspond to everyone's understanding of deferential
behaviour). But, whatever it is called, it was this phenomenon
which made the power of the old proprietary classes what Kitson
Clark identifies as the 'most important single political fact' in mid-
Victorian Britain, and beyond.[7]

Doubtless Whig historians placed too much emphasis on change
and tended to see liberal and democratic implications where they
were not. But it seems likely that the work of historians in the last
twenty years or so has placed too much stress on continuity. And,
in fact, the kind of evidence on which they have mainly relied to
prove the continuing dominance of the landed classes in the
electoral system does not necessarily prove anything of the sort.
It is true that aristocrats and landed gentlemen and their near
relations continued to be returned in large numbers to the House

of Commons, and probably constituted a comfortable majority of members throughout the period with which this book is concerned. More than that, it is true that in a very large number of constituencies members of these same classes—not infrequently the same families—played the most conspicuous roles in political leadership throughout the period. These undoubted facts have convinced most recent historians, as they convinced many contemporaries, that the landed classes continued to hold the balance of electoral power in the country firmly in their own hands.[8] But there were, of course, very good reasons, apart from control of the electoral system, why in an age when politics were primarily an expensive avocation and the landed classes the only leisured classes, they should have continued to play most of the most prominent roles in politics. In a competition in which the landed classes probably provided most of the contenders, it would hardly be surprising if they also produced most of the victors. The crucial question, then, is probably why one aristocrat or country gentleman succeeded and another did not. Because we know *who* was elected to parliament, we must not suppose that we necessarily know *why*.

Professor Aydelotte, whose exhaustive research into the social class and economic interests of MPs who sat in the parliament of 1841–47 has illustrated the overwhelming numerical superiority of the landed classes in post-1832 parliaments, has concluded that social class and economic interest are not very helpful guides to members' votes on the Corn Laws. He suggests that explanations must probably be sought in their constituencies.[9] This seems a sensible suggestion, and will very likely help to clarify other issues besides the Corn Laws. At present, we really know very little about how candidates were chosen, by whom, and how they went about getting themselves elected. We have no solid knowledge, in other words, about where power in the constituencies actually resided, or how it was divided. It may well be that when we have, notions about the degree of control exercised by the landed classes, and therefore about the 'important facts' in nineteenth-century politics, will have to be revised.

As has been suggested above, the case for the continuing political dominance of the landed classes is primarily based on the assumption that they continued to exercise firm control of most of the county and small borough constituencies. This study will

examine this basic assumption by examining the politics of several
such constituencies—the county and six (after 1832, four) borough
constituencies of Buckinghamshire. As will be seen, this examination suggests that to consign such constituencies wholesale to the
control of the landed classes is to do a grave injustice to the independence of mind and action of many drawn from other classes in
village and small-town society. In 1847 the vicar of Horsenden
fumed to Mrs Disraeli about the 'army of petty-fogging [sic]
Attorneys and Cheesemongers' that was blocking the Duke of
Buckingham's attempt to oust a Conservative member for Aylesbury whom the duke considered too Peelite.[10] They were the kind
of people John Wilkes, MP for Aylesbury from 1757 to 1764,
would have described as being of the 'middling class'. And John
Gibbs, pawnbroker-turned- auctioneer, was still describing them
in the same way when, after a narrow defeat for the Liberal
candidate in 1835, he

> alluded to the backwardness of Reformers of landed property . . .
> With a few honourable exceptions they had not appeared, and
> the election had been entirely conducted by the middling classes
> (cheers).[11]

Judging from this election, besides attorneys, cheesemongers, and
pawnbrokers, included in this middling class were, among others,
bankers, surgeons, brewers, corn dealers, chemists, wine merchants, innkeepers, cabinetmakers, carpenters, and shoemakers.
Such people had played an increasingly active and vital role in the
politics of Aylesbury and other Buckinghamshire constituencies
from the days of Wilkes onwards. They were not very different
from the kind of people one would find among the leading inhabitants of county and market towns and larger villages today.
The carpenters would be called builders; the cabinet-makers
would own a furniture shop and the shoemakers a shoe shop, but
they would be recognizable types. Today they would call themselves middle class.

    D. C. Moore is right that historians have too long tended to see
reform almost solely against a background of increasing industrial-
ization, but it is a stricture that applies equally as well to recent as
to Whig historical writing. Whig historians had a tendency to
ascribe to the middle classes everywhere the motives and interests

of their urban and industrial representatives. Recent historians, on the other hand, tend simply to dismiss as unimportant those members of the middle classes who were not urban or industrial. Either way, the role of the small-town and village middle classes is ignored. Moore assures us that the Reform Act of 1832 did not mark 'the arrival of the urban middle class to political power.'[12] Indeed it did not, but why must we confine our attention to the role of the urban middle classes? It is probably a grave error—it certainly is in Bucks.

Thus far nothing has been said about the working classes, and they will not occupy an important place in this study. This is in part because those who might conventionally be considered working class, skilled craftsmen and artisans, were indistinguishable from the middle classes in most Bucks constituencies. There were certainly members of the working classes who were clearly distinguishable from the middle classes, that is, the agricultural and other unskilled manual labourers. But their political role was largely a passive one. Indeed, it seems likely that the effect of their enfranchisement after 1867 in the 'ruralised' boroughs (and all the Bucks boroughs had substantial rural areas within their boundaries after 1832) was to increase the role of influence—though not necessarily the influence of the landed classes—and possibly even to create a large genuinely deferential electorate, which voted for its superiors because it believed in their superior ability. As we shall see, George Howell, the secretary of the Reform League and an undoubtedly working-class candidate, made a very creditable showing in Aylesbury in 1868 and 1874. But his vote came almost exclusively from the towns and larger villages—and probably from much the same kind of people who had possessed the franchise before 1867. In Buckinghamshire, before 1885 at any rate, the working classes did not play a creative role in politics.

It may well be asked what the study of one county can prove or disprove. No county, after all, is exactly like any other county. neither is one borough ever exactly like any other borough, even if only a few miles separate them—a fact which will be illustrated amply in this study. All this is true, but it is necessary to start somewhere; and, as it is unlikely that one county and six boroughs would have been unique unto themselves in every respect, to study them may suggest possible lines of investigation elsewhere. In short, I would argue that some knowledge is better than none, and that some may be capable of broader application.

Beyond this, to study more than a fairly limited area over the period of time I have attempted would take an immense time and would probably not be practicable for one scholar. And yet I think it critically important that we know more of local politics in length, as it were, as well as in depth and breadth. Our present view of politics in the localities might be likened to one's vision of a mountain range shrouded in mist. A number of peaks are visible, and occasionally a new one comes into view. But one has no idea of the terrain that lies between, and in the shifting mists one peak is easily confused with another. So with the history of politics in the provinces. We know something about several limited periods, usually in times of intense popular interest, but little is known of the long spaces of time intervening. Doubtless this is a large part of the reason why historians of one period often seem to take little account of work on earlier periods. Each new period stands isolated from the one preceding it, and the same processes are seen as starting anew—or not starting! In a study of a century and a quarter, it may be possible to tie some loose ends together, and perhaps to begin the process of clarifying a distorted vision of politics in the localities.

Finally, it may be asked why Bucks was chosen as the area to be studied. There are several answers. One is that Bucks undoubtedly belonged to the world of the small town and the countryside, which continued to have an enormous weight in the political system up to 1885 and the politics of which I think have been both neglected and misunderstood. Another is that the history of the county and its boroughs is extremely well documented. A third reason is that the county is often cited as an instance to prove precisely those generalizations about the continuing dominance of landed influence which I wish to call into question.[13]

Clearly, whatever may emerge from a study of one county and six boroughs is not going to disprove, or to make completely irrelevant and outmoded, the work of the last couple of decades. Historians build on one another's work, as Kitson Clark doubtless wished to recognise when he dedicated his reappraisal to George Macaulay Trevelyan. And, if Trevelyan was not the fool that some seem to suggest he was, neither obviously are the recent historians whom I have cited fools. There is, however, an unmistakable tendency in all their work, and it is one that I think needs correction. Professor Gash remarks in the introduction of his *Politics in the Age of Peel* that he willingly exposes himself

> to the criticism and correction of local historians. Such criticism must not only be risked but be invited. Only on an established basis of local history can national history of this kind be written.[14]

I agree with Professor Gash, and accept his invitation. I hope others will.

Chapter 1 BUCKINGHAMSHIRE SOCIETY AND POLITICS BEFORE THE GREAT REFORM BILL

Tis our lace trade, our Farms,
Our labour—our arms
In Militia too th'ant be forgotten,
Which this County partakes,
Who those Int'rests forsakes
Is no Buck, but a true misbegotten.

THUS RAN a song in support of W. W. Grenville, the future premier, when he stood for this county in 1784.[1] Making some allowances for poetic licence and for the fact that Grenville's brother, Earl Temple (later the first Marquis of Buckingham), was Lord Lieutenant and thus commanded the county militia, this would seem to have been an accurate identification of the county's primary interests as contemporaries saw them.

It is doubtless mainly poetic licence that accounts for the lace trade being put before agriculture; but contemporaries did put a great stress on it, and, until the 1830s at least talked a good deal more about its fortunes than about those of agriculture. The trade and its tools played a leading part in the ritual and panoply of county politics. The Grenvilles, who by 1760 were consolidating their position as the leading family in the county, ostentatiously associated themselves with the trade. In 1761 the first Earl Temple, the Lord Lieutenant, presented George III, on behalf of the lacemakers, with a pair of exquisite ruffles of Bucks lace.[2] In 1784, as we have just seen, his nephew emphasized the family's solicitude for the trade. And in the eighteen twenties and thirties the latter's great nephew, the Marquis of Chandos (second Duke of Buckingham) similarly stressed his role as champion of Bucks lace. At elections a lace-pillow (ie the hard round pillow on which the lace was made) was mounted on a pole and carried at the head of processions, followed by banners hung with the lace itself.[3]

Though lace had been made in the county for a century and more before 1700, the period of its greatest prosperity came after that date and lasted until about 1815. In 1717 the large lacemen of Wycombe kept several hundred workers constantly employed. The lacemen went up to London weekly and sold their goods to the London milliners at the lace markets held in Aldersgate inns. They took back to Wycombe a stock of thread and silk, which they put out to their workmen to be made up to their specifications. In the northern part of the county Newport Pagnell was the centre of the trade, and the town by itself was said to produce more lace than any other place in the country. A lace market was held every Wednesday at which great quantities were sold. Besides the lace taken up to London and that sold in the Newport Pagnell market, lace-buyers came round from the London houses, usually monthly, met the lacemen at some inn in one of the market towns, and bought their stock of lace there.

The trade seems to have been fairly uniformly distributed throughout the county. Aylesbury was also noted for the fine quality of its lace, and during the eighteenth century lacemaking supplanted spinning as the task for women in the workhouse. It was undoubtedly much more profitable. Indeed lacemaking was so profitable that in the later eighteenth and early nineteenth century, there was a general lament that women refused even to consider agricultural work, and that men too were being weaned away. The Earl of Bridgewater told the representative of the Board of Agriculture around 1810 that when he first went to Ashridge he was shocked to find that the boys knew nothing of farming, 'nothing but the straw-plaiting and lacemaking their mothers had taught them.' The earl immediately set himself 'to root out this effeminacy and instil into them manly principles.'[4] But elsewhere the rot continued. In Hanslope, in 1802, 800 people out of a population of 1,289 were employed in lacemaking, and both men and women made it their regular employment.

Prosperity, however, did not outlast the war. In August 1816 the 'Association for the Relief of the Manufacturing and Labouring Poor,' whose committee met at the City of London Tavern, wrote to the Marquis of Buckingham, as Lord Lieutenant, offering to place at his disposal the sum of £300. The committee had been 'apprised of the peculiar distress under which some of the Manufacturers in the County of which your Lordship is Lord Lieutenant (more especially those employed in the manufacture of lace) at present labour.'[5] The post-war slump was common to industry generally, but, if there was a revival of the lace trade, it was a brief one. By the middle of 1824 the newspapers were full of correspondence about the decline of the trade. It never really recovered. In 1826 the editor of the *Buckinghamshire Chronicle*, commenting on subscriptions which were being taken up for the relief of distressed industrial districts, hoped that the state of the county's own manufacturers would not be forgotten. He was speaking of lace and straw plait, used for the making of hats and bonnets, and the manufacture of which also flourished during the war due to the lack of foreign supplies. 'Some measure,' he urged, 'should certainly be adopted to support the latter.' He had apparently already given up the lace trade; probably because, as was explained later, it had become almost impossible, to compete profitably with machine-made lace. He was well aware of the social and economic consequences of the decline of the trade. There had been an early harvest in 1826, and thus there would be an unusually long interval before spring field work brought a renewal of any significant demand for agricultural labour. This would almost certainly throw many on the parish, and the

> burthen is likely still more to be augmented about Aylesbury and many other parts of the county of Bucks, from the rapid decline of the lace-trade, which had used to afford much profitable employment to the female inhabitants.[6]

The lace trade had provided a buffer against the uncertainties which plague an agricultural economy: it did so no longer.

Lacemaking in Bucks did not disappear completely, and even had occasional modest revivals. Straw plaiting declined less rapidly at first, but after mid-century, with the removal of protective duties, probably a good deal faster. Both industries survived into this century, but to a large extent their survival was an artificial one. It is probably indicative of their former importance that hereafter when philanthropic people turned their thoughts to bettering the lot of the poor, their minds usually turned to these trades, particularly the lace trade; and as late as 1897, with the formation of the North Bucks Lace Association, a major effort was made to revive the trade. But though the trade survived, never again after 1830 could it be mentioned in the same breath with agriculture.[7]

Agriculture was to remain, as it always had been, the greatest industry in the county. As elsewhere, farming in Buckinghamshire began to change fairly rapidly after 1760. The number of enclosures by act of parliament increased markedly after that date,[8] and with enclosure came different kinds of farming. The least change came in the chalklands of the Chilterns, whose soil was most suited to corn; that district remained one of mainly arable farms. The great changes came in the Vale of Aylesbury, roughly the broad central portion of the county lying between the Chilterns and Watling Street, and the area to the north.[9] There, there was a pronounced shift from arable farming to dairy and grazing farms. The Vale, particularly the area north of a rough crescent based in Thame at one end and Tring at the other and passing through Aylesbury, had long been noted for its lush pastures, devoted mainly to the grazing of sheep. This was another change: the prime emphasis changed from sheep to cattle.[10]

There was also an improvement beginning in the breed of cattle by the turn of the century. During the eighteenth century the ordinary Midland Longhorn seems to have held sway. But by the turn of the century the phenomenal success of the famous grazier Westcar of Creslow with his Herefords began to popularise that breed. Westcar also pioneered (though probably not very many followed) in shipping cattle by water. In December 1799 he shipped an ox to the Smithfield Christmas show via the recently opened Wendover branch of the Grand Junction Canal. Having lost no flesh in its two day journey, the ox weighed its full 241 stone, won first prize, and sold for the astounding price of £100.[11]

Many local farmers, however, seem to have felt that the London market had established too tight a hold. In December 1804 the graziers and feeders of cattle in the Vale held a meeting in Aylesbury and decided to establish regular markets there. Their reasoning was that many fat cattle sold in the London market were afterwards driven back to supply districts to the north, and that it would be much cheaper to the consumer and more profitable to the farmer to eliminate this unnecessary wastage and expense.[12] This reasoning would appear to have been correct, since the Aylesbury cattle markets then established have flourished ever since.

A relatively few men were only graziers (only five called themselves such in an 1835 pollbook[13]). Most were also dairy farmers, and did some arable farming as well—a point to bear in mind for the post-1832 period. But, however diversified they were, the most important source of the prosperity of the farmers of the Vale, at least from the beginning to the middle of the nineteenth century, was the golden butter they sent up to London. The butter was made twice weekly, packed in 2lb lumps in osier baskets, and carried to central collecting points, where carriers picked it up.[14] The need for milk as well as meat doubtless accounts for the increasing popularity of Shorthorns, the first apparently being those bred at Broughton, Aylesbury by the Seniors (relatives of the famous economist) from the second decade of the century onwards.

There can be little doubt that the effect of these changes in agriculture, combined with the high prices for corn, was to make the farmers richer. It is impossible for me to say whether the changes made for fewer farmers. But it is possible to say that a great many small farmers were left; and, while most would not have owned the bulk of the land they farmed, neither would most have been tenants of large landowners (though they might well have been the tenants of two or three small ones).[15] Enclosure and the changes that went with it, then, would seem not to have been disastrous either to small landowners or to small farmers. What the effect was for the cottager and the squatter is again impossible for me to say. Probably, it was not good. It is not, of course, with their fate that we shall primarily be concerned. But we shall naturally be concerned with their fate as it affected the independent, which usually meant the rate-paying, electors—and by the 1820s the suffering of the poor was affecting them very severely.

As will be seen, when contemporaries talked in the twenties about 'the unparalleled distress existing among Agricultural Interests, Landlords without Rents, Tenants continually sinking, and the labouring classes reduced to the lowest pittance able to support nature,' they attributed their difficulties mainly to the enormous burden of taxation, local as well as national.[16] And, in so

far as the problem was a local one, the main burden was the poor
rates, which it was claimed consumed the value of the land and
made farming unprofitable. Bucks was one of the Speenhamland
counties, where wages were in one fashion or another subsidised
from the rates; and there were the usual charges by ratepayers that
the system made the poor lazy and idle, and by non-farmers that
farmers were taking advantage of the system to keep wages low.
But, as has been seen, more thoughtful observers attributed the
problem to what was certainly one of its main causes, the decline of
alternative employment for women, and, to some degree, for men.
The possibility for women and children to supplement substantially the earnings or poor relief given to the main breadwinner, a
possibility which had existed until the end of the war, would
obviously have been an important factor in alleviating distress.
After 1815 the alternatives were increasingly removed, and nothing
arose to take their place. Thus, for most people it was agricultural
employment, or none at all.

The other important factor in the situation was that, as economic
opportunity declined, the population rose dramatically. Bucks was
among those counties where there was a rise of about 50 per cent
in the thirty years between 1801 and 1831.[17] The result could have
been nothing but disastrous for labourers; and until the New Poor
Law of 1834, at any rate, their disaster touched all other classes as
well. For the upper and middling classes, for the most part, it
meant no more than losing some accumulated fat. Probably they
should have been grateful that they had fat to lose. But people
rarely are, and the upper and middling classes of Bucks were no
exception. Their anger and irritation were to be one of the main
bases of political controversy until the prosperous middle years of
the century restored their economic good humour.

In 1760, however, the years of anger, frustration, and, for some,
real suffering were still far in the future. What lay ahead for most
people were several decades of unexampled prosperity, which
included the poor as well as the middling and the rich. And for
many of all classes there was yet another economic resource on
which we have not yet touched—politics. From the great peers, to
the corporations of Buckingham and Wycombe, to the humbler
householders of Aylesbury, Amersham, Marlow, and Wendover,
the fruits of politics were likely to play a not unimportant part in

their domestic economies. For some it played a very important part indeed. It was calculated that the first Marquis of Buckingham and his brothers William (later Lord Grenville) and Thomas had in half a century drawn about £900,000 of public money from offices and sinecures which they had held.[18] Some of this, however, was shared with their Buckinghamshire neighbours; and they were able to tap other resources as well. Lords and gentlemen and wealthy merchants undoubtedly dominated the politics of Buckinghamshire, as of most of the rest of England in 1760—but they paid dearly for the privilege.

One who did so was John Wilkes. In 1761, at the time of his second election, he had lived in the Prebendal House in Aylesbury for over a decade, lavish in his hospitality, generous in his charity, the closest approximation the town had to a resident squire. It did him little good with the electors. As he wrote to John Dell:

> I have well weigh'd every thing respecting my affairs at Aylesbury, both as member, and as a private gentleman having an estate in the Borough. After so many and so various acts of Kindness to many individuals, I found what I had to trust to from the majority. I never thought my interest at A. of any consequence: I have found it not of the least. I was worked up to the high-water mark of [Welbore] Ellis, and shall be of Delaval or Clive, if I expect to carry the borough again, and either of them attempt it.[19]

The truth was that Wilkes *had thought* his interest at Aylesbury of some consequence. He had worked hard and spent much to build it up. And he was very bitter, instructing Dell to have the gates of his spacious gardens locked so that townsmen could no longer walk in them, and threatening in future to spend as little time as possible in residence. But he had at last faced the fact that the majority of the electors in the county town could only be bought for hard cash. Ellis' intervention had forced Wilkes to pay five guineas each to 300 electors on this occasion; and he was quite right, as they subsequently proved, that there was nothing they would like better than a wealthy East Indian to drive the price of a vote still higher.

Corruption was organized into a system at Aylesbury, and one which prevailed and carried every election until the widening of the borough's boundaries after particularly ostentatious corruption in the election of 1802. The system was described in a memorandum drawn up at about that time:

> The gratuities given at Aylesbury have been of two kinds: one subsequent to every Election is remuneration of the services of Electors; the other Donations at XMas given prospectively with a view to keeping up Interest.
> The former used to be five guineas but over the last forty years have been 7 guineas. The latter used to be only 5s given regularly every XMas, but latterly it has been a guinea given at the XMas preceding the Election.[20]

This description is substantially correct, though the higher figures in both cases were not in fact reached until a particularly heated conflict between Scrope Bernard, representing the Grenville interest, and Col Gerard Lake, backed by the Portland Whigs, commencing in a by-election in 1789.[21]

The franchise was vested in all householders in the town not receiving alms, and until 1804 (when the borough's boundaries were extended beyond those of the parish of Aylesbury, and the 40s freeholders of the Three Hundreds of Aylesbury were also given the vote) the electorate varied from about four to five hundred. Aylesbury, as the county town, a bustling market town, and the centre of a thriving lace trade, was not a poor place; but throughout the period up to 1802 at least three quarters of the electors, and sometimes more, received the candidates' profferred gratuities. More than that they came to organize their expenditure in anticipation of them, treating them as a regular form of income.[22] The sums were not, of course, inconsiderable at a time when a labourer's wage would have been something in the neighbourhood of 1s a day.[23]

The electors of Buckingham played for rather higher stakes; but there were fewer of them, and, as a whole, they were a rather more select group. Unlike Aylesbury, whose local governmental arrangements were a combination of manorial and parochial elements, Buckingham was governed by a corporation, consisting of the Bailiff and twelve Burgesses. The same corporation returned members of parliament, the Bailiff serving as the returning officer. Buckingham was a small market town, with few trades not connected with the agricultural community save for the ubiquitous lacemaking; and, according to Lipscomb writing in the 1840s, it had long 'chiefly been supported by the advantage of some great and affluent families residing in its immediate neighbourhood . . .'[24] The greatest and most affluent of these were the Grenvilles at Stowe and by 1760, the first Earl Temple, head of the family, seems to have had the borough safely in his grasp. This situation was fairly recent; for as late as 1742 Temple (or Richard Grenville as he was then) had had to hurry down from London to deal with 'violent commotions and divisions among ye antient and Loyal Corporation of Buckingham,' apparently stirred up by the antiquarian Browne Willis.[25] Six years later, however, Temple appears to have felt fairly secure, writing to his brother George:

> As to the Bayliff I do not know any thing very certain about it, but I suppose it must be one of our friends, I only know that I have a great deal to pay there in different shapes. The old gaol is pulled down, but the new one is not begun.[26]

The corporation had a taste for civic improvements, paid for by the earl, and besides the new gaol, they got from him a bridge, and a heavy contribution towards a new church—using this to extort the hill to place it on from Lord Verney! Verney's reward in this case was to be votes for the county. But he also meddled in the affairs of the borough, attempting in 1782 to promote a petition couched in language calling for broad parliamentary reform, but specifically requesting a forfeiture of the Buckingham charter and an extension of the franchise to all the inhabitants.[27] By that date some such drastic reform would have been necessary to break Stowe's hold on the borough. In 1806 Thomas Grenville, MP for Buckingham, could write to his brother the first marquis: 'I enclose to you the letter which you desired me to write to Buckingham because you will know to whom to send it, & I forget whether it be Mr Box or who that is the present Bailiff.'[28] The marquis did indeed know the members of the corporation: he had handpicked every one!

Like the corporation of Buckingham, that of Chipping (now High) Wycombe had a taste for building at other people's expense: in their case at the expense of the Earls of Shelburne. It is to that family that Wycombe owes its fine guildhall and market house. The second and more famous earl (or first Marquis of Lansdowne as he would have been then) probably had Wycombe in mind when he wrote towards the end of the century:

> Family boroughs (by which I mean boroughs which lie naturally within the reach of cultivation of any house or property) are supposed to cost nothing; but I am sure from my own experience and observation that if examined into they will be found to cost as much as the purchase of any burgage tenure.[29]

He may well have been right—and Wycombe at any rate was far from being so secure. It had appeared to be up to 1790, long returning without a contest one nominee of Earl Shelburne and one of the Wallers of Beaconsfield, who shared the interest, apparently without such a heavy investment. But in 1790 no Waller stood, and Lansdowne put up two candidates. A bitter struggle ensued, and one which did not end to Lansdowne's advantage, as we shall see.

The franchise in Wycombe was vested in the burgesses; but like their freemen equivalents elsewhere, the burgesses were created by the corporation, and, as often happened, the corporation had used is power to create burgesses to secure electoral power firmly in its own hands. In the early part of the century this had necessitated the creation of new burgesses to swamp the old; but from the 1730s onwards it had no longer been necessary, and the total electorate had dwindled to the fifteen members of the corporation and about thirty-five others. Unlike Buckingham's electors, however, those of Wycombe never ended in anyone's pocket. The corporation (or Common Council as the mayor, bailiffs, and aldermen were collectively called) always included substantial and independent local residents, and so did the burgesses. And, close corporation though Wycombe's was, in times of crisis it always responded to strong feeling in the town—and the town was against becoming a pocket borough of the Marquis of Lansdowne, or anyone else.[30]

There may have been strong feeling in the other Buckingham-shire boroughs, but it was generally not strong enough to be effective. Wendover, as Oldfield said, was 'a poor mean place, and possesses no trade or manufacture of any consequence.'[31] Lacking very many local residents of substance and independence, so long as its patron was strong and determined, Wendover was docile.

The other two boroughs were not inconsiderable places: Amersham being a thriving little market town, Marlow enjoying a bustling river traffic and several local industries. But in the former local landed influence exercised apparently unquestioned control, and in the latter a combination of industrial and landed influence long appeared equally secure.

For most of the eighteenth century, Marlow had no established patron. The closest approximation were the Claytons of Harleyford, who owned a substantial number of houses in the borough: and William Clayton sr held one of the seats from 1761 to 1783, followed by William jr, who held it until 1790. In that election, Thomas Williams, who had recently acquired the nearby Temple Mills where he carried on a brass and copper manufacture, first appeared as MP for Marlow. Around 1791 Williams purchased some of the Clayton property in the borough,[32] and by adding other properties in the intervening years, it was reckoned that he owned about half of Marlow by the 1820s.[33] In 1796 he was joined in the representation of Marlow by his son, Owen, and from that time until 1831 the Williamses or one of their close associates held both seats.

The Williams' influence at Marlow was based on the fact that they were large local employers and became large landowners in the area; but, most of all, it was based on the houses they owned in the borough. Their tenants were given advantageous rents if they voted for their landlord's candidates—and were turned out if they did not. And these considerations weighed sufficiently with the 250 or so scot and lot electors (ie those paying local rates) of Marlow. In Wendover, where the vote was vested in some 150 householders, the ownership of a majority of the houses was all important; and the houses, and with them the nomination of members for the borough, passed from patron to patron.

At the beginning of the period Lord Verney, who had purchased the Hampden property in the borough, was the patron. Verney, however, was careless and slack in his management; and in 1768 one of the seats was lost to Sir Robert Darling, according to Oldfield a candidate introduced by 'Mr Atkins, a considerable lace manufacturer in this place . . .'[34] Thereafter, Verney seems to have tightened his discipline and had no further trouble until 1784, when the electors took advantage of his severe financial difficulties, and the knowledge that he would have to sell, to revolt once more and return two members in opposition to his interest. And in 1787 when Verney was attempting to sell, his attorney wrote to a political ally that 'we have not a day to lose to break a combination which has been so well formed amongst the independent electors that it threatens to defeat the principal end of the purchase.'[35] But the independent electors were unsuccessful; and the borough passed to another patron and finally by 1796 to Lord Carrington, in whose family it remained for the rest of its career as a parliamentary borough. There was only one contest in the latter period. In 1830 the Marquis of Chandos strained every effort to wrest the borough from the Carrington interest, but the voting was two to one against his candidates.[36]

Opposition to the Drakes seems never even to have occurred to the some seventy scot and lot voters of Amersham. The Drakes of Shardeloes had been patrons of the borough since the seventeenth century, and they were to remain its patrons until the end in 1832. Probably by 1760 they owned the majority of the houses in the borough (though as late as 1742 they had not[37]). It is unlikely, however, that it would have made a great deal of difference if they had or not. They certainly owned most of the land around the borough, and they took their responsibilities as large resident landowners seriously. In 1824 an advocate of parliamentary reform, not likely to over-state the case for the Drakes, remarked on 'the gentlemanly conduct, great liberality and hospitality' of Amersham's patron.[38] The praise was well merited. Pocket borough though it may have been, the electors of Amersham were treated with as much respect as the electors of Westminster; and all the forms of electioneering were meticulously adhered to, from addresses and speeches to the entertainment of the voters after the election. Considering that no election during the period was contested, the cost of the entertainments, which ranged from about £350 in the eighteenth century to almost £600 in the 1820s, might be considered excessive.

The Drakes gave a great deal, and perhaps no less important they gave graciously. There seems little doubt of the respect and affection in which they were held; it manifests itself in all sorts of ways. Perhaps one of the most charming evidences is in an address from the town in 1784 thanking its representatives for their 'endeavours to defend the Constitution of this County from alarming and dangerous innovations.' This imposing document ended: 'and we must not omit to return to you our grateful thanks for your generous and liberal benefactions to the Poor of this Parish, in the course of the last and preceding Winters.'[39]

The Drakes used their secure tenure to pursue an independent line in politics. As William Drake sr said in the House of Commons in 1790, he was one of a 'chosen band' who 'thought for themselves, who were neither the spaniels of ministers, nor the followers of parties.'[40] The Drakes were not the only ones who prided themselves on their independence. There were men less socially exalted who, in their own sphere, had similar notions.

Chapter 2 PORTENTS OF CHANGE

E. P. THOMPSON HAS said of the great Radical victory that returned Sir Francis Burdett and Lord Cochrane for Westminster in 1807 that it:

> was a halfway house between the patrician techniques of Wilkes and more advanced forms of democratic organization. The gains were important. A new meaning had been given to the notion of 'independence'. Hitherto, the word had been a synonym for opulence and landed interest: Whig and Tory candidates were often recommended on the hustings on account of their wealth, which, it was supposed, would render them 'independent' of the need to curry favour or place from the Ministers or King. Cobbett's notion of independence insisted upon the duty of the *electors*, whether freeholders, tradesmen or artisans, to free themselves by their own exertions from patronage, bribery, and deference.[1]

Mr Thompson is quite wrong in believing that this latter meaning was a new one. Wilkes himself had used it when he wrote to his Aylesbury friend and political agent John Dell in 1757:

> I know the nature of Aylesbury perfectly, and I feel at my heart the kindness of the Independents to me; but for the mercenaries I am to buy them.[2]

The 'Independents' he referred to were certainly not men of opulence and landed interest. Dell was a farmer and surveyor who would later turn brewer. John Stephens, the vicar, was another 'Independent' supporter. Two other brewers, a draper, an innkeeper, a schoolmaster, and a large farmer were among the others.

Though the pollbooks sometimes dub them 'gent' or even 'Esq', they were, in fact, all men of the 'middling sort'; substantial men certainly, and leaders of the town, but hardly representatives of landed society. They were 'Independents' precisely because they disdained patronage and bribery and gave their votes of their own free will.

When men talked of the independence of electors, or the independence of boroughs, as they did in Bucks from the beginning of the period, it was always with reference to this kind of notion. Sometimes, it is true, the cry for 'independence' became but a thin cloak for the desire for freedom only to be bribed by all comers, as opposed to falling under the influence of one patron, but this was a conscious perversion. As has been seen, it would be quite wrong to believe that most electors or boroughs in eighteenth-century Bucks valued 'independence' in the sense that Cobbett used it. But some did, and as it was from these elements that a new kind of politics was to emerge in the second and third decades of the next century, we might examine a few characteristic examples of their political attitudes and activities.

On the morrow of Wilkes' first triumphant return for Middlesex in March 1768 an Aylesbury attorney wrote to Sir William Lee of nearby Hartwell House:

> Here was great rejoicings last night—Bonfires, Illuminations & every thing of the Sort. The Bells began ringing at 12 yesterday & are ringing now. Windows all broke that did not illuminate on account of Mr Wilkes being elected for Middlesex.[3]

And on the first intimation that Wilkes might be deprived of his seat, thirty-four of his former constituents wrote urging their MPs that both 'from your connexion with us, who are sincere in our friendship for him' and 'from your regard to the public' they oppose any such attempt, and take the side of 'justice to his constituents.'[4]

This was in April 1768. In September 1769, when the general petitioning movement, calling for the dismissal of a corrupt ministry and parliament, had got under way, there was strong pressure in the borough to join and an attempt was made to secure the co-operation of Lord Temple. Temple apparently considered it; and this horrified his brother George, who sent a hasty note

> entreating you most earnestly not to compromise yourself with
> the Electors of Ailesbury [sic], as I cannot but think it derogatory
> to your high rank and Character . . . No Borough in the Kingdom
> has hitherto thought themselves considerable enough to engage
> in a measure of this Importance & surely considering the notorious
> Venality of this Borough at the very last Election, it throws a
> great Ridicule upon the whole for them to be the first to apply
> for a new Election in such Terms. If however They are determined
> to do it let them do it by themselves but do not sully the rest of
> your Proceedings by taking Part in this which in every light is so
> objectionable. Wait at least till you see farther, but do not I
> beseech you let this Borough set the Example under your Direction
> or Patronage.[5]

Temple was Wilkes' former patron and at this time one of the
leaders of an opposition that was attempting to make political
capital out of the Middlesex election issue; but, as the above letter
makes clear, Wilkesite sentiment in the borough was not the product of Temple's 'direction or patronage'. There was an independent Wilkesite opinion in Aylesbury. How extensive it was is not
easy to say. It certainly did not include all those who lit bonfires
and broke windows in Wilkes' honour. As George Grenville
suggests, at the last election the scale of corruption—though not
its extent—had reached unexampled heights, and the ordinary
elector's dream had come true, with one nabob, John Durand,
driving another, Eyre Coote, from the field by the superior weight
of his metal.[6]

Durand may have enjoyed the support of Wilkes' independent
friends. At any rate, his first recorded votes were with opposition in
support of Wilkes at the end of January and the beginning of
February 1769. But on 3 February he did an abrupt about-face
and voted with the administration on the expulsion of Wilkes. This
was followed by consistent support for the government, which was
rewarded by a contract for victualling troops in the West Indies.
And, whatever the importance of Durand's principles in securing
his initial return, it seems likely that his reversal of them was one
of the factors in his not being re-elected. In 1774 he was defeated
by John Aubrey of Boarstall (and later Dorton), a consistent

supporter of Wilkes and opposition, by only eighteen votes. In such a close contest Wilkesite sentiment probably told. But it was not strong enough to prevent Wilkes' successor in 1764, Anthony Bacon, a wealthy merchant and munitions contractor and generally the opponent of Wilkes' causes (though he voted against government on the issue of the general warrant), from a remarkably secure tenure of the seat until he retired twenty years later. The 'Independent' electors were in a distinct minority, generally reckoned at between eighty and ninety (out of about 500)[7] in the latter half of the century. And, of course, not all of them were of one opinion.

Independent opinion probably played a more decisive role in the county, but it was longer in making itself evident. Until 1784 probably the most important issue arose out of Grenville pretensions to county leadership. From the time when Richard Grenville, who was to succeed his mother to the earldom, succeeded his uncle Lord Cobham to the Temple estates, thus uniting them with those of the Grenvilles, it was evident that a new county magnate had emerged. But it was some time after the union of Stowe and Wotton in 1749 that the fact was marked by a seat for the county, not least because of gentry distrust of this new agglomeration of aristocratic power. Thus in 1754 and 1761 two substantial gentlemen, Sir William Stanhope and Richard Lowndes, were returned unopposed. By 1768 Temple had become distinctly restless, and when Stanhope retired he was most anxious that his brother George should get the seat. But on this occasion Earl Verney, his neighbour and rival at Claydon, out-manoeuvred him by declaring early and receiving a good deal of support from leading gentlemen;[8] so the Grenvilles had to wait until 1774 when the younger George Grenville was able to claim a seat unopposed.

In 1779, however, Lord Temple died, and his nephew succeeded him, thus vacating the seat for the county. It was the new Lord Temple's intention that his brother Thomas should succeed him. But the opposition sprang a surprise, and at a dinner preceding the county races proposed, and carried by fourteen votes to four, a county meeting to nominate a candidate to fill the vacancy. The meeting was duly held and Thomas Hampden, the heir to Viscount Hampden, was chosen as the candidate to uphold 'the Independency of the County.' But the Grenvilles stood firm and, by exposing some private negotiations that had preceded the race

meeting, managed to raise grave doubts as to whether it was not
Hampden and his friends who were trying to force a candidate on
the freeholders; with the result that Hampden finally stood down. [9]
So far as one can tell, these manoeuvres were confined to the
aristocracy and leading gentlemen of the county. The freeholders
were invoked, but what the ordinary freeholders thought of the
question it is impossible to say. Neither is it easy to say with precision what they had thought of the Wilkesite petitioning ten years
before. Burke reported that at the commencement of the campaign
at the races in September 1779 Temple found 'the freeholders in
general totally ignorant of the question, and but very little affected
with it.' But a week later he was able to report a highly respectable
meeting of 400, 'many of them substantial people, who came forward to the work with a great countenance and an alacrity equal to
that of the Third Regiment of Guards.'[10] The petition itself proved
an outstanding success, with 1,800 signatures, representing four-
fifths of the freeholders. It would be rash, however, to attribute
this success entirely to the enthusiasm of the ordinary freeholder;
for the leaders of county society were united on this occasion as
perhaps never before or afterwards, with the Grenvilles and their
leading opponents in the county like Verney uniting to promote the
petition.

The Association movement of 1780 appears to be more revealing
as to the existence of an important opinion independent of that of
the greater landowners, however. Two divergent views emerged in
the course of the agitations in the county. Lord Temple and Burke
opposed the extension of the objects of the movement from economical to parliamentary reform, and their ˙view dominated at a
county meeting on 13 April, which endorsed economical reform
only. Their position was, however, opposed by Lord Mahon (later
the radical third Earl Stanhope), MP for Wycombe; and at a
second county meeting on 27 May he was able to secure endorsement of the principles of more equal representation and shorter
parliaments. Contemporary newspaper accounts fail to report any
remarks at meetings save those of prominent politicians and substantial country gentlemen—if indeed anyone else addressed such
meetings.

Thus, though one can know that a majority of hands favoured
one side or the other, one cannot know whose hands they were, save

sometimes by a process of elimination. In this respect, it is significant that Mahon took a leading part; for, as he had written to Shelburne at the beginning of the month, he was reluctant to be forward in 'a county where I am not resident and where I have not enough property to assume any kind of lead.' Yet a fortnight later he was taking the lead, strongly suggesting that no one else would. Apparently the only county influence that supported him was Shelburne's and that would hardly have been sufficient to have produced what is reported to have been a 'prodigious majority in [Mahon's] favour upon a show of hands' at the 27 May meeting.[11] This strongly suggests that he had substantial support among the ordinary freeholders. But if so, the reforming zeal had either dissipated or deprived of the kind of leadership Mahon had given was incapable of coming to the surface in 1782-3 in the second attempt to launch a purposeful parliamentary reform campaign.

Bucks was not among the twelve counties that petitioned for parliamentary reform in 1783, and there is no sign that any attempt was made to get up a petition.[12] But, whatever the depth of feeling for parliamentary reform, the experience of 1780 would seem to suggest a significant body of opinion in the county which was not a mere reflection of that of peers and country gentlemen.

This impression is further strengthened by the tumultuous proceedings which surrounded the contested election of 1784. As the historian of the Fox-North coalition has remarked, one of the most impressive displays of public opinion on the coalition and its policies came in Bucks.[13] A county meeting was held on 20 March, attended according to *Jackson's Oxford Journal* by about 2,000 freeholders. There waš no question of where the great weight of opinion among the freeholders lay. Everyone—Sir William Lee, Coke of Norfolk, and Burke—who attempted to speak against an address thanking the king for dismissing his late ministers was shouted down. And when Mahon finally secured Burke a hearing, the latter freely admitted that popular opinion was against the coalition and its India bill:

> He rallied Mr Aubrey upon not having delivered his Sentiments in Parliament on the India Bill: that was the proper place to discuss Questions of so delicate a Nature, and not popular Assemblies like the present. He said the people were not com-

petent to decide on such points: they had approved of the
American War in the same senseless manner they now disapproved
of the India Bill.[14]

Other reports agree about the sense of the meeting. Verney's agent
(ie his general factotum) at Claydon informed him that at the
'County meeting the People seemed violent against those that
opposed the address.'[15] Sir William Lee and his son would appear
to have agreed about the state of popular opinion, if not its cause.
The Duke of Portland wrote to Sir William that 'I understand
from Mr Lee that several of the Freeholders & substantial Yeomanry
of Bucks were induced to put their names to the Address by an
expectation of being relieved from their Taxes. . . .'[16]
   The opinion of the leaders of county society was more mixed,
though not necessarily less strong. Indeed the intensity of feeling
was such that in several cases long-standing alliances were broken.
Lord Verney, who had supported the coalition, stood against
W. W. Grenville and Aubrey, two supporters of Pitt. The Earl of
Abingdon, expressing his personal preference for Verney and
mourning the loss of Lord Rockingham who would never have
tolerated such iniquity, declared that he could not support 'a Man
who has joined Charles Fox and Lord North . . . to pull down the
Constitution of this County.'[17] Thus he could not support Verney.
Sir William Lee, on the other hand, who had long had ties of
personal friendship with the Grenvilles and supported their pretensions to one of the county seats, now deserted them. He was
aghast at the way in which the king and Lord Temple had brought
down in the Lords a government which had an ample majority in
the Commons. Sir John Borlase Warren, in response to a con-
ventional request for Lee's interest at Marlow, received the reply
that 'in this awfull crisis' he would give no one his support without
knowing their sentiments fully. And to one of Warren's friends who
attempted to get him to ease his unseemly rigidity Lee answered:
'The existence of the Constitution of this Country is now in Question . . .' There was therefore nothing for Sir William to do but to
offer his whole interest and support to a somewhat surprised, but
certainly pleased, Duke of Portland.[18]
   Lord Abingdon and Sir William were by no means unique.
There were others who altered long-established habits. It is

interesting, for example, to note that of the five who had taken the leading part in upholding the 'Independency of the County' by the attack on the Grenville seat in 1779, three supported W. W. Grenville in 1784. These were Robert Waller, MP for Wycombe, who moved the county address in 1784, and a Mr Hopkins, both of whom supported both Pittites, and Lord Inchiquin, who supported Grenville alone. The two others were Verney supporters, Viscount Hampden and Burke.

The feeling at the county meeting was both clear and decisive against the Coalition, and opinion among the leaders of county society was at least clear, if divided.[19] The results of the April–May election might, in contrast, appear both ambiguous and indecisive. The poll commenced on 21 April, just a month after the county meeting. At its close on 6 May Grenville was more than comfortably ahead, with 2,264 votes, Aubrey came second, with 1,740 votes. But Verney came only twenty-four votes behind him, with 1,716. This was the more impressive in that Verney had laboured under the most severe handicaps. On the eve of the election the results of a life of expensive indulgence and extravagant generosity to his friends, combined with particularly bad investments, came to rest on Verney's head; and the sheriff's officers arrived to seize the very furniture at Claydon House. As a consequence, Verney never appeared in the county throughout the crisis, and the canvassing was done completely by his friends and supporters. Under the circumstances, he would seem to have done very well. And, according to local tradition, save for a cruel twist of fate, he would have won. On the morning of the last day of the poll, so this account goes, Verney was ahead by thirty votes; and only fifteen minutes of the required hour without a vote, which would close the poll, remained. At this point, a loyal supporter from Buckingham galloped into town, rushed to the hustings, and recorded a plumper for Verney, thus allowing Lord Bridgewater's tenants to arrive and cast the votes which cost Verney the election.[20] However this may be, the election was clearly not a complete rout for the Foxite Verney—but then Verney had not been run as a Foxite.

Verney's address to the electors, like Grenville's, avoided specific issues altogether. Verney stressed his 'Independence,' in the patrician sense that no office or place had corrupted his judgement.

Grenville talked mostly about his family, and the county's gracious
recognition of their claim to one—and he stressed, only one—seat.
Only Aubrey spoke of the great controversies of the day:

> At the late Meeting of the County at Aylesbury, your senti-
> ments respecting the great Constitutional Questions which have
> justly excited the Anxiety of the Nation, were so distinctly declared,
> as to be subject neither to Mistake nor Misrepresentation. This
> decisive Declaration on your Part points out the Political
> Principles on which alone a Candidate can properly propose
> himself . . .[21]

Verney appears to have accepted the justice of this assessment—at
least to the extent that it was impossible to run on any other
principles. In his absence his chief spokesman was Joseph Bullock
of Caversfield (then an enclave of Bucks in Oxfordshire), former
MP for Wendover. And Bullock was willing to state emphatically :
'I can venture to Pledge myself that he is not connected with Ld
North or Mr Fox but is totally independent of them.'[22] This was
meant to reassure Lords Abingdon and Wenman, and with them
it did not succeed; but it may have with others.

Another possible explanation of the ambiguity of the election
results is that by the time of the poll there had been a reassertion of
influence, with Verney's supporters marshalling their dependants.
It is interesting that both the results of the election and its close-
ness could have been predicted from the way the gentlemen of the
county divided. In the Spencer Bernard Papers is a list of sixty-
nine men who were obviously thought to be the leading gentlemen
of Bucks, with their preferences. Forty-six supported Grenville,
twenty-five supported Aubrey, and twenty-four supported Verney
(there were nine mixed Foxite-Pittite preferences, all divided
between Verney and Grenville.)[23] This evidence might seem to
argue for the predominating influence of the landed classes. On the
other hand, if one takes the fifteen signers of the Aylesbury
requisition in support of Wilkes in 1768 who voted in the 1784
county election—electors who were almost certainly not under any
consistent influence—one would get very similar results: thirteen
votes for Grenville, eight votes for Aubrey, and six votes for
Verney. This suggests that county opinion was not necessarily
made from above.

And, whatever the effects of obfuscation and of influence, there were some who were neither deceived by the former nor swayed by the latter. The behaviour of the electors in the Newport Hundreds provides an example. On 4 April Bullock wrote ecstatically to Sir William Lee of the success of the canvass in that northern district of the county:

> On Friday Mr Wright met us at Newport Pagnell where there are 70 & 3 only refused. On Saturday we were at Olney where Mr Throgmorton [ie Throckmorton] joined us. *All promised us there except some of ye Dissenters.* In these great towns we have many single votes. All the adjoining smaller towns have been canvassed by Mr Wright's, Mr Throgmorton's, & Mr Chester's agents.[24]

Optimism would have been justifiable too on the basis of the list of gentlemen and their preferences; that is by the reckoning of the opposition, since it had been drawn up by Grenville supporters. Adding the head of the old and influential Catholic family of Throckmorton (the one significant omission I can find in the list), three, and these the largest and most prominent, gave their undivided support to Verney. Two gave theirs to Grenville. And one split between Grenville and Aubrey. But at the election, the Newport Hundreds put Grenville first, with 387 votes; Verney second, with 344; and Aubrey third, with 300[25]—a not unrespectable showing, which he clearly did not owe to the weight of influence behind him. Judging from Bullock's remarks, it seems likely that Aubrey owed his support instead to the votes of Dissenters, who were strong around the old nonconformist centres of Olney and Newport Pagnell (it might be noted parenthetically, that the population of these 'great towns' in 1801 was about two thousand each). This meant that he probably owed it to his opposition to the coalition and support of Pitt. And in an election which was decided by twenty-four votes, only thirteen Dissenting votes could have made the difference.

The events of 1784 suggest, what was certainly the case, that county politics rested on more than the decisions of cosy little caucuses of country gentlemen. No contemporary would ever have dreamt that they did. From the Duke of Portland downwards the leaders of Bucks politics were aware of the importance of 'the

Freeholders and substantial Yeomanry,' as the duke called them; or the 'principle People,' as they were called by Verney's Claydon agent.[26] These people made up a substantial portion of county opinion, and peers and gentlemen could be swayed by the violence of 'the People' on an issue, as Verney and his friends clearly were.

County opinion could be mercurial, which made county contests highly uncertain. It was partly for their uncertainty, partly for their enormous expense, that the leaders of county society strove to avoid contests. And it might be argued that their considerable success in avoiding contests is proof of their ultimate predominance. But it was not only the great landowners who had to be considered if the peace of the county was to be preserved. Almost half a century after the 1784 election, commenting on the High Anglican antics of the then county member, his great nephew Lord Chandos, Lord Grenville (the candidate in 1784) recalled his own experience: 'I always knew the strength of the Dissenters in this County & took great pains to conciliate them . . .'[27] If his successors as members for the county had been as solicitous of Dissenting feelings there might not have been cause in 1820 to lament the seizure of one of the seats by a family new to Bucks and to the nobility, Pitt's banker friends, the Smiths. There was always someone willing and anxious to fish in troubled waters, which is why the leaders of the county devoted considerable time and thought to keeping them untroubled. They were politicians— not autocrats.

One other aspect of the 1784 election requires comment—the beginnings of Whig organization, which have so fascinated Professor Ginter.[28] There is no doubt that the election marked the beginning of a highly organized campaign, which continued through a scrutiny, to the next election and beyond. In Verney's financial embarrassment, much of the election campaign had to be financed by subscription, and when local contributions fell behind a plea was sent up to the Duke of Portland, who either on his own behalf or that of others seems to have contributed £1,800.[29] And following the election, on 29th May, forty-three peers and gentlemen headed by the duke met at the Star and Garter, Pall Mall, formed the Buckinghamshire 'Independent Club,' and agreed to dine together on the 'first thursday in every month after her Majesty's birthday, during the meeting of Parliament at 5s per head.'[30] It

was hoped that the club would grow, and every member was to
subscribe a guinea annually to be expended under the direction of a
committee of seven. In addition the members seem to have been
expected to provide among themselves for a dinner for the freeholders, which was to accompany the annual anniversary meeting
at Aylesbury on the Saturday preceding the summer assizes in
July.

The club was very active for the next few years. In June 1784
Lord George Cavendish (of Latimer, Chesham, and the future
Earl of Burlington) presented a petition against Aubrey's return
and supervised a scrutiny that took place in the following year.
Meanwhile the government put off the hearing of the petition, and
one postponement followed another until 4 April 1786. Then a
committee sat on the matter for a week, when the petition was
finally dropped and Aubrey declared duly elected. Doubtless the
point of the postponement on the government's part was to wear
out the opposition, particularly financially. If so, the attempt
would seem to have backfired; for, while Verney's expenses were
once again largely covered by subscription, Aubrey had to meet
his out of his own pocket, to the tune of £50,000 according to one
account.[31]

The efforts of Verney's friends paid off. In May 1789 Verney
announced his intention of standing in the next election. Aubrey,
after addressing a letter asking for support 'to each individual
Freeholder of the County,' announced in October that he had
'not met with such an extensive Encouragement as will justify a
Perseverance in offering himself for the County for a new Parliament . . .' Verney took the occasion to thank his 'numerous and
respectable Friends for their very honourable and indefatigable
Support.'[32] Well he might. Aubrey had been forced from the
field, in large part at least, by their finance and organization, and
no one else dared to come forward. Verney was returned unopposed
in the election of 1790.

He died in 1791, whereupon his supporters put forward the
Duke of Portland's son and heir, the Marquis of Titchfield, who
was likewise returned unopposed. How long the London meetings
survived it is impossible to say, but those in Aylesbury continued.
After a 'very numerous and respectable Meeting of the Club' in
July 1795 'a Committee of Gentlemen' was appointed to 'carry

into Effect the Objects of the Club in preserving the Rights of the
Freeholders and the Freedom of Election.'[33] The annual dinners
seem to have lasted until about 1810, and the members of the club
still acted as a political group at least until November of 1809. Then
one of its founders, Lord George Cavendish, wrote to another, Sir
John Dashwood King, about the son of a third, their recent
representative who had now succeeded his father, the late Tory
premier, to the dukedom:

> I acquainted the Duke of Portland with the wish that had
> been expressed that Ld William Bentinck should stand for the
> County. I have received a letter from him in which he states
> that he has no desire to interfere in the Election. From the
> indisposition which he had before expressed to his brother being
> proposed I had little doubt of such being his determination.[34]

This was an attempt by two Whigs—long overdue some might
think—to substitute a Whig Bentinck for a Tory one.

For some of its members, support of the Club had probably
never had much to do with Whig principles. In the 1830s it was
generally remembered, and often invoked, as having been founded
'to restrain Grenville ambitions within reasonable bounds.'[35]
From the election of 1796 onwards it can have had little other
common purpose, for Portland had been in Pitt's government since
1794 and Titchfield was not surprisingly a supporter of that
government. So of course were the Grenvilles, but in 1804 they
entered into alliance with the Foxite Whigs. And Lord Grenville
was the head of the Whig-Grenvillite-Addingtonian 'Ministry of
All the Talents' which George III dismissed in 1807—and re-
placed with one headed by Titchfield's father! It was the latter's
death in 1809 which raised his son to the dukedom and thus
caused the vacancy. The failure to get the new duke to back his
Whig brother would seem to have marked the effective end of the
club—and probably not before time.

By the time the club finally died the spirit which had lain behind
much of its success, the dislike of aristocratic domination—though
in this case on the part of the gentry, since there is no indication
that 'middling' people ever took a leading part in the club—had
shown itself of decisive importance in two other Bucks constituencies, Wycombe and Aylesbury. As was suggested in the last

chapter, in 1790 Robert Waller, whose family had long shared the representation of Wycombe with nominees of Lord Lansdowne, did not stand again. Lansdowne thereupon nominated two candidates, his son Lord Wycombe and Sir John Jervis (the famous admiral who became the Earl of St Vincent). They were elected, but only after a severe contest with a third candidate, John Dashwood King of Halton and West Wycombe Park, son of Sir Francis Dashwood's half-brother, and successor to the baronetcy in 1793. It was a close thing, with Jervis polling only twenty-six votes to Dashwood King's twenty-two.

As the recent historian of Wycombe has pointed out, Dashwood King's support can fairly be described as wholly local.[36] Seventeen of his votes came from burgesses who lived in the town, two from those who lived in the parish outside the borough boundaries, and three from Londoners who were sons of Wycombe men. Twelve of his votes were plumpers. In contrast, of the twenty-three electors who supported only Lansdowne's candidates, only eleven were Wycombe men. These latter, however, included a majority of the Common Council, and after the election a meeting of the Council with Lansdowne and Wycombe attending in their capacities as aldermen, created fifteen new burgesses to bolster the Lansdowne influence. These fifteen were made up of six Londoners, five country gentlemen, and only four Wycombe men. The new voters proved useful in the 1794 by-election caused by Jervis' elevation to the peerage; but Sir John was still only seven votes behind Lansdowne's candidate, the great London banker, and soon to be a burgess of Wycombe, Sir Francis Baring. Lansdowne alleged the most colossal bribery:

> What can you say to a blacksmith who has seven children or to common labouring man who is offered £700 for a vote, or to two misers who are offered £2,000, which are instances directly on record since Mr Dashwood's election?[37]

Presumably, particularly in view of the reference to 'Mr' Dashwood, Lansdowne meant the former's first candidacy rather than election. Nor would there have been a need for such bribery when Dashwood King finally secured one of the seats in 1796. There may have been bribery earlier, but this does not mean that the bulk of Dashwood King's supporters were what Wilkes would

have called 'mercenaries'. Quite the contrary, it would seem.
Dashwood King's supporters in 1790 included no less than ten
'esqs' (though significantly only three of them appear on the 1784
list of influential country gentlemen), six 'gents,' a London
stationer, a brewer, a brandy merchant, a miller, a carpenter and a
blacksmith (who also cast a vote for Lord Wycombe). Lansdowne's
voters, in contrast, were rather less select. The Wycombe men
who voted only for his nominees included only two 'esqs,' two
clergymen (Lansdowne was patron of the living), 2 'gents,' an
attorney, two apothecaries, a farmer, a gardener and a blacksmith.[38]

There would seem then to be little question of where the weight
of opinion among Wycombe's more substantial inhabitants lay.
And popular opinion would seem to have supported them. We
have it on Landsdowne's own testimony that Lord Wycombe was
severely manhandled by 'the multitude' in 1794;[39] and according
to local tradition it was about this time that 'Earl of Wycombe was
taken to town pump & pumped upon.'[40] In the face of this strong
local opinion, Lansdowne gave in. A compromise was worked out
through the good offices of a retired London cutler, a Quaker,
whereby Lansdowne and his allies on the Common Council were
no longer to attempt to pack the electorate with 'foreigners' and
were to unpack it forthwith by bringing in forty-three new town-
burgesses. Apparently implicit in the 1794 compromise was the
understanding that Dashwood King should have one of the seats at
the next election. In any case this is what happened, he and Lord
Wycombe being returned unopposed in the 1796 election.[41]

In 1831, when Dashwood King had offended both his constituents and popular opinion in Wycombe by his refusal to support the
Great Reform Bill, Robert Wheeler, alderman and several times
mayor of Wycombe, soon to become a leader of the popular party
in the town, 'could not help lamenting the cause of the resignation
of Sir John D. King, who, nearly forty years since, had been the
champion of the independence of the borough . . .'[42] Dashwood
King himself had said the same thing at the time.[43] It was a healthy
municipal pride and dislike of aristocratic dictation that substituted
one Whig for another as MP for Wycombe in 1796.

Chapter 3 THE TRIUMPH OF 'INDEPENDENCE' IN AYLESBURY, 1802-1818

THE FIRST two decades of the nineteenth century saw a struggle, in some ways very similar to that in Wycombe, to vindicate the 'Independence of the Borough of Aylesbury.' Other themes that have been evident throughout the last chapter also converge in the Aylesbury experience of these years, making it a useful one to study in the greater detail which is possible.

Until the eighties Aylesbury's venality had maintained its independence of a patron. But in this decade new struggles began. In 1789 a vacancy was caused by the death of one of the sitting members, Sir Thomas Halifax. Two candidates emerged. One was Scrope Bernard, son of Sir Francis Bernard of Lower Winchendon. Besides his local connexions, Bernard was wealthy, having married an heiress to a banking fortune. And, to add to his other advantages, he was an intimate friend and close political ally of the Grenvilles. Bernard entered the lists with impressive credentials. He was opposed by another local gentleman, the soldier Gerard Lake (later Viscount Lake of Delhi) of Aston Clinton. Lake probably had less money than Bernard, but he was quite ready to part with what he had; he was notorious as an inveterate gambler. One of his patrons was even more exalted than Bernard's—the Prince of Wales—but more important for Bucks, Lake was one of the founders of the 'Independent Club' and was supported by the interest of its members.

The Grenvilles won the first round, and Bernard was returned in 1789. But there was an agreement soon afterwards, and Lake was returned unopposed for the other seat in the general election of 1790.[1] He retained his seat until 1802 when he did not stand again.

The Grenvilles do not appear to have had designs on the other

seat, but others had designs on Bernard's seat. The first new
candidate to appear was James Du Pre of Wilton Park, Beaconsfield. He was soon followed by a third candidate, Robert Bent, a
wealthy West Indian. Many years later a prominent local resident
and politician, John Gibbs, recalled the election, which he had
observed as a boy. The candidates, he said, were 'Scrope Bernard,
Esq, on the Buckingham interest, Robt. Bent, Esq as a Whig, and
James Du Pre, Esq, who professed to be independent of both
parties.' 'A strong body of the leading tradesmen of the town and
several lawyers joined the Whig party,' Gibbs continued, and 'a
simultaneous effort was made to shake off the yoke of Buckingham,
and it succeeded.'² This would seem to be a most accurate description of what happened. Du Pre may or may not have been invited
to the town by local residents. Bent was; several of the leading
inhabitants of the town had wanted a third candidate, and significantly—they had gone to the Whig Club to find one.

Who were these local politicians? Later, one of their friends,
explaining to a parliamentary committee why he was sure that
fifty of Bent's supporters had not received bribes (he thought at
least 150 had!), said that 'they were the Gentlemen of the Town;
they did not wish to receive any Donation from anybody.'³ The
remarks of their enemies were both less flattering and more
detailed. According to a memorandum in the Spencer Bernard
Papers, 'those who opposed Mr Bernard chiefly consist of—'

1) the old opposition, who on all occasions were adverse to the
   M of Buckm & his connections
2) those tradesmen, who took up the cause of the quered men,
   having money owing to them by those men, which they had
   expected to recover out of their gratuities
3) those who were partizans with Messrs Neale & Dell in the
   contest between the two Banks
4) those who thought or pretended they had not been sufficiently
   noticed by Mr Bernard, such as Hickman the apothecary,
   Lathwell a retired Tradesman.⁴

Two comments might be made immediately. Of the names
mentioned, all were certainly among the leading 'gentlemen of the
town.' The fine and substantial old houses of Henry Hickman,
surgeon, and Daniel Lathwell, gent, still stand in Church Street,

as does that of Robert Dell, now Barclays Bank in the Market Square. The other observation is that all these names appeared on the 1768 requisition in support of Wilkes; and Hickman and Lathwell were probably the very same who put their names to that document. This suggests a more complicated explanation than Bernard's supporter advances, though it does not of course disprove the validity of any of the factors he mentions. It would be very surprising if all those factors had not played some part in the opposition to Bernard. The question is, how much part?

A list of nominations for Land Tax Commissioners, submitted to Lord Verney in 1791 and identified as 'General Lake's friends from Aylesbury'[5] may give the clue to who comprised the 'old opposition.' There were eleven names on the list. Eight voted in 1802, all save one of whom had also voted in the last borough election for which a pollbook exists, in 1780. Four, all of whom had voted against John Smith, the Grenville candidate in 1780, again voted against the Grenville candidate in 1802; John Parker, 'Esq, gent', who as he lived just across from the Dells' brewery in Waterhouse—now Bourbon—Street, was evidently not a country gentleman; Charles Lucas, gent; Thomas Duncombe, gent; and Daniel Lathwell—which suggests that his bruised feelings went back some way! John Turvey, brewer, who had signed the Wilkes requisition in 1786, had voted for Smith in 1780; he now split his vote between Bernard and Bent.

The remaining three on the 1791 list had all shifted their allegiances to the Grenville candidate in 1802. The Rev William Stockings, master of the grammar school, was a close political ally of the Lees, who were now once again supporting the Grenvilles (though in 1780, before Sir William broke with the Grenvilles, Stockings had voted against the Grenville candidate). William Eagles, draper, had not voted in 1780. His son, Woodfield Blake Eagles, supported Bent in 1802; and the whole family, who were prominent supporters of Du Pre, were suspect to Bernard's friends. William Rickford, who had also not voted in 1780, was the Rickford of Rickford's Bank, the rival of Messrs Neale and Dell.[6]

It is immediately evident (perhaps the only thing that is!) when one looks at local politics in terms of the actions of real people over a period of years—as opposed to the usual way of looking at the votes of occupations, election by election—that they are full of eddying tides. But it is also fairly clear that Aylesbury politics, at least, had a certain integrity of their own, and that all the participants did not merely register the dictates of influential outsiders. What uses their independence was put to, is another question. There is probably more than a grain of truth in the second allegation of Bernard's supporter concerning tradesmen who backed opposition in order to get their bills paid. It would appear that voters incurred debts in anticipation of their gratuities. [7] A householder who received 'alms', however, disfranchised himself for the year in which he received them; and this provided an excuse, if a candidate wished to use it, to refuse a gratuity. Since poor relief was a form of 'alms', a large number might be affected. It appears that Bernard had chosen to be stringent in the Christmas donation of 1801.

Certainly the electors were very ready to believe any allegation of a lack of generosity on the part of the Grenville party. In April 1802, when the contest had begun to get heated, it was rumoured that Lord Buckingham had prevented a promised distribution of money by Du Pre by buying out the latter's interest for £9,000! William Rickford jr reported to Bernard that one of Bent's supporters had 'angered the populace with these words—'

> The infamous conduct of Bernard, and a certain Peer, is such as ought to disrobe him—we are once more call'd upon to exercise our Liberty and Independence. I therefore entreat you to repair to the Bulls Head and shew yourselves Independent.

His last remark was an invitation to join a meeting of Bent's major supporters who were planning to introduce a fourth candidate. [8] The invitation was accepted and another candidate decided upon, though one never materialized. In any event ,it is clear that, whatever meanings of the terms to the leading citizens and prosperous tradesmen of Aylesbury, for the bulk of the electorate 'Liberty and Independence' had a fairly specific connotation, and not the usual one! If Aylesbury was transformed from a venal borough into a proprietary borough under the constant influence of the Marquis of Buckingham, or anyone else, the bulk of the electorate would feel it in their pocketbooks. For them, interest dictated independence of a patron so that they might continue to be at liberty to sell themselves to the highest bidder.

To most electors, this is what independence connoted—but not to all. The leaders of the town were certainly not moved primarily either by influence or by interest. The Rickfords are an example. They had been supporters of Lake, but by 1802 they were hand in glove with the Grenville party. The alliance was certainly cemented by business interests. There was a close association between Morlands Bank, in which Bernard was a partner, and the Rickford bank in Aylesbury; and Bernard and Rickford were partners in the purchase of Lord Spencer's considerable property in the Kimbles at just about this time. They also looked after extensive purchases of property in Aylesbury and surrounding parishes being made by Lord Buckingham and almost certainly lent him the money to make them.[9] But despite his grand associations William Rickford had his roots firmly in the town. His sister was married to Zachariah Hunt, a grocer in the Market Square; and it was as a townsman, independent of aristocratic connexions, that he was to be triumphantly returned for one of the borough seats in 1818. Rickford had extensive business interests, but they put him in nobody's pocket. He was his own man.

The same can be said of his main adversaries in 1802. In February, the Rev John Rawbone, probably the junior master at the grammar school, an active partisan of Bernard, wrote advising him how he thought some of the leaders of the opposition might be brought around:

> I think Mr Pitches & the Dells may be influenced by their Landlords, although rich men they would not like to leave good bargains, Neale & Wilson by Sir John Russell, Sir George Lee & Revd Mr Goodall with whom they have very considerable dealings; Dell, Robt by Mr Du Pre under whom he rents a bargain at Aylesbury; Pitches, Joseph by Mr Rickford of whom he rents a little compact grass farm.[10]

It did not work. James Neale, draper and banker, his banking partner Robert Dell, wine merchant, the latter's brother, Thomas, who followed his father, Wilkes' old friend John, in the brewing trade, Joseph Pitches, farmer, and John Wilson, whitesmith, all continued to lead the opposition to Bernard and cast their votes for Bent at the election. And they continued to lead the opposition to attempts at aristocratic domination for the next five years. Such men were neither bought nor influenced. They were some of 'the gentlemen of the town' who disdained money and influence and hated its purveyors. At least they hated would-be aristocratic patrons. Aylesbury was their town, and they meant to dominate its politics. This was another meaning of 'Liberty and Independence'.

In 1802 they were successful. Bent bought his way into the hearts of the electors, and he was returned at the election of 8 July, receiving 271 votes to Bernard's 180. Du Pre, who benefited from the split votes of both sides, headed the poll with 336. This, however, was just the first round. Lord Buckingham seized the gauntlet that had been thrown down. A petition was lodged against Bent's return, and the best talents of the family, headed by Lord Grenville, watched and advised on its progress at Westminster. Meanwhile the marquis was marshalling his resources and intensifying his campaign of land purchase. In January 1801 he wrote to his brother Tom: 'My sales in Somerset added to those of Eastbury have enabled me to *look at* Weedon . . .'[11] He looked, and bought. At the same time he was negotiating with Lord Dillon about the latter's estate at Bierton, which he also bought. In April 1802 he concluded the purchase of the Manor of Aylesbury and extensive property there from Sir John Pakington. And sometime between then and 1804 he bought up large amounts of the unredeemed land tax in Aylesbury as well as that of the Lee estate at Hartwell, the Lee estates being in disorder after the death of the elder Sir William.

The marquis then proceeded to create 40s freeholds, the unredeemed Aylesbury land-tax by itself yielding fifty-one.[12] The point of all this soon became clear. The Aylesbury election committee finally met in February 1804 and quite rightly unseated Bent for bribery—though of course he was not the only one guilty of it. An act of parliament swiftly followed 'for the preventing of bribery and corruption in the election of Members to serve in Parliament for the Borough of Aylesbury.' The marquis' nephew C. W. W. Wynn managed the bill in the Commons and his brother Lord Grenville in the Lords. The object of the bill, which largely succeeded, was to make general bribery prohibitive. It extended the parliamentary borough to include the three hundreds, about one-fifth of the whole county; and it enfranchised the 40s freeholders, more than doubling the electorate. The bill became law on 29 June, just in time for the by-election on 10 July.[13]

That must have been a bitter disappointment. Bernard, whom the marquis felt had made too many enemies, was politely shoved aside, and Tom Grenville brought down to uphold his brother's interest. But the Independent Club still functioned, and apparently saw its opportunity. William Cavendish, the eldest son of Lord George, was put up on its interest. Whether the independent electors in the town had anything to do with his standing cannot be said with certainty, though C. C. Cavendish claimed in 1818 that the family had answered a 'call which was made on them upon a former occasion to support your independence, at a time when you considered it in danger. That call was obeyed,—and your independence established.'[14] It was indeed, Cavendish beating Grenville by 485 votes to 418. And, whether or not the Aylesbury independents had had anything to do with bringing him forward, they gave Cavendish strong support.

It is interesting that there was remarkable consistency in the behaviour of town electors on both sides in the two elections of 1802 and 1804 (there would, of course, have been no electors in the hundreds until 1804). Of the 240 electors who voted in both elections, 118 who had supported Bent also supported Cavendish, and ninety who had supported Bernard voted for Grenville. Only twenty-three changed sides. Nine votes rejected as coming from disqualified inhabitants make up the total.[15] The Grenvilles, who had their own influential supporters in the town (besides Rickford and the Rev Mr Stockings, the Rev John Harris, the Presbyterian minister, and a number of others), clearly commanded considerable loyalty. But there were more who, for their different reasons, did not wish them well.

Cavendish also got strong support from the newly enfranchised electors in the hundreds. Despite the fact that Lake had always been more the Prince of Wales' friend than a Whig, and at the end of his career in the Commons was supporting Pitt, he must have given his Foxite fellow member of the Independent Club his full backing. Of the thirty-two Aston Clinton freeholders, thirty-one voted for Cavendish. Support for Fox's friend also came from another quarter which might be thought odd. For whatever William Cavendish might be expected to do when he got to

Westminster, in Bucks he was 'a Mr Cavendish on the Portland Interest . . .'[16]

But there was another reason besides conflicting local ambitions and jealousies for party confusion in Bucks; conflicts of principle also cut across party lines. Sir John Dashwood King, for example, was by most criteria a good Whig, even a radical one, as is instanced by his support for Thomas Brand's parliamentary reform motion in 1810. On one question, however, on which almost all Whigs were united, Dashwood King demurred; from the time when the question was first introduced into parliament he was a firm opponent of Catholic Emancipation. Thus though he was in the minority on the motion deploring the change of administration on 13 April 1807, supporting the late government headed by Lord Grenville, on the question on which it had been turned out, Catholic relief, he was in sympathy with the new administration headed by the Duke of Portland. He was not therefore being as inconsistent as might at first appear when at the county election on 11 May he nominated the duke's son Lord Titchfield.[17] Indeed, in terms of principle, he was being quite consistent; for, to the extent that the 1807 elections turned on a national issue, it was 'no-popery.'

In his address of thanks after the county election Lord Temple, eldest son of the Marquis of Buckingham and himself to become the first duke, averred that he had been returned 'in spite of a Cry the most malignant, raised for Purposes the most mischievous, and amidst Attempts, the most artful, to make religious Animosities subservient to the political Objects of Individuals, to influence the Passions and to blind the Judgements of the People . . .'[18] Since the county election was uncontested, Temple must have referred to the one that had just been concluded in the county town. And it was certainly that election that had been the focus of the family's anxieties. On 4 May Temple had written to W. H. Fremantle, one of the members for the marquis' Cornish pocket borough of St Mawes:

> I do not know in what situation this may find you as to your election. But I take my chance of letting you know that a Contest has unexpectedly started up in Aylesbury. A Mr Williams whom the disaffected here have picked up has started. The Election

begins on Friday. If there are any means by which you, Tom Fremantle, and Mansel can come up in . . . Time pray do, as we shall want all our strength and all three have votes.[19]

Just who William Thomas Williams was, I cannot discover. He did not, however, state the issue in the election in the same way Temple had. According to Williams' address, the question was

> now reduced to this, Whether your Representative shall in effect be chosen by any Noble Family, or by yourselves? and that unless you continually and actively exert yourselves your Fate is sealed, you become enslaved for ever.

He made no reference at all to the Catholic question; and Sir George Nugent, a Grenville relative and the family candidate, while complaining like Temple of the rousing of bigotry, exonerated 'my Opponent, who was only the Instrument of others . . .'[20] There were certainly some of the opposition, like the Dells, who would have been quite willing to use the 'no-popery' cry, and probably they did.

It is not easy in this election either to determine the weight of issues generally or their relative importance. One issue, as Williams made clear, was aristocratic nomination of candidates. And his address was therefore aimed as much at George Cavendish, who succeeded his brother as a candidate, as against Sir George Nugent. The other issue was 'no-popery,' and this could have counted for or against either of the aristocratic candidates; for both the Foxites and the Grenvilles, who had sat together in the Talents, were firm for Catholic (and Dissenting) relief. But, as the following lists will show, no very clear patterns of electoral behaviour emerge. One hundred and ninety-two electors voted in all three elections.[21] Their votes are indicated below, divided into two main groups according to whether they showed themselves to be Grenville or opposition supporters in 1802 and 1804, and with the more prominent voters in each sub-group listed by name, occupation, and Dissenting denomination, if any is known.

116 OPPOSITION

50 *Cavendish & Williams*	**28** *Nugent & Williams*
Philip Payne, currier, Independent	Francis Farmborough, farmer & maltster

Thomas Dawney, grocer
George Ing, innkeeper
Richard Dukes, chinaman,
  Methodist
Thomas Ivatts, cordwainer,
  Dissenter

19 *Williams*
Thomas Dell, brewer
Thomas Hatten, attorney
Richard Kirby, farmer &
  butcher

3 *Cavendish*

James Grace, miller

15 *Nugent & Cavendish*
John Rolls, curriei, Independent
Robert Gibbs, clothier,
  Independent

1 *Nugent*

78 *GRENVILLES*

41 *Nugent & Williams*
Thomas Deverell, grocer,
  Methodist

25 *Nugent & Cavendish*
Rev Mr Stockings
Rev John Harris, Presbyterian
James Fell, laceman & farmer
Michael Russell, liquor
  merchant
Robert White, draper
Benjamin Loader, draper &
  laceman, Dissenter

9 *Nugent*
Rev William Lloyd, vicar
William Rickford jun, Esq
Robert Fell, laceman
James Dixon, hairdresser,
  Methodist

1 *Cavendish & Williams*

2 *Williams*

As was suggested above, these lists are mainly significant for what they do not show. They do not, for example, suggest any distinct lines of political cleavage between Churchmen and Dissenters. These would come later. Neither do they show any distinct cleavages between Dissenting sects. There would have been no reason at this date for either sort of cleavage. As will be discussed in more detail in the next chapter, both the Grenvilles and their opponents, usually Whigs, took a liberal line on religious questions.

Another thing which the lists do not show is any very distinct socio-political cleavage. It will be noted that the opposition had no monopoly of substantial townsmen, though they had the bulk of them.

When one turns to the question of issues, one is on uncertain ground. The actual poll ended with Nugent leading with 567 votes, Cavendish second with 490, and Williams losing with 413. This suggests that either the Grenville influence was greatly increased since 1804 or that they roused much less intense opposition. The latter explanation is probably the more important, as is suggested by the forty-three split votes they got from former opponents. One can only speculate as to why. Perhaps the fifteen who voted for both supporters of the Talents were indicating approval of the ministry's principles. The measure on which the Talents were ousted would have removed Dissenting, as well as Catholic, disabilities; and this may have been why the most prominent Dissenting layman in the town, John Rolls, gave Nugent a vote, which may have influenced others, like his niece's husband Robert Gibbs. On the other hand, the twenty-eight who voted for Nugent and Williams, withdrawing support evidenced in 1804 for Cavendish, may have been operating on the principle that the independence of the town dictated shifting alliances—a balance of power concept.

The other striking point about the poll is that Williams did so well. So far as I can determine, he had no prominent supporters outside the town. This of course would explain why he did well there, as is indicated in the lists (which, it will be remembered, include only town voters). In the actual poll, he received 209 votes in the town, which means that almost half his votes came from outside it. Though I have not done a systematic study of voting in the hundreds in this election, spot checks of parishes like Aston Clinton, which was virtually unanimous in the previous election, and a cursory survey of the others suggests that splitting there was as common as in the town. This might reflect attempts at strategic marshalling of second votes, but there is no evidence of it. The marquis' 40s freeholders, for example, whose votes would have been the most easy to manipulate, all plumped for Nugent. It seems more likely that no attempt was made to interfere with second votes, and that it was a matter of catch as catch can. The most likely reason for Williams to have caught votes, at least outside the town, was the association of his name with anti-popery.

But when one deals with issues in this election it is, as has been suggested, largely a matter of speculation. The patterns are too complicated, and the data too uncertain. But there is perhaps one vote where one is on fairly certain ground. Thomas Dell had supported Bent in 1802. He had remained ostentatiously neutral between his two aristocratic neighbours in 1804. And in 1807 he plumped for Williams. Anti-catholicism may have had something to do with this, but anti-aristocratic notions almost certainly had as much to do with it, as Dell's future actions would further confirm.

For the time being, however, the anti-aristocratic party bided its time, and the Grenvilles and the Cavendishes, in political alliance at Westminster, amicably shared the representation of Aylesbury. There were some bad moments. In January 1809 George Cavendish, a major in Moore's army in Spain, died in battle. Lord Temple addressed an urgent letter to W. H. Fremantle, the unofficial Grenvillite whip:

> I write this without any communication *with a soul*. In consequence of poor Cavendish's death I have written an ostensible letter to Aylesbury notifying our intention of *not* interfering with the nomination of his successor. I have however received an express from thence to tell me that the same people who last time brought down Mr Williams to oppose Cavendish & Nugent, have already set off probably in search of the same man. Unless some immediate steps are taken by the Cavendishes, the seat will *inevitably* fall into the hands of some adventurer which will plunge the Borough again into hot water. I know how horrible a thing it is to be called upon to make exertions in a moment of agony and distress, but unless Ld George does exert himself without a moment's loss of time the mischief will now & ultimately be very great. The nature of this communication shews how private my name must be kept, but for God's sake see Tierney directly to whom, but to whom *only* under sacred promise of secrecy you may shew this note, & urge him to take any means which may occur to him to see the Cavendishes & to press upon them the absolute necessity of not losing a *single moment* in sending down one of their family or their immediate connexions to Aylesbury. Tierney must be made fully sensible of the vast importance of my name not being mentioned in this, but I have full confidence in his prudence, especially too as he will see in this note only an

anxious wish to keep the Borough quiet & their seat to the Cavendishes . . . *Burn this letter*.[22]

It is evident that the Grenvilles did not underestimate the strength of the opposition in the town and were fully aware that any attempt on their part to interfere with the second seat would be political dynamite. There is no other explanation of the elaborate precautions and enjoinders of secrecy; for, as Temple points out, it was quite evident that *all* he wanted was to keep the Cavendishes in their seat and the borough quiet. Neither Tierney, as a leader of the Whigs, nor the Independent interest in the county would have been frightened by that. It was opinion in the borough and the charge of interfering that concerned Temple.

On this occasion all passed off quietly. Thomas Hussey of Fulmer, stressing that he was a freeholder in the hundreds and long a resident in the county, duly made his appearance, having as he said 'been called upon by several Gentlemen of the Independent Interest of the County to come forward as a Candidate . . .'[23] The election passed off quietly, as did the next general election in 1812 when Hussey and Lord Nugent (George Nugent—Grenville, Baron Nugent in the Irish peerage, second son of the Marquis of Buckingham and not to be confused with his predecessor in the seat) were returned unopposed. And in 1814 there was another smooth transition when Hussey stepped down in favour of another of Lord George's sons, Charles Compton Cavendish.[24] Aylesbury appeared to have become a nomination borough under the joint patronage of the Marquis of Buckingham and Lord George Cavendish, and so Oldfield described it in 1816.[25]

The description was premature. In the general election of 1818, almost before they realized what was happening, the Cavendishes were ousted. A requisition was started for William Rickford, and in a few hours it had 219 signatures.[26] As C. C. Cavendish put it, the opposition was 'clandestinely excited' before it was made public, which is another way of saying that the ground was well prepared. The polling lasted for four days; and at the end of it Nugent stood first with 854 votes, Rickford second with 573, and Cavendish a poor third, with 420.[27] One does not have to search far for the sentiment that made the difference between Rickford and Cavendish. It was the overwhelming feeling for the former in the town, which gave Rickford 188 votes, Nugent 185, and Cavendish only 43.

Neither does one have to search far for the most important issue. Rickford summed up on one of his banners the theme which he had hammered relentlessly in addresses and newspaper advertisements—'May Voters be Free and Representatives Independent.' The good old cause of the liberty and independence of the borough had triumphed at last, vindicated by one of the town's own residents.

Broader political principles had had nothing to do with deciding the outcome as between the three candidates—which is not to say principles were unimportant. In fact, there was not a great deal to choose between the political principles of the three. All were good Whigs. Cavendish hotly, and quite rightly, defended himself against the charge of having supported the suspension of Habeas Corpus—suggesting that the opposition had attempted to bring his liberalism into question. Rickford proclaimed it the duty of all representatives in these critical times 'to defend the rights and privileges of their Constituents, to reform all public abuses, and to enforce strict economy in the expenditure of public money.'

Nugent was even more specific. The times, he said, called for parliamentary reform, triennial parliaments, a reduction of the influence of the crown, and of 'the undue influence of individuals at Elections.'[28] Coming from the brother of the head of the house of Grenville, standing in the borough of Aylesbury, such a political testament is somewhat startling. But, as Nugent broadly hinted, he and his family were drawing further and further apart. If he did not exactly stand under Rickford's banners, he could—as in fact he did—appeal to much the same kind of support.

Doubtless not all the electors of Aylesbury were interested in these questions of political principles. The *Bucks Advertiser* commenting some years later on this contest between three candidates 'all of the Whig stamp,' remarked that Rickford was 'liberal in his opinions as he was large in his generosity.'[29] To many it was probably the largeness of his generosity that counted most. This is not to say that Rickford bribed, at any rate not in the generally understood sense of that term. Indeed in this election, according to Lord Buckingham, it was the Cavendishes who sinned in this way: 'As a last recourse, *there were attempts made to bribe, of which I have evidence.*'[30] In another form of expenditure also the Cavendishes were not backward, spending close to £1,000 at the White Hart alone to provide food and drink for the electors.[31] This latter form of expenditure was to continue and to be the most common form of corruption in Aylesbury elections for many years to come. How many ordinary electors were corrupted by food and drink is never an easy question. People have been known to get drunk in a cause they believe in! But one very large class of electors could hardly have been indifferent to the sums expended on entertainment, the publicans and beershop keepers. Rickford was never to be backward in his hospitality at elections; and in the years to come he was to give annual dinners to the electors at numerous inns and public houses throughout the constituency. He was also generous in his charity, becoming famous for his Christmas gift of beef and coal to the poor. The Cavendishes had been charged with ignoring the borough save at election times. Rickford lived in the borough and was constant in his attentions. It certainly did him no political harm, and it undoubtedly did him a great deal of political good.

None the less it will not do to over-estimate the importance of such factors. We have followed the cause of the 'Liberty and Independence' of the borough of Aylesbury and its electors through some peculiar twistings and turnings, but it all ended with two Whig MPs. And it is difficult to see how it could have ended any other way; for there were lines of continuity throughout, and most tended in the direction of the party of reform. There were four stewards for the dinner celebrating Rickford's victory.[32] One was Thomas Dell jr, son of the man who had backed Bent in 1802, Williams in 1807, was probably the main architect of Rickford's victory in 1818, and whose own father had been Wilkes' agent. Another was W. B. Eagles, colleague of the elder Dell in the struggles of the first decade of the century and of the younger in the struggles to come in the third and fourth decades. A third was a newcomer, one who was to play a leading role in the years ahead, John Churchill, grocer. It was these men—a brewer, a draper, and a grocer—who were mainly responsible for bringing down a Cavendish.

Lord Buckingham was left distinctly uneasy by the election;[33] and, as the events of the next decade and a half would prove, he had very good reason to be. While his brother grew more radical, the marquis was growing more conservative. The Grenville connexion pretty definitively cut itself off from the Whigs as a result of arguments over government measures to deal with popular unrest in 1817. Five years later, its head became a duke and his party joined the supporters of the Tory government of Lord Liverpool. There was no great inconsistency involved, for Buckingham reserved the right to press the great family principle of Catholic emancipation, and on other questions he had never been a reformer. Now, however, without the moderating influence of the Whigs, it was easier for him to indulge his conservative prejudices.

The result was not to his political advantage in Bucks. There the tides of reform were running strong. Buckingham would not ride with them, and therefore they had to sweep over him. The times called for men of 'the Whig stamp'. At any rate, the brewers, drapers, grocers and their like called for them—and that was enough.

Chapter 4 THE COMING OF REFORM, 1820-1832

TOWARDS THE end of the second decade of the nineteenth century, there was an important shift of emphasis in Buckinghamshire politics. The influence of national issues, which heretofore had been only occasional, now became constant and critical. The precise turning point is not easy to pinpoint. It may well have come in the great agitations following the end of the war, marked in Bucks by two meetings at Aylesbury following hard one upon the other in February and March 1816. The first, of 'persons interested in agriculture', protested against the property tax and the enormous military establishment that added to the burden of taxation. The second took up the theme of large military establishments, also denouncing them as subversive of the principle and spirit of a free constitution. The increase of civil expenditure and of pensions and sinecures was also protested, as was 'the unnatural and mischievous operation of an artificial paper capital and currency'.[1] (Unlike the other two issues in the famous trinity of 'Cash, Corn, and Catholics', 'cash' was not to be an issue in Bucks in the twenties; since, of course, it arose from the reversal of the very policy which was here being protested against.) It seems likely, as has been suggested, that Rickford's candidature at the next general election as an exponent of retrenchment and reform was not unconnected with the local sentiment expressed in these meetings; but the lack of local newspapers before the twenties makes it impossible to speak with complete confidence.

There can be little doubt, however, that after 1820, when the evidence becomes rich and full, the influence of national issues became of crucial significance. The questions that exercised governments and parliaments in the 1820s—the campaign for the abolition of slavery, the battle over Catholic emancipation, the

59

agitation for the repeal of the Test and Corporation Acts—were all lively questions in Bucks as well, creating controversies that prepared the way for the great struggle over parliamentary reform in the years 1830 to 1832. And one cannot fail to be struck during this period by how the most seemingly trivial issues came to assume a broader significance.

An early evidence of this is a bitter controversy commencing late in 1821 over where official county newspaper advertisements should be placed. Until this date, there had been no difficulty deciding, as the *Bucks Gazette*, founded a few years before, had been the only county newspaper (though, unfortunately, no issues before the 1820s survive). The *Gazette* was at this time generally favourable to the Grenville party. But in July 1821, the *Buckinghamshire Chronicle* was founded, espousing the advanced whiggery coming to be represented by Lord Nugent, and bitterly critical of the Duke of Buckingham (as he would soon become) and his party. When Nugent and some of his allies on the county bench proposed to have advertisements placed in the *Chronicle* as well as the *Gazette*, they were defeated by the Grenville majority at the autumn meeting of quarter sessions. Nugent and his friends thereupon set about getting up a protest from as many members of the bench as possible. The Rev Sir George Lee, who had succeeded his brother to the family baronetcy and estates, had assumed the leadership of the protest, and he and Nugent missed no one likely to be favourable to their cause. On 12 November Nugent informed Lee that he had written to Lords Spencer, Althorp, and Blandford (interestingly, in Bucks in the twenties and thirties the Churchills always appear on Whig lists). The Duke of Bedford, Coke of Norfolk, and several other Whig gentlemen had already promised their support. Nugent had just remembered the Duke of Somerset, who had 'large property in the county, and is a staunch Whig. He ought on every account to be communicated with. Whether this should be done at once from yourself, or through Smith [the Hon Robert Smith, MP for the county since the last election] you will be able to judge better than me . . .' Nugent went on to say:

> I should consider myself wanting in every proper sense of what
> I owe to private friendship and publick virtue, did I not say how

warmly and sincerely I feel your handsome and gallant conduct in relieving *me* personally, and the whig cause in the county generally, from the embarrassment which must have been felt if you had not nobly volunteered to mount the breach first and lead the phalanx of protesters. It has never been out of my mind since, that in no other way could the difficulty have been avoided of, on the one hand, having it imputed to us that we were covertly making ourselves Smith's partizans in the county, or, on the other, bringing the D. of Bedford for the first time into the county to head a personal opposition to my brother—Among all those who on publick grounds will have reason to thank you for your manliness in cutting this Gordian knot, I do feel that I have the most reason, on private grounds too, to be grateful to you.[2]

The Hon Robert Smith was the eldest son of the first Lord Carrington, Pitt's friend and a London banker, who, as Thomas Grenville was to complain when the second Lord Carrington became Lord Lieutenant on the duke's death in 1839, 'thirty years ago was a stranger to the County without an acre in it!'[3] This was something of an exaggeration, since Carrington had acquired Lord Lansdowne's Wycombe property in the late nineties. Still, the Smiths were relative newcomers, and as rich and powerful ones, constituted a threat to the Grenville influence. This obviously concerned Nugent, but not sufficiently to deter him from close political co-operation with Robert Smith.

Nugent and Lee might wish to distinguish between the Whig cause and Smith's, as indeed the Smiths themselves did; but it was not a very meaningful distinction. The point of the protest in which they were at that very moment heartily co-operating was obviously not the ostensible one of getting advertisements for the *Chronicle*, as Nugent went on to make even clearer:

> Nothing I think will remain for us to do, after our protest, but to endeavour to persuade Sabin [the proprietor of the paper] not to weary the generality of his readers by pushing to too great length a question, personal to himself, with which it may be difficult to convince him that people in general will cease, after much repetition, to take interest.[4]

It was quite evident, not least from the long list of allies they called to their assistance, that the point was to strengthen the Whig cause in the county by making the duke's party look arbitrary and high-handed in their proceedings. And whatever qualifications and distinctions his adversaries chose to make, the duke had not the slightest doubt that that was the point. His cousin Sir H. W. Williams-Wynn wrote: 'I am truly sorry to see Election Politics running so high between you and Smith. I think you are under a mistake as to his being a Radical . . .'[5] But the duke was right; Smith continued to be part and parcel of every Whig or 'radical' (as their enemies were apt to call the Whigs) manoeuvre against him.

Indeed the following year it was Smith who led the Whig pack, successfully moving at the autumn meeting of quarter sessions for an inquiry into county expenditure. It was a provincial version of the economical reform movement, clearly aimed at the duke whose appointees controlled the county administration. It was also evident that it was a party fight; among Smith's supporters were Nugent, Lee, Col Thomas Aubrey (the heir to the baronetcy), Rickford, and Dashwood King, the leading Whigs in the county. In the end, there was little reduction of places or emoluments, as the duke successfully rallied his forces to stave off the attack. But during the several months that the inquiry went on the Whigs had been able to advertise their concern for economy, and to cause the duke severe embarrassment.[6]

The rivalry even extended to the election of a new clerk to the trustees of the Bicester and Aylesbury Turnpike in 1825. James James, an Aylesbury solicitor, was nominated by Rickford and supported by Nugent, Smith, and Aubrey, among the Whig gentry, and by such leaders of the middling classes as John Rolls, Thomas and Robert Dell, W. B. Eagles and a number of other familiar names. The opposing candidate, Henry Hatten, another Aylesbury solicitor, was nominated by Major Robert Browne, JP, and backed by many more of the duke's party, including Sir S. B. Morland (formerly Scrope Bernard), two Dayrells, John Grubb, three Pigotts, the duke's steward, and a phalanx of clergymen who held his livings. On this occasion the opposition candidate won, which caused a correspondent of the *Chronicle* to rejoice in the defeat of the 'arrogant faction of this county,' and to remark that this was not 'a meeting of Quarter Sessions, where they carry everything their own way.' And he rejoiced 'the more, because I think it ominous of the result of a contest for the

county, if such a thing there should be.' 'Though the contest was
not to come until 1831, the omen proved accurate in so far as the
same parties would again be ranged against one another, James'
supporters backing two pro-Reform Bill Whigs, Hatten's backing
Chandos, the opponent of the bill.

Many of those who had backed James for the clerkship in 1825
were also among Smith's party at the uncontested general election
the following year. Sir George Lee nominated him, and would
doubtless have chaired a celebration dinner. But Lord Carrington
wrote begging that none be held: 'a public dinner at the present
moment, whatever may be proper hereafter, might be considered
merely as an invitation of a political Party from which my Son is
entirely distinct.'[8] Lord Carrington, who was never a Whig,
might choose to think that his son was not; but few could have
guessed it from the latter's actions, or from the fact that he was
nominated by one leading Whig and seconded by another,
Rickford.

Neither could anyone have guessed from Smith's principles,
which were distinctly whiggish from the beginning. Shortly after
the 1820 general election the Rev J. L. Dayrell had written to a
friend in another county:

> Our Elections have passed off very quietly—although the
> new Member is much disapproved of—the honble Mr Smith son of
> Lord Carrington, as being of the dissenting Interest & a Friend
> to Roman Catholic emancipation.[9]

Indeed, Smith had espoused the Whig principles of 'civil and
religious liberty' before he acquired many Whig friends, at least
in Bucks. As was seen above, Lee and Nugent were still suspicious
of Smith at the end of 1821, and the only prominent figure in the
county to support his candidacy in 1820 had been Lord George
Cavendish.

Unfortunately not much information exists about this election.
It would appear that William Selby Lowndes, member for the
county since 1810, had, without consulting anyone, simply decided
not to stand again. This is suggested by correspondence a few
years later. In 1829, it was thought that the differences that the
heir to the Grenville dukedom, the Marquis of Chandos,
experienced with his father over Catholic emancipation would

lead to his accepting the Chiltern Hundreds. In dismay, the vicar of West Wycombe wrote to Sir John Dashwood King, long a leading opponent of emancipation: 'surely he will not take such a step without consulting you? or we shall be placed in the same situation we were when Lowndes thought proper to take the Step which threw the County into the power of the Smith Party.'[10] Since the dissolution of the Independent Club interest a decade before, there had been no one to organise candidacies for the second county seat (the Grenville seat continued to go to the heir); and the Smiths obviously profited by the resulting confusion.

But Robert Smith would also seem to have established a popular following to make up for his lack of support among the nobility and gentry of the county. As was seen above, Dayrell identified Smith as being 'of the dissenting Interest', which suggests that the latter had made an evident effort to associate himself with that interest; and in the years that follow there is abundant evidence that he made every effort to identify himself with Bucks Dissent.

The first occasion was in the late summer and autumn of 1824, when a bitter religious controversy disturbed the peace of the county. As Robert Plumer Ward, author and friend of Canning, wrote to the Duke of Buckingham: 'As to the county, by very far the most momentous thing that has happened is Lowndes' famous committal of the Methodist parsons, and Smith's meddling activity upon it.'[11] In fact, the two unlucky preachers called themselves Baptist Revivalists, not Methodists. They were collecting money to pay for a new chapel for a congregation at Raunds, Northants, when the Rev Mr Lowndes (probably a brother of the former MP) put an end to their activities by clapping them into Aylesbury gaol as vagrants, for a month at hard labour. Since they were duly registered preachers on legitimate business, the case caused great excitement. The Protestant Society for the Protection of Religious Liberty flew to their assistance. Smith was their ardent champion on the county bench. And the final result was that the Rev Mr Marshall, who had lodged the original complaint before Lowndes, was forced to make a generous settlement in restitution.[12]

It was by such protection of Dissenting interests in Bucks, as well as by championing their claims in parliament, that Robert Smith established a special relationship with his Dissenting constituents. He publicly and ostentatiously took pride in that relationship. In 1832, when he had retired from the county seat and was standing for Wycombe in the first election after the Reform Act, he spoke of

> the dissenting body through the county, whose representative he certainly no longer was, but whose confidence, he was proud to say, he still had reason to think he possessed, and whose friendly opinion, and intimate alliance, he should ever seek to preserve (cheers).[13]

It seems reasonable to suppose that that 'intimate alliance' with Dissent had been another reason for Smith's unopposed return in 1820, providing him with a popular appeal that discouraged opposition. For politicians who knew the county well, like Lord Grenville, were well aware of 'the strength of Dissenters in this County . . .'[14]

A separate and distinct Dissenting interest is something that has not been encountered before in this study; and, as it was to be a critical element in Bucks politics henceforward, it is worth pausing to speculate as to the causes of its emergence. As has been seen, Dissenters had not voted as a block at least as late as the Aylesbury election of 1807. In 1818 the Dissenting vote in the town went to Rickford and Nugent. The only exception, so far as I can determine, was the Rev William Gunn, the Independent minister, who voted for Cavendish and Nugent. But, except that the Independents did not defer to their minister, this proves very little; an overwhelming majority of townsmen of all religious persuasions voted for their fellow townsman, Rickford, and all three candidates were sympathetic to Dissenting causes. After 1820, however, Dissenters did tend to vote as a group, and leading Dissenters played prominent roles in a party who usually called themselves first 'Reformers' and later Liberals, and supported candidates who called themselves by one of these names, or as often Whigs. What was it that made Buckinghamshire Dissent into a political interest, and forged the link between it and whiggery? The answer I think is that the Dissenting interest emerged in response to persecution and that the alliance between Dissenters and the Whig friends of 'civil and religious liberty', like Smith and Nugent, was a most natural one.

It seems likely, though the lack of detailed evidence makes it impossible to speak with certainty, that controversies in the first decade of the century lay behind the emergence of political Dissent in Bucks. The Bucks magistrates had been among those who had anticipated Lord Sidmouth's proposed legislation to limit the registration of Dissenting ministers, and also among those with whom he had consulted before framing his bill. The case of one of those refused registration, the Rev Peter Tyler, the Baptist minister at Haddenham, had become part of the manoeuvres by the Dissenting leadership in London to block the introduction of the bill.[15] Tyler himself was later to be a leader of the movement for the repeal of the Test Acts in the county, a pillar of the Reformers, and of Liberalism into the 1860s. The chairman of the quarter sessions that had refused him registration was William Selby Lowndes, MP, whose clerical relative was to commit the two unfortunate Baptist preachers in 1824. And it seems likely that, as these individual cases suggest, the divisions of the twenties had their roots in the earlier period.

The case of one William Carr who was refused registration early in 1809 is the first one I find mentioned in the records of the Dissenting Deputies. But, according to a history of the Aylesbury circuit, there had been disturbances of Wesleyan Methodist meetings as early as 1805–6, with the consequence that their preachers were forced to seek protection as Dissenting ministers under the Toleration Acts.[16] It would be strange if these disputes had not created bitterness, and it was probably this that lay behind the emergence of a distinct Dissenting interest in Bucks.

Certainly there is no evidence of the existence of one before the second decade of the nineteenth century. As has been seen, Lord Grenville testified to his anxiety to conciliate the Dissenters during the time when he was MP for the county in the eighties.[17] His efforts would appear to have been successful. Though there was controversy in neighbouring Oxfordshire and the corporations of both Oxford and Woodstock passed resolutions against repeal of the Test Acts in the agitation of 1789–90,[18] neither side seems to have stirred in Bucks. (Grenville was perhaps not sorry that, as Speaker, he was necessarily neutral in the debates of May

1789.) And the Grenville candidates had no steadier adherent than the Rev Mr Harris, the Presbyterian minister in Aylesbury. Harris came from an old Dissenting family in London, was educated at Homerton, and, according to his obituary in the *Gentleman's Magazine*, was a man of considerable polish and charm, as well as piety. Lipscomb tells us that he was 'sincerely respected by his neighbours and acquaintances, Churchmen as well as Dissenters.'[19] He was clearly no hot-gospeller (his piety is described as 'unostentatious'), but a cultivated Dissenting minister of the old school. Like his clerical counterparts in Aylesbury, Harris was a loyal supporter of the Grenvilles—and on broad grounds of principle there was no reason for him not to be.

Until Chandos took a radically different line in the 1820s, the Grenvilles were always on the liberal side of religious questions. In 1807, for example, they went out of office on a question of easing the disabilities of Protestant as well as Catholic non-conformists. And it was Selby Lowndes, not the Marquis of Buckingham, who was the spokesman of quarter sessions in the attempts to restrict registration: the marquis' role would appear to have been that of mediator between quarter sessions and the Dissenting leadership. Indeed, judging from the correspondence quoted above between the vicar of West Wycombe and Sir John Dashwood King in 1829, Selby Lowndes' great attraction as second county member, in terms of principle, was precisely his High Church notions, which served to balance the liberal position of the Grenvilles.

It was neither Dissenters like Harris nor grandees like the Grenvilles who were responsible for the initial acrimonious divisions between Church and Dissent in Bucks. Rather it was the children of the evangelical revival whose enthusiasm and zeal, and apparent success, in the cause of Dissent were equally repugnant and frightening to the High Church loyalties of squires like the Lowndeses.

The latest and most impressive authority on the impact of the evangelical revival on the numbers of Dissenters places Bucks among seven counties where, because there was no decline of Dissent in the eighteenth century, as happened elsewhere, there was also no absolute increase in the number of Dissenters in the two generations between 1772 and 1827 (Methodists are not included in these calculations).[20] This may well be. But, even if it is true, contemporaries might well have believed that the numbers of Dissenters were growing faster than perhaps they were. For, while the Quakers were certainly in decline and some old Dissenting congregations were disappearing or merging with new ones, what probably impressed contemporaries was the enormous activity of the evangelicals.

The Methodists must of course be included. They seem to have taken root in Bucks about 1770, the first society being at Weedon. Thereafter societies fairly quickly sprang up all over the central part of the county (the only part for which there are adequate records). In 1784 a society was founded in Aylesbury, and in 1786 one in Bierton. In 1805 the first regular chapel in the district was opened at Waddesdon. In 1808 another was built in Whitchurch, and by 1810 Whitchurch had become the head of a circuit which by 1813 included Aylesbury, Bierton, Waddesdon, Aston Clinton, Stoke Mandeville, the Kimbles, Weston Turville, Bishopstone and North Marston. The first decade of the century therefore would appear to have been one of considerable activity, and doubtless it was activity of this sort that frightened and angered the magistrates. In fact, the numbers of Methodists were not enormous. By 1823, by which time Aylesbury had become the head of the circuit, ten societies had a total membership of only 223.[21] But until late in this decade, when there was a rough local survey made, the magistrates would probably not have had a very firm idea of numbers of Dissenters. They could, however, see the strenuous activity of the Methodists, which did not of course end with those who became actual members of the societies. And the activity was not confined to the Methodists.

In both Aylesbury and Buckingham new evangelical congregations of Independents were founded in 1789 and 1792 respectively. In both cases there were older congregations of the same persuasion still in existence. More information exists about the congregations in Aylesbury, and its case may serve as an example. The congregation served by the Rev Mr Harris was Presbyterian mainly by virtue of the fact that their minister chose to call himself one. But, unlike most of that denomination by this date, he and his congregation remained orthodox and the minister was partly supported by a trust set up by Mary Cockman in 1734 to provide a stipend for a minister of either the Presbyterian or Independent persuasion.

A new congregation calling itself Independent launched itself in December 1789, with thirteen signing the original convenant. By 1797 the new church had forty-four members who had signed the covenant, but the congregation was certainly larger than that. Among others, it included the Aylesbury Baptists. In 1801 John Rolls wrote to the Independent Board, which had been assisting in the support of the minister since 1796, requesting more aid as the Baptists had just called their own minister and thus their pecuniary support had been lost. Difficulties continued until 1816 when 'the Church having been in a most disorganized state a few of the friends determined to begin a new foundation.' In that year they took over the Presbyterian chapel in Hale Leys, and the Rev William Gunn came in the following year, taking over Harris' stipend.[22]

Thereafter the church prospered. In 1830 it had 132 members and a congregation of some 900. Meanwhile the congregation had spawned another in Wendover in 1812 and in 1830 was on the point of spawning another in Bierton. At the same time the Baptists were estimated to have a congregation of 350 and the Methodists one of about 500. These figures include those attending from outside the parish of Aylesbury. In the parish itself the total number of Dissenters (including only one Quaker) was put at about 600. These figures seem to have been for adults only and they could probably be at least doubled by Sunday-school scholars. Thus there were probably some 1,200 Dissenters in a population of some 5,000 in 1831.[23] Dissenters were a minority, but they were a powerful minority, and there was almost certainly a much higher proportion of them among the ratepayers and electors. Evangelical Dissent was firmly established in the town of Aylesbury, as it certainly was as well in the towns and villages of the hundreds (though the figures for the parishes in the hundreds would need much more careful scrutiny than I have been able to give them, and thus I quote none), and in the county as a whole.

There were probably several important results. One was that it became politically dangerous to trifle with Dissenters—as, for example, the Rev Mr Lowndes trifled with them—for not only were their numbers substantial, they were also remarkably united. As was seen above, gentlemen like Plumer Ward could not tell a Baptist from a Methodist, and in Bucks, at any rate, this confusion was pardonable. Independents, Baptists, and Methodists shared one another's pulpits and chapels and supported one another's missionary societies with a fine disregard of sectarian distinctions.[24] And, though a few Methodists hung back, this co-operation was largely extended to politics, with important consequences.

Probably another important result of the spread of zealous Dissent was to decrease the corruption of politics and to increase the 'independent' element in the electorate. Certainly Dissenters were leading critics of bribery and corruption, and occasionally congregations acted against erring members. The most Draconian measure recorded was that taken by the Aylesbury Baptists who are supposed to have expelled half their congregation for taking bribes in the notorious 1802 election.[25] Doubtless a point made in this way did not have to be made too often.

Political Dissent had a marked impact on Bucks politics in the 1820s. In 1822 the *Buckinghamshire Chronicle* begins to bring into clear relief what has heretofore been a local landscape for the most part shrouded in obscurity;[26] and indications of the objectives and influence of the Dissenting interest soon become apparent. The first important manifestation was in the launching of the anti-slavery campaign early in 1824. At a meeting in Aylesbury on 4 April, the Rev Mr Gunn and John Rolls took a leading part, as did half a dozen other prominent Aylesbury Dissenters. In January 1826 when a Buckinghamshire Anti-Slavery Society was formed with Lord Nugent as its president, among the ten vice-presidents was John Rolls, 'Esq,' currier and patriarch of Aylesbury Independency. One of the two joint secretaries was the Rev E. Barling of the Old Meeting House, Independent, of Buckingham. The treasurer was William Richardson, a Quaker corn dealer of the same town. The society was certainly not the closed preserve of nonconformists. Far from it, the vice-presidents also included Sir George Lee, James Stephen, the great evangelical lawyer whose son was vicar of Bledlow, Thomas Dell, and the vicar of Aylesbury and five other clergymen.[27] But significantly absent from the meeting, which was held in Buckingham, was any representative from the great ducal house nearby at Stowe; for its master was also the owner of the Hope plantation and some 300 slaves in Jamaica, and Chandos was to be chairman of the West India Committee, the pre-eminent spokesman of the slave-owning interest.

Slavery was not the only issue on which Chandos, at any rate, was headed on a collision course with Dissent. Lord Grenville's remark about the power of Dissent in Bucks, referred to several times above, was made on 6 March 1828, a week after his great-nephew had recorded his vote against the repeal of the Test and Corporation Acts. And, whatever the case in the 1780s, there can be no doubt of the strength of Dissenting feeling for repeal this time. Excited meetings were held all over the county in 1827-28, and petitions rained in upon MPs from every corner of it. Significantly perhaps, besides Chandos, only T. T. Drake, secure at Amersham, opposed this tide of popular feeling. The other Bucks MPs voting all supported repeal—Smith for the county, Nugent and Rickford (Aylesbury), Dashwood King (Wycombe), George Smith (Wendover), and T. P. Williams (Marlow).[28]

But, while Bucks Dissenters were angered by Chandos' vote against repeal, many would have agreed with him on the other great question of civil and religious liberty then at issue. Many Dissenters shared his ardent opposition to Catholic emancipation, and his leadership of the high Protestant party, as such, would not have been an unattractive role. If his Protestant notions were attractive to Dissenters, they were also attractive to fellow Anglicans, like Dashwood King and Rickford (though both disagreed with him on the repeal issue) and others outside parliament, like Thomas Dell. On the other hand, Chandos' position on religious questions ran dead against the traditions of his family and the strongly held opinions of his father, his uncle, Lord Nugent, and his great-uncles. But for Chandos this was probably a recommendation, rather than a cause for dismay.

In 1827 the Duke of Buckingham remarked of his son: 'Chandos thinks himself the head of a Protestant Party instead of his Father's.'[29] So far as Bucks was concerned, it would probably be truer to say that Chandos became the head of the Protestant party so that he could head the Grenville interest and lead the county in his father's stead. There can be no doubt whatever that he pursued the latter objectives. And, if he did not take up the 'malignant cry' (as his father had called it in 1807) that had condemned his family to years in the political wilderness and shaken its influence in the county, to advance those objectives he could hardly have chosen a better one. For the first—but by no means the last—time, Chandos appealed to popular opinion to advance his political ends.

The duke and his son had never got on well, but for four or five years after the latter's first election for the county in 1818, when he had just turned twenty-one, political differences were not added to personal ones. By 1823 however Chandos was causing the duke considerable embarrassment by absenting himself on a number of important issues, because, W. H. Fremantle reported to the angry father, 'he is hampered & connects all these questions with Catholic emancipation . . .'[30] In 1825 the split became open. Chandos not only did not stay away from the debates on Sir Francis Burdett's Catholic emancipation bill in April and May—he appeared and twice recorded his vote against emancipation, in opposition to Fremantle and the rest of his father's connexion.[31]

The rejoicing in some Bucks circles was great. The Rev Mr Dayrell wrote:

> I will give my Vote at an ensuing Election with all my heart to Lord Chandos, for the County, because he is I verily believe a staunch Churchman—And if I cd throw Lord Nugent out for Aylesbury I would do it most cordially—he is such a decided Radical.[32]

But the duke was placed in a terrible quandary. On his death in 1839 his cousin Lord Braybrooke put his finger on what had always been the duke's great guiding principle:

> The poor Duke amongst his many good qualities inherited one from his father which I always admired, that of an anxious wish to keep well with all the numerous members of the Family . . .[33]

This may have been all very well for his father; but for him, with his son pulling in one direction and his brother in exactly the opposite direction, the strain was almost unbearable. Yet the duke

clove to his family—all of them, the dead as well as the living—
until his dying day. Nugent almost begged to be repudiated at
Aylesbury, but the duke would not do it; and in the end Nugent
had simply to declare himself independent of his brother's
support.[34] As for Chandos, however much he had hurt and insulted
the duke, however extravagant his demands on his father's
strained resources, here too the duke could never bring himself
to a definitive breach. The consequences for Bucks politics in the
twenties were bizarre.

Chandos seems to have begun his popular politicking early. In
1822 the young Sir Thomas Fremantle complained to his uncle:
'If we were farmers & clowns, instead of gentlemen, we might
have a chance of being favoured with his company.'[35] And in
1824 a ball and dinner for a thousand people at Stowe to celebrate
the christening of the young Earl Temple[36] launched a series of
extravagant entertainments that were to be a prominent feature
of Chandos' electioneering for the rest of his political career.
This great event coincided with the yeomanry exercises and
annual races at Stowe, which in future would almost always be
accompanied by dinners for hundreds, if not thousands. Chandos
spent a great deal of time and money courting popularity, and he
was not unsuccessful. He seems to have had a considerable talent
for popular politics. His worst enemies conceded that he had
immense charm when he chose. And there is no doubt that he
had an eye for popular issues.

With opposition to Catholic emancipation, an excellent choice
for his purposes, he was further aided by the fact that his father,
in order to reduce expenses and recover from financial difficulties
that stemmed in large part from Chandos' extravagance, set off
on his yacht in June 1827 for an extended cruise in the Mediter-
ranean. He was away until the end of 1829, with Chandos serving
as Vice-Lieutenant—and continuing his reckless expenditure![37]
Thus throughout the most intense agitation of the emancipation
question, while Chandos led the Protestant party in the Commons,
helped to direct the application of public pressure through the
Brunswick Clubs, and presided over the founding of one in Bucks
at the end of September 1828 (the second provincial club to be
formed[38]), the duke could only protest from a distance and after
the event—usually, of all places, from Rome! (The vicar of West

Wycombe firmly believed that the duke was negotiating for a cardinal's hat![39])

The climax of these extraordinary events was a great public meeting at Buckingham in February 1829 to oppose Catholic emancipation. The meeting was of the three neighbouring hundreds. In a letter to Lord Nugent received at the beginning of the month the duke had, Sir George Nugent reported to Sir Thomas Fremantle, enclosed one to his agent 'Parrott, which he [Lord Nugent] is to deliver himself & which gives him positive Directions to prevent his Tenants from attending any County or other Meeting . . .' But he had not expressly forbidden meetings of the hundreds—which is hardly surprising, as no one had ever thought of them before—so Chandos simply substituted four of these for one county meeting.[40] And on the morning of the Buckingham meeting he rode in from Wotton at the head of a party of some 300 'gentlemen or farmers' who had breakfasted with him, to be received by a cheering crowd of some 3,000.[41]

In fact, save for the clerical ones, the gentlemen were not conspicuous. The meeting was chaired by George Morgan of Biddlesden, and the Rev Mr Dayrell's brother, Richard, of Padbury, was there, but neither were major landowners in the area.[42] Sir Alexander Croke, a distinguished admiralty lawyer, and Major Macdonald, a retired naval officer now an officer in the yeomanry, were also in attendance. Beyond them, Philip Bartlett, 'Esq' was a large tanner in the town; and George Nelson, 'Esq' was a former clerk who had been taken into the partnership in the bank headed by Bartlett's brother, Edward. Both the latter were old opponents of Chandos' father. Edward Bartlett and Nelson had had the temerity to oppose one of the duke's candidates for the corporation some years before, and Bartlett seems to have resigned subsequently; but Nelson had stayed on. Nor did he join Chandos, Dayrell, and another member of the corporation who resigned at an 1827 by-election rather than vote for the duke's pro-Catholic candidate, Sir Thomas Fremantle— Nelson simply refused to vote for Fremantle. The only other laymen noted as present were Lord Nugent, advocating his brother's views and twitting the town on having two pro-Catholic MPs, and Mr P. Box, auctioneer, who replied that the burgesses might well rectify their mistakes at a subsequent election.

Nugent alone opposed the petition against concessions to the Catholics. He invoked the memory of his dead father and the authority of his live brother, but all to no avail. Chandos had claimed ninety-seven petitions from Bucks, with above 7,000 signatures. Nugent ridiculed these claims, charging that paupers had been bribed to sign and that names had been duplicated and even forged. In any case, Nugent claimed, few people of consequence had lent their support. Chandos more or less admitted the latter allegation, but, he said, the 'mass of people' were behind him.

The duke was beside himself with fury—and anguish. As he wrote to Sir Thomas Fremantle:

> . . . *Whilst I live* I will maintain my father's fair fame and the principles of my family, let them be attacked by whom they may. No one can accuse me of having intemperately or hastily interfered with my Son's political sentiments or opinions. But when he breakfasted and headed my own tenantry and brought them under the walls of my own house to hold up my principles and those of my family to the detestation of the County, it was high time to shew that *I was still alive*.[43]

He showed that he was still alive by writing a letter addressed to the 'Gentry, Clergy, and Freeholders of the Hundreds of Buckingham, Ashendon, and Cottesloe,' which was published in the local newspapers on 11 April. In it he made his sentiments crystal clear, and made it clear as well that no one who wished to remain his friend would have anything to do with anti-Catholic activities.[44]

All the meetings were over, and the resolutions passed. But it is difficult to believe that anyone who opposed emancipation had ever been in any doubt that he was acting in defiance of the duke. His principles were well known. He had reiterated them in his letter of instructions to his agent.[45] But many seem not to have cared. When Nugent appealed to the tenantry to remember his brother's principles (and, with the family weakness for maudlin sentimentality, the principles of their old master his father, whose casket they had together followed to its grave on this very day sixteen years before) he was booed for his pains. Doubtless the fact that the duke's son led the rebellion made it easier, but it was rebellion none the less. The discreet would have stayed at home, as some of their betters did.

Sir Thomas Fremantle and his father-in-law, Sir George Nugent, MPs for Buckingham, had not appeared at the meeting to support Nugent. They had no desire to get involved in the family squabble. Furthermore, as Sir George delicately reminded Lord Nugent, 'in all other respects I have constantly been of what is called Tory Principles'. And, speaking of Chandos, Sir George went on to say: 'In all other political Questions I should probably agree with him in Principles (as I think his Father would also) . . .'[46] Sir George had no intention of compromising the party interest in the county.

Nor did anti-Catholic views get much more support among the nobility and gentry of the county as a whole than they had received at Buckingham. Most of the Protestant party would probably have appeared at the great Brunswick Club dinner on 21 October 1828, when the club was publicly launched.[47] Great claims were made. It was asserted that the club had 1,200 members, forty-five per cent of whom were present at the dinner. Thirty-five were supposed to have been magistrates of the 'county and towns'—a vagueness that was probably significant. The figures for total attendance at the dinner were largely confirmed by a hostile observer, who counted 457. But the suggestions that the club had the support of the majority of the nobility and gentry of Bucks drew from the editor of the *Buckinghamshire Chronicle* the dry comment that 'Lord Kirkwall of Ireland, Sir John Chetwode of Staffordshire, and Mr Grubb, of the landed interest, and Captains Badcock and Baldwin, half-pay RN' did not quite add up to that! This was unfair, but only a little. Lord Kirkwall was the heir of the Earl of Orkney, who had only a house and about an acre of pleasure grounds at Marlow. Sir John Chetwode of Chetwode, though he lived mainly in Staffs, had some seven hundred acres of Bucks land. And Mr Grubb actually existed, though as was perhaps being unkindly suggested, the parish of Horsenden which he owned produced only the votes of Grubb and a friend. In addition, John Blackwell Praed of Tyringham, one of the family of London bankers and Bucks landowners and subsequently MP for the county, was at the dinner; as were Sir Alexander Croke and Robert Sutton of Cholesbury, the gentleman farmer who was later to found the Bucks Agricultural Society. Beyond these, Sir John Dashwood King, a most important addition, would have been in the vice-presidential chair had illness not prevented him. But most of the thirty-five magistrates claimed must have been clergymen, and magistrates of the towns, who did not enjoy the prestige of members of the county bench.

All in all, it was not a terribly impressive showing of landed influence behind the anti-Catholic cause. It is true that other prominent anti-Catholics did not join the club, probably because they did not wish to associate themselves so closely with Chandos —the Drakes, because of their proud independence, Rickford and Col. William Clayton, because they were Whigs, and Thomas Dell, for both reasons. Still, though these names add interesting complexities, they do not greatly alter the heavy balance of landowning influence against the Protestant party. Ultra squires would seem to have been few and far between in Bucks; and the movement was largely a popular one, or, at any rate, made up of elements below the gentry. Certainly the evidence of great public meetings in Aylesbury, in Wycombe, and in Marlow, as well as the flood of petitions from all over the county, strongly suggest that for the 'mass of people', Chandos' was indeed the popular side of the question.

As Sir George Nugent had predicted, the breach in the Tory ranks in the county did not long outlast the settlement of the emancipation question. The duke's anger with his son never lasted long, and, as Sir George had remarked, on all other questions, the duke, his son, and the rest of the party were generally agreed. Thus the Grenville party was firmly united behind the marquis' candidacy in the following year. The Whigs too were largely re-united, with Rickford seconding Smith's nomination. Dashwood King, it is true, as a leader of the Protestant party in the county, nominated Chandos, as he had nominated the anti-Catholic Titchfield in 1807; but, on the other hand, he remained true to the principle of parliamentary reform, which he had supported at least since 1810. But, though the latter question had already been raised early in the year, it did not dominate the election. The question that occupied the candidates almost exclusively at the nomination on 5 August 1830 was the abolition of slavery. Smith stated his unequivocal support for abolition; and Chandos, clearly attempting to trim his sails before a popular wind, protested his own desire for the same end, so long as it was achieved with fairness to all parties. Since there were only two candidates, there was no opportunity for the electorate to indicate its opinions on this occasion. But contests were not far off, as parliamentary reform quickly moved to the centre of the political stage from which the Catholic cause had recently made its triumphant exit.

The juxtaposition of the two issues raises the question of their connexion, discussed several years ago by Professor D. C. Moore. The time has come to examine 'the other face of reform' in Buckinghamshire. As I understand Professor Moore, his contentions would run something as follows. Too much attention has been paid to the 'urban' agitation for parliamentary reform, and not enough to the 'country' agitation which pre-dated it and in the end was more influential. This 'country' agitation is seen most clearly in the counties, where effective opinion time out of mind had been that of the landed classes (ie the aristocracy and gentry). It was elements of this opinion that created a parliamentary reform movement in the summer and autumn of 1829. The prime movers were the ultra-tories who, already infuriated by government monetary policy and tampering with the Corn Laws, found Catholic emancipation the last straw. The governments which had perpetrated all these iniquities had been able to do so because of the support of that relatively small group of noble borough patrons and other boroughmongers. The only solution was a reform of parliament which would eliminate the rotten parts of the constitution and put power where it belonged—in the hands of the landed classes as a whole.

In the endeavour to bring about such a reform, the ultra-tories were joined by the 'rural' Whigs, and together they formed a 'country party'—and not surprisingly it was this 'country party', much more congenial and understandable to them than the urban radicals, to whom the aristocratic Whigs listened and whose political influence they attempted to strengthen in their reform bill. More than the 'urban middle classes', then, it was the 'country party' ('these squires') who were responsible for the triumph of reform, and they certainly profited much more by it.[48]

This, as I understand it, is Moore's position. I must confess there are things in it I do not understand, and to remove all ambiguity, I might comment upon them. What does he mean, for example, by 'urban middle classes'? I am not sure, but I think he would exclude—and I certainly would—anyone one would have met in the market towns of Buckinghamshire (Wycombe, the largest, had a population of only 6,300 in 1831). I understand what he means by ultra-tories: those concerned with cash, corn and Catholics. I am not sure, however, what a 'rural' Whig was, though, presumably, it was someone who was concerned with cash and corn, but not with Catholics (ie not opposed to emancipation). Having constructed what I hope is a reasonable approximation of Professor Moore's model, so far as I understand it, how does it apply to Bucks?

The answer is, not very well. The iniquitous support of government by members for pocket boroughs, for example, would hardly have been overwhelmingly apparent to Bucks residents. Buckingham, it is true, was controlled by a great boroughmonger, and its MPs did support emancipation. But Amersham was a pocket borough whose patron-members' views closely approximated those of Moore's alleged 'country Party'. The Drakes were concerned both about the easing of the Corn Laws in 1828 and Catholic emancipation in 1829. (As I have already suggested, no one in Bucks was concerned about 'cash'.) The Williamses of Marlow voted for emancipation—but they were members of the Whig opposition. The MPs for Wendover split on the emancipation question; Abel Smith opposed emancipation, while his brother, George, voted for it. The members for Wycombe also split, Baring voting for emancipation and Dashwood King against (though they were, in fact, the nominees of a close corporation, contemporaries were apt to class the two MPs as patrons[49]). And, if anyone still thought that Nugent was his brother's nominee at Aylesbury, he of course voted for emancipation, while Rickford voted against it.

If the flunkeys of governments that offended against ultra susceptibilities on cash, corn and Catholics were not numerous among Bucks MPs, neither do the issues themselves seem to have been uppermost in the minds of Bucks reformers. Certainly no ultra 'squires' appeared at the 'very large and respectable meeting of agriculturists and tradesmen residing at and in the neighbour-

hood of Aylesbury' in February 1830, which was close to being
a county meeting—certainly as close as Bucks ever got to one
during the parliamentary reform agitation—and was undoubtedly
a part of Moore's 'country' reform movement. The meeting was
chaired by John Churchill, grocer. The five resolutions, embodied
in a petition, were moved by Thomas Dell, brewer. A farmer and
corn merchant, a surgeon, and another farmer who called himself
a 'yeoman' (he meant a substantial freeholder) also spoke; and
the latter gave a rousing anti-aristocratic, anti-clerical speech, in
which he attacked the game laws, tithes, and absentee landlords.
It is safe to say that he at any rate was not the pawn of ultra
squires! Lord Nugent concluded the proceedings with high
compliments for the radical Mr Maydwell, and jibes, greeted
with much laughter and applause, at the 'reformers of the
Quarterly Review' (ultras?).[50]

None of the five resolutions speak to any of the supposed ultra
concerns. They demanded a reduction of taxation and a reform
of the abuses that it was believed contributed to the crushing
burden—pensions and sinecures, and bloated army and navy
establishments. These latter were once again, as in 1816, denounced as subversive of a free constitution. There was a demand
for a revision of the existing laws so that there could be a more
equitable contribution by *all* property towards the poor-rates.
And, finally, there was a call for a reform of parliament, made
necessary, the petitioners said, by the 'apathy and indifference
with which their petitions are received', which they attributed
to 'the notoriously corrupt and imperfect state of the representation . . .'

Most of the demands give no conclusive proof of the broader
political allegiance of the petitioners. Though a few years before
such notions would have been whiggish, by this time concern for
a reduction of swollen national expenditure and the belief that
much of it sprang from enormous corruption were no longer
Whig monopolies. Neither is there any significance in the concern
about the poor-rates, beyond the fact that they were undoubtedly
a heavy burden in Bucks and counties like it. The strictures on
large military establishments is another matter. Their alleged
threat to liberty had been a Whig cry since 1815, and Lord Nugent
had led the halloo. In this, as in all political questions, Nugent

had taken great pains to educate and inform his constituents, with effects that had been evident since 1816. His arguments had clearly convinced the sixty-four men who signed the requisition for the meeting in 1830, and a study of these individuals throws added light on the question of the validity of Professor Moore's assumptions.

The list of requisitioners is especially valuable in that many whose names appear on it had also expressed their views on the question that provided the touchstone of true ultra opinion— Catholic emancipation. On this question too, Nugent had apparently been persuasive, in Aylesbury if not at Buckingham. At a meeting of several hundred of Nugent's supporters before the 1826 election, John Gibbs, the Independent pawnbroker and auctioneer, had said:

> His Lordship was the advocate of general liberty, and particularly in the cause of religion. He (Mr Gibbs) was aware that a particular point—the Catholic Question—had been much contested; and, though on that head, had he had the same opportunity, he might probably have voted contrary to his Lordship, he still admired him for his consistency and liberality.[51]

That consistency and liberality continued. In May 1827, in pledging general support to Canning, Nugent specifically reserved his freedom to press two questions on which he disagreed with the new premier, parliamentary reform and repeal of the Test and Corporation Acts.[52] And Nugent showed his willingness to embarrass both Canning and the Whigs, who mostly joined or supported him, by appearing at a large meeting at Aylesbury at the beginning of June called to petition for repeal.[53] Nugent was indeed consistent in his liberality, and by 1829 he would appear to have converted Gibbs fully to his views.

At any rate when a requisition appeared at the end of February for a meeting to oppose emancipation, Gibbs' name appeared on a list of the friends of 'civil and religious liberty' who opposed such a meeting and called on those who believed in 'universal liberty of conscience' to sign a counter-petition.[54] Most who signed were, like Gibbs, Dissenters. John Rolls' name headed the list, that of the Rev William Gunn was not far behind, and the names of most of the prominent Dissenters in the town followed. Their stand was, so far as any significant body of opinion (as opposed to isolated individuals) was concerned, unique not only among Bucks residents generally, but among Bucks Dissenters. But, for present purposes, the information given by the two lists, of friends and opponents of emancipation, is invaluable. The friends of 'universal liberty of conscience' clearly were not ultras; the opponents of emancipation may have been.

SIGNERS OF THE REQUISITION FOR THE FEBRUARY 1830 PARLIAMENTARY REFORM MEETING

	Occupation	Votes in Parliamentary Elections		
		1831	1832	1835
Signers Anti-Cath Req (27 signed)				
	Publican	Ref	Ref	Ref
	Gentleman	NV	Ref	Ref
	Clergyman	Ref	dead	
	Grocer (John Churchill)	Ref	Ref	Ref
	Gentleman	Ref	Ref	Ref
	Miller	Ref	Ref	Ref
	Innkeeper	Ref	NV	Tory
	Brewer (Thomas Dell)	Ref	Ref	dead
	Brickmaker & farmer	Tory	Tory	Tory
	Coal Merchant	Ref	Tory	Tory
	Unknown	NV or dead		
	Unknown	NV or dead		
	12			
Signers Pro-Cath Handbill (34 signed)				
	Farmer	Ref	Ref	Ref
	Currier	Ref	Ref	Ref
	Schoolmaster	Ref	Ref	Ref
	Solicitor	Ref	NV	Ref
	Ironmonger	Ref	Ref	Ref
	Publican	Ref	Ref	Ref
	Cabinet-maker	Ref	Ref	Ref
	Auctioneer (John Gibbs)	Ref	Ref	Ref
	Draper	Ref	Ref	Ref

Occupation	Votes in Parliamentary Elections		
	1831	1832	1835
Farmer (Abraham Wing)	Ref	Ref	Ref
Brewer (John Dell)	Ref	Ref	Ref
Cabinet-maker	NV	NV	NV
Unknown	NV	NV	NV

13

Others

	1831	1832	1835
Watchmaker	Ref	Ref	Ref
Esquire (farmer)	Ref	Ref	Ref
Esquire (farmer)	Tory	NV	NV
Esquire (grazier)	Ref	NV	Ref
Gentleman (china dealer)	Ref	Ref	Ref
Gentleman (solicitor)	Ref	dead	
Gentleman (W. B. Eagles)	Ref	Ref	Ref
Wine Merchant (Robert Dell)	NV	NV	NV
Carpenter	Tory	Tory	Tory
Collarmaker	Ref	Ref	Ref
Farmer	NV	NV	Ref
Farmer	Tory	Tory	Tory
Farmer	Tory	Tory	Tory
Grazier	Tory	NV	Tory
Grazier	Tory	NV	NV
Farmer	NV	Ref	Tory
Farmer	Ref/ Tory*	Ref	Ref
Farmer	Tory	Tory	Tory
Unknown	Tory	NV or dead	
Unknown	Tory	NV or dead	
Grazier	NV	NV or dead	
18 Unknown	NV or dead		

39

Totals of those voting		1831	1832	1835
	Refs	26½*	23	24
	Tories	10½	6	9

KEY—Ref, Reformer; NV, not voting.

*The elector voted for two Reformers in the borough and plumped for the Tory candidate in the county.

But there is one further means of checking the accuracy of Moore's views. He seems to suggest that many 'country'—as opposed to parliamentary—ultras still supported reform in the persons of pro-Bill candidates at the general election of 1831. In Bucks prominent 'Protestants' mostly opposed the Bill, and candidates who supported it, because of the reduction of the number of English members, which would result in increased Irish, and thus Catholic, influence; and, though oddly enough Moore ignores it, this would seem a sensible position for an ultra to have taken. At any rate, it is highly unlikely that any ultra would have continued to support Reformers in 1832, after the ensuing reform agitation and the anti-clerical form much of it had taken had raised fears for the safety of the Church. And it would have been a very peculiar ultra indeed who would have supported Reformers in 1835, after those fears seemed to be justified by threatened Whig depredations against the Irish Church, and Peel had just been brought in to save the Church's cause. Thus pollbooks for the county election of 1831 and borough elections of 1831, 1832, and 1835[55] provide useful additional information.

All this information has been brought together in the accompanying table. The evidence is clear and needs only brief comment. It is evident that anti-Catholics were well represented among the reformers, but their voting records show that only a couple could have held ultra opinions. The reforming enthusiasm of the friends of civil and religious liberty is at least equally evident (and the issues were probably much more closely connected in their case).

It is also clear that there were no ultra squires among the reformers. Indeed, in the usual sense of the word, there were no squires at all. J. T. Senior, the cattle breeder and grazier who would later become a member of the county bench, came closest. But though he was undoubtedly a 'gentleman' (he was related to the famous economist of the same name), he worked his own land and had no tenants. The two other 'esquires' had a tenant or two, but were not exactly 'gentlemen'. Both were working farmers (and the pollbooks sometimes describe them simply as 'farmer') who also rented some of the land they owned to other farmers. The gentlemen on the list were large tradesmen or farmers who had generally retired from the active pursuit of trade or farming. Some of the signers of the parliamentary reform requisition were large tenant farmers, like Richard Rowland, the famous grazier of Creslow. This probably includes most of those who, also like Rowland, do not appear in the pollbooks (if they were not freeholders they would not appear in the 1831 county pollbook, and most lived outside the borough boundaries).

To describe the leadership of the parliamentary reform movement in Aylesbury in a few words, then, one might say that it was drawn from prominent members of the middling classes, some of whom happen to have opposed Catholic emancipation. And far from being dominated by 'squires', ultras or any others, one of the primary motives behind the movement was an intense dislike of landed and all other sorts of exclusive influence. The 1831 Aylesbury borough election provides an example of the strength of this kind of feeling. From the time of the emancipation agitation, Chandos had bragged that his father was a cipher and the family influence his. And just before the duke's return to England late in 1829, Chandos told Sir William Fremantle that Lord Nugent must be turned out at Aylesbury, and that if the duke would not co-operate 'he Lord Chandos, would at any rate set up any man to oppose his Uncle, (this is certainly affectionate) . . .' But stronger family affections than those of Chandos prevailed. Fremantle believed that the duke would never be able to resist the pressure from his son, to which the duchess had added hers.[56] But resist he did, and in the general election of 1830 and a by-election late in the year caused by his appointment to the Treasury Board, his brother was returned unopposed. But, as the reform crisis grew, the duke retired more and more to Avington, his house near Winchester, brought up the guns from his yacht, and resolved to fight when the revolution came. While his father thus occupied himself, Bucks politics were increasingly left to Chandos, with only an occasional intervention from the duke. And in 1831 the marquis made good his threat to oppose his uncle.

There were two issues in the election. One was the question of parliamentary reform on which the government had dissolved. The other was the issue of Grenville influence. Chandos brought down his old Brunswick Club friend, Lord Kirkwall, to oppose

Nugent and the Reform Bill. Nugent denounced this 'combination, the most unnatural and tyrannical'. And it was tyranny to
which the Aylesbury electors did not propose to knuckle under.
Though the marquis appeared in person and led some hundred
faggot voters to the poll to cast their votes against his uncle,
Nugent was triumphant. Rickford, who got the second votes of
both parties (for reasons that will be examined in a later chapter),
headed the poll with 983, but Nugent was almost a hundred votes
ahead of Kirkwall, with 604 votes to 508. But this was not because
Nugent had great landed influence behind him; for among his
former staunch supporters, Sir John Dashwood King was neutral
on this occasion, Nugent's great friend Sir George Lee was dead
and the Hartwell influence now against him. Some large local
landowners, like the Cavendishes and Sir R. G. Russell of
Chequers, remained in the Nugent camp. But the great majority
of the 'esqs' and 'gents' among his supporters were of a kind we
have met before, brewers, surgeons, solicitors, large farmers etc—
and they supported Nugent because he supported the Reform Bill
and 'abhorred Aristocratic influence.'[57]

Abhorrence of aristocratic influence, as well as other sorts,
played an important part in reforming sentiment all over the
county, and gave it a keen local edge. The residents of Buckingham
deeply resented a corporation made up of the duke's flunkeys and
excluding all the leading townsmen. Many substantial inhabitants
of Wycombe had very similar feelings about the close corporation
of that town, though it was Whig and returned two Reformers in
1831.[58]

A similar sentiment flowed strong even in Marlow and helped to
break the Williamses' hold on that borough. In 1826 an opposing
candidate, James Morrison a wealthy Londoner, had been
introduced through the good offices of Wooler, the editor of the
Black Dwarf. The story was that Wooler was simply passing
through Marlow, which seems unlikely; but I can substitute no
more satisfying account. Morrison would seem to have had good
radical credentials, John Bowring and other prominent London
radicals coming down to support him. He also received the support
of several leading local tradesmen and Dissenters. Though he was
defeated, he made a creditable showing, with ninety-nine votes to
T. P. Williams' one hundred and twenty-eight. The frightened

Williamses thereupon clamped down and began a policy of whole-sale eviction of the disobedient. Morrison assisted the evicted and continued to stir the troubled waters for a while. But the ultimate beneficiary was a neighbouring Whig gentleman, Col William Clayton of Harleyford, son and heir of Sir William Clayton a former MP for the borough. Clayton took up the Morrison cause and was taken up by the Morrison party. Though it was Sir William's sale of houses to the Williamses around 1790 that had established their influence in the borough, the Claytons retained a good deal of property in the town as well as around it, which was now put to good use. Clayton received 171 votes to T. P. Williams' 192 in 1830, and 187 (170 plumpers) to Williams' 192 in 1831. In the last election Owen Williams was only four votes ahead of his son; and when the elder Williams died shortly afterwards Clayton was allowed to assume the seat without a contest. Reforming sentiment and hatred of the Williams' influence, and Clayton's own influence and money, combined to give a reform candidate a seat for Marlow.[59]

Reforming sentiment in Bucks, then, far from being a product of the discontents *of* the landed classes, was rather largely a product of discontent *with* the landed classes, springing from an intense resentment against landed influence; though the resentment extended to all sorts of exclusive influence, of close corporations, for example. Anti-Catholicism—but in the middling rather than the upper classes—probably played a part in the building up of discontent. The reforming party in Aylesbury would seem to have been unique in its pro-emancipation views. As has been seen, local opinion in Buckingham was strongly against the duke's pro-Catholic views. The pro-Catholic views of the Williamses were likewise resented in Marlow, where Clayton gave a lead to a vigorous Protestant sentiment, as well as to the reforming party. On the other hand, in Wycombe, which seems to have been pretty well united in its anti-Catholicism, Baring's vote for emancipation did not deprive him of the town's continued support. Nor did Dashwood King's Protestant opinions save him from the town's wrath when he refused to support the government's Reform Bill in 1831, and the violent reaction both of the corporation and of public opinion caused him to stand down in the election of that year. And even where anti-Catholicism was an important element in discontent, it was not the only, nor the most critical, issue. In Buckingham, for example, though prominent anti-Catholics like the Bartletts and Geroge Nelson played a leading part in the anti-Grenville, pro-reform coalition, the issue that dominated in 1831 and 1832 was the abolition of slavery. Anti-Catholicism was but one issue among several.

To sum up, it would appear that 'the other face of reform' in Bucks is an hallucination. The reform movement was not primarily a movement of the gentry, ultra or any other sort. There were anti-Catholic gentry in Bucks, but, save for Chandos, the most prominent were Whigs—Dashwood King, Rickford and Clayton—though in this Bucks was probably unusual. And, if there were few ultra gentry, neither would there seem to have been much that can meaningfully be called ultra opinion. Though there were anti-Catholics among the reformers of the middling classes who were the backbone of the movement, many were probably Dissenters—and ultra-tories were High Anglicans as well as High Protestants. Not all anti-Catholics, of course, were Dissenters, and by no means all reformers were either. But, as the Rev John Morley, the vicar of Aylesbury, who chaired the great reform meetings in the crises of March 1831 and May 1832 and played a prominent part in the formation of an Aylesbury Independent Union in October 1831, said of himself, 'he had ever been a whig'.[60]

We shall briefly return to Professor Moore in the next chapter, when we discuss the implications of his notions of party, in general, and specifically in Bucks in the context of the important 1831 county election. His ideas on the genesis of parliamentary reform, however, can be dismissed from our minds at once, so far as Bucks is concerned. The model—and a careful reading of his evidence will, I think, reveal that it is no more than that—is an intriguing one, but unfortunately, it bears no relation to reality.

Chapter 5 PROSPECT
AND RETROSPECT

In the preface to his study of politics in the age of Disraeli and Gladstone, Professor Hanham tells us that one of his themes is 'the contrast between the old political world of the counties and small towns, which looked back to the years before 1832, and the new world of the big industrial towns with their masses of working-class electors and their penchant for Birmingham Radicalism.'[1] Doubtless a contrast existed, but probably not of the sort Hanham envisions. In an ascending scale of genuine political activity and consciousness, he places the counties and the small towns before the 'provincial backwaters,'[2] and the contrast he clearly means to suggest is one between the old oligarchical politics that preceded 1832 and the more popular politics that followed, or were meant to follow. It is a contrast that is in the minds of most recent historians, but it may well be an imaginary one, and one that has led to a good deal of misunderstanding.

The main burden of work in the last twenty years is that much of the old system of oligarchical politics carried over into the period after 1832 and continued to be the dominant factor in English politics right up to the reforms of the mid-eighties. But in Bucks at any rate one does not find this kind of continuity. To the extent that they had ever actually existed, oligarchical politics had begun to weaken significantly before 1832. As has been seen, several factors contributed to the process. One was certainly the jealousy of aristocratic dominance by substantial people of the middling sort. The Dells of Aylesbury are an example of this kind of attitude from the beginning of the period dealt with in this book. It is manifested in Wycombe in the 1790s and in Buckingham and Marlow somewhat later. In its purest and most disinterested sense, the cry for 'Independence,' for the individual elector or for the borough, was a plea for freedom from aristocratic influence.

The men who talked about 'Independence' in this sense referred to themselves and were referred to by others as 'middling class' or some variation of that term. Hence it would not seem to be doing violence to the facts of the situation to describe one of the forces for change as, to use more modern terms, a middle-class desire for a recognition of what they conceived as their rightful place in the political system. But it was not only social tension that weakened the power of the landed oligarchs. Issues played a part as well. As has been seen, great national issues had been capable of influencing Bucks politics from the time of Wilkes. But not until the 1820s does their influence appear to have become fairly steady and consistent.

Doubtless this impression is heightened by the fact that local newspapers before this period have not survived; but it seems unlikely that even if they were available for earlier periods the broad picture would change much, though it would obviously be possible to trace the emergence of issues in local politics with much more confidence and precision. One could, for example, know more about the growth of a powerful Dissenting interest, which was an accomplished fact by 1820, and thus about the emergence of what was probably the most important force behind liberal and reforming movements from that time forward. As it is, one can only say that the appearance of political Dissent seems to have been the product of new Dissenting fervour and aggressiveness after about 1790 and of resulting conflicts with conservative Anglicans like the Lowndeses and other Bucks supporters of Sidmouth; that is, that political Dissent was a product of the stresses and strains created by the evangelical revival.

The new religious fervour doubtless also increased the zeal for another cause which had a strong appeal for the middling classes, Anglican as well as Dissenting. That was the movement launched in the mid-twenties for the abolition of colonial slavery, an issue which certainly heightened the dislike of the slave-owning Grenvilles' influence. That the two issues were connected in people's minds was illustrated by chants which often greeted Chandos in his 1831 canvass, in this case in Chesham. ' "No West India Chairman." "No slavery of any kind." "Down with borough-mongering." '[3] The other great religious issue that stirred the public during the period, Catholic emancipation, had contradictory effects. It undoubtedly increased the dislike of the pro-Catholic duke's control of the corporation in anti-Catholic Buckingham, and probably added to the opposition to the Williams influence at Marlow. But, as will be seen, it is very likely that the Catholic issue also strengthened the position of the duke's anti-Reform-Bill son in the 1831 county election, giving him supporters to whom his opposition to the Reform Bill would have been no recommendation.

All these issues of power and principle took a strong hold on Bucks politics in the twenties. Economic issues were also undoubtedly important, and, like the Catholic issue, they probably told in Chandos' favour. As has been suggested, 'cash' was not an issue in the twenties. Indeed if the 1816 Aylesbury petition is indicative of opinion on the question, the decision in 1819 to return to the gold standard was precisely what was desired in Bucks. As has been seen, one of the complaints in the petition was against 'the unnatural and mischievous operation of an artificial paper capital and currency.'⁴ In presenting the petition against the property tax shortly before, from 'persons interested in agriculture' in Aylesbury, Nugent had explained:

> They are in general graziers and dairy farmers who hold in their hands highly valuable old grass lands, at a very high rent, and who are obliged to stock their pastures with a very expensive sort of stock . . . They complain that they can neither make their rent, nor stock their farms. They are consuming their capital in the means of life.⁵

What they do not appear to have needed was cheap money to pay off debts they do not seem to have contracted!

But if 'cash' was not an issue in Bucks, 'corn' was. As Professor Spring has suggested, the reasons for its importance are highly complicated.⁶ Corn had never been as important in Bucks as in some counties, and it was growing increasingly less important. From the late eighteenth century onwards the tendency in Bucks agriculture was away from arable farming and towards grazing and dairying, particularly the latter. The area of the county lying in the Chilterns was an exception, its thin chalkland being unsuitable for much but corn; but in most of the county butter became the most valuable product in the first half of the nineteenth century. As a consequence, corn-growing became increasingly less crucial to the Bucks economy as the century progressed. It had, however, started out as fairly important, so it had some way to decline. In 1810 there were 184,000 acres of arable to 169,000 of meadow and pasture; and in 1862, it was still reckoned that about half the county consisted of arable farms (ie with not more than one-fifth of grassland).[7] Most Bucks farmers therefore would have had some interest in the Corn Laws. In the Chilterns it would have been a consuming interest; but even in the other two-thirds or so of the county most dairy farmers and graziers would also have grown some corn and thus have had a vested interest in the question. There can be no doubt that Bucks farmers were deeply concerned about it.

I agree with Professor Spring that the concern would probably not have been so great had Chandos not chosen to take up the issue. To be effective, popular movements usually still required the adherence and leadership of a leading county politician. But, if there was political advantage to be derived, such adherence and leadership was usually not long in making its appearance. Robert Smith's emergence as the champion of Dissent in 1820 is one example. And I think that, as he had done on the Catholic emancipation issue, Chandos once again sensed a good cry in the Corn Laws. As with emancipation, Chandos' advocacy of the Corn Laws had the distinct advantage of attracting allies who on other questions were suspicious of him, or strongly opposed.

The issue seems to have first emerged in 1826 when the government had released corn in bond to relieve the distress of the poor. Chandos had opposed this action as a threat to the principle of the Corn Laws. Sir John Dashwood King noted Chandos' stand with approval at the county elections of that year. T. T. Drake did not mention Chandos, but while dismissing the government's action on bonded corn as of minor importance, he told his constituents at Amersham that he would oppose any basic change in the existing law.[8] The next reference I can find to the question is in April 1829, when, at a meeting at the George Inn in Aylesbury, the radical Mr Maydwell protested against the alteration of the Corn Laws (ie the substitution of a sliding scale for a fixed duty in 1828), and the easing of the regulations on the importation of foreign

wool and, apparently as a consequence, talked of offering himself
as a candidate for the borough at the next election. [9] A cause which
could unite the whiggish Dashwood King, the independent Drake,
and Maydwell the radical 'yeoman' was one worth espousing, as
Chandos certainly realized. As will be seen, his Whig opponents,
to their cost, do not seem to have sensed its importance; and a large
part of the impressive Conservative success in the county and
boroughs in the eighteen thirties and forties must be attributed not
so much to Chandos' influence as to his political shrewdness.

   To a certain extent, as has been suggested, Chandos' stand on
the Catholic question had had a similar effect. For example, such
prominent anti-Catholics as Thomas Dell of Aylesbury and George
Nelson of Buckingham, who were also among the strongest of the
opponents of the Grenville influence in their respective boroughs,
served on Chandos' committee in the uncontested 1830 county
election; and though they did not serve on his committee in 1831
when he ran against two Whig supporters of the Reform Bill,
neither can I find that they voted against him; apparently they did
not vote at all. Two of the Bartletts, while bitterly opposing the
Grenvilles in Buckingham, actually plumped for Chandos in the
county election. And similar sentiments may account for similar
votes on the part of a number of humbler Buckingham electors,
and of some Aylesbury voters who split between Rickford and
Kirkwall (ie against the pro-Catholic Nugent) and then voted
Liberal in elections through 1841.

   This kind of split voting raises the question of the place of party
in Bucks politics. Many recent historians have tended to de-empha-
size parties, especially in the localities. Professor Moore, for
example, asserts that 'clearly defined parties . . ., as distinct from
factions, simply did not exist.' And in what he sees as a 'general
picture of non-party, factional politics' the organizing principle is
supplied by the influence of important individuals. True, he says
that issues were not entirely unimportant, but the picture which
he then proceeds to unfold seems to leave precious little room for
them. For example:

   Even in May 1831 when all of electoral England is supposed to
   have been divided on the Bill, a large proportion of pro-Bill
   candidates stood as individuals and were supported as individuals
   . . . In Buckinghamshire, as *The Times* of 10 May 1831 complained,

some two hundred voters whom they described as 'Smith votes'—
the name of a local squire—plumped for one of the two pro-Bill
candidates instead of polling for both. As a result of Smith's
instructions to his voters, and the instructions of others similarly
inclined, the county returned one pro- and one anti-Bill Member.[10]

Perhaps Moore was misled by *The Times*, but, as it happens, his
description of what happened is wrong in almost every detail, and
the election exemplifies the very opposite of what he intends. As it
was in many ways not untypical of county elections all through the
century, it is perhaps worth examining in some detail.[11]

John Smith was not a local squire. He lived in Sussex, though he
was the brother of Lord Carrington. More important, as it turned
out, he had been Lord John Russell's second-in-command in the
parliamentary struggle to repeal the Test and Corporation Acts in
1827–28, seconding Russell's motions and otherwise acting as his
trusted lieutenant. The other Reformer was Pascoe Grenfell, a
partner of the Williamses in copper mining and manufacturing and
long MP for Marlow. Grenfell was seventy years old and had
retired from parliament in 1826. He came forward again only a
week before the polling began, to give the electors an opportunity,
he said, to cast their votes for two Reformers; but he made it clear
that he would not put his family's inheritance at hazard by incur-
ring any election expenses. The third, and only Tory, candidate
was Chandos.

The polling commenced on Thursday, 5 May and Chandos had
a commanding lead from the beginning. For the first two days the
Reformers showed a high degree of unity, mostly splitting their
votes for Smith and Grenfell. On Saturday, however, with Chandos
still in the lead, Smith's supporters began to plump for him.
Grenfell's committee protested, and towards evening Smith's voters
began to split once again. But over the weekend Grenfell decided
the game was lost and withdrew on Monday, leaving Chandos and
Smith the victors. Chandos received 1,594 votes: 1,287 plumpers,
287 split with Smith, and 18 split with Grenfell. Smith received
1,284 votes, including 191 plumpers and 806 split with Grenfell.
Grenfell received 826 votes, only two of them plumpers.

The total number of electors casting votes in the election was
2,593; and of these 2,095, Chandos' plumpers and those who split
for Smith and Grenfell, gave a clear vote as between the supporters

and the opponents of the bill. That is, 81 per cent of those voting gave a 'party' vote, which seems rather too high a proportion to make one very confident about sweeping statements concerning the absence of party feeling. But how does one explain the 191 plumpers for Smith? Were they Lord Carrington's faithful retainers? Carrington's main estates lay in Wycombe and in the rural parishes of Bledlow and Bledlow Ridge, where he was the major landowner. Among some 125 Wycombe voters, there were only three plumpers for Smith; and not one among the twenty-six voters in Bledlow and Bledlow Ridge, who mostly followed Robert Smith in splitting their votes between his uncle and Grenfell. The largest number of Smith plumpers, eighty-two, came from the Newport Hundreds, where, as yet, the Smiths possessed little property. A characteristic the Newport Hundreds had, however, was a large Dissenting element, which had given the doughty champion of civil and religious liberty a warm welcome during his canvass—which suggests the most likely explanation for the strong support he received there.[12]

The main explanation for Smith's plumpers, then, seems rather different than Moore supposed. As has been seen above, the decision to plump came only after two days of polling during which Chandos had maintained a commanding lead. That is, the decision was taken only when it became evident that two Reformers could not be returned, and when the question thus became which one it would be. In these circumstances, Smith's close supporters, drawn mainly from the Newport Hundreds and including prominent Dissenters like James Millar, not surprisingly decided that it should be their candidate. Doubtless they were not deterred in making their decision by the fact that Smith and his committee, like Chandos, were spending a great deal of money. Among other things, they were paying to bring Grenfell's voters to the poll! At any rate, they were paying for most of them. Wycombe, which was a great centre of Reforming enthusiasm, sent some 200 electors to Aylesbury free of charge, but this was unusual.[13] Those who would be asked to subscribe towards Smith's expenses doubtless did not wish to make them higher than necessary.

The electors whose principles might be suspected to have been most flexible are the 305 (12 per cent) who split their votes for Chandos and a Reformer, all but eighteen for Smith. Doubtless the principles of some were pliable, like most of the fourteen Wendover freeholders who followed the lead of Abel Smith, Tory MP for the borough and brother of John Smith and Lord Carrington (whose Wendover property Abel Smith would soon acquire), who voted for Chandos as well as his brother. Some, however, certainly split their votes on principle—or, more precisely, because of conflicting principles. The most prominent person to do so was Rickford, whose Protestant principles conflicted with his reforming principles on this occasion. Others evidenced the same concern; for example, an elector who asked Grenfell at the nomination whether he would support that part of the bill that would 'reduce the number of English Protestant members.'

The fact that 139 of the Smith and Chandos votes came from the Aylesbury Hundreds might suggest Rickford's 'influence'. But if the word is used in the sense that the 'deferential' school usually use it, it is unlikely that this is the primary explanation. Rickford always stoutly maintained that even in borough elections he only asked his friends for one vote, leaving them quite free as to the use of the other; and, as will be seen in a subsequent chapter, in later elections his own tenants availed themselves of this freedom. Nor does the evidence of the pollbooks during this period suggest the existence of a Rickford 'faction' in the sense that Moore seems to use the word, that is, a group of electors unquestioningly following their leader's every political shift and turn.

Among electors who voted in all three Aylesbury borough elections between 1831 and 1835, there were fifty who demonstrated an especial preference for Rickford by giving him a plumper at at least one of those elections. Thirty-one of these electors also voted in the 1831 county election. Thirteen followed Rickford's lead on this occasion. Ten voted for both Reformers. Two plumped for Smith. One divided his vote for Smith and Grenfell. And five plumped for Chandos. It is impossible here, or from other evidence, to discern the existence of one of Moore's 'factions.' There was undoubtedly a group among Aylesbury Reformers who were Rickford's especial partisans and generally followed his political lead, but for many at least the explanation was simply that they shared his political views. This seems the most likely explanation of the split voting in 1831.

There were at least two good reasons why Bucks electors might have wished to give a vote to Chandos. One was Rickford's main reason for supporting the Marquis on this occasion, his strong Protestant churchmanship. Another, which also weighed with Rickford, was Chandos' continued vigorous advocacy of the 'agricultural interest.' The apparent popularity of parliamentary reform among the farmers might seem to weigh against the importance of this latter consideration in the 1831 election; but though Chandos was against the 1831 bill, he took great pains to make it clear that he was not against reform. As he told the electors at the nomination, and on many other occasions, he differed from his opponents 'in degree rather than in principle.' He favoured the extension of the franchise to large and populous towns and disfranchising boroughs proven to be corrupt. Indeed, he approved of many points of the government bill, and he had no doubt that a bill would be formed that would meet the 'approbation of constitutional reformers, of whom he was one.' Then the chairman of the West India Committee proceeded to tell the electors that he also favoured the abolition of colonial slavery! Since there is no reason to believe that Chandos was fired either with reforming or abolitionist enthusiasm, it would appear that he was bending to popular enthusiasm for those causes. Would anyone have taken him seriously? A number of electors in the agricultural and anti-Catholic county of Bucks might well have done. And so far as many of the parliamentary reformers, at least, were concerned, they would have had little cause to be disappointed by his performance: it was Chandos' clause, after all, that gave the vote to the tenant farmers.

The above survey of the 1831 Bucks county election suggests what I think are several of the errors in the approach of Professor Moore and those who agree with him. Moore contends that there was a lack of party voting, assumes that this indicates a lack of principle, and concludes that therefore the electors must have been behaving deferentially (as he would say, or—as I would term it— that they were under influence). As has been seen, the evidence for this election does not support either the contention, the assumption, or the conclusion. In fact, some 80 per cent of the electors gave a party vote, registering a clear preference between the supporters and the opponents of the bill. And principle is a much more likely explanation than influence for those electors who did not do so. There is every reason to believe that most of those who plumped for John Smith voted not for Lord Carrington's brother, but for the champion of the repeal of the Test Acts. The evidence on the split votes for Chandos is not so conclusive; but, in view of the fact that most of the 'gentry' had very strong views for or against the bill, principle seems a more likely explanation than influence. Thus, this particular example that Moore has chosen to illustrate his ideas, in fact, confounds all of his assumptions. And, as I shall attempt to demonstrate more fully in succeeding chapters, this election is by no means untypical in the evidence it gives on the questions of party, principle and influence.

I do not mean to suggest either that party was all important or that the elector always made his decision on the basis of principle, much less that influence was never important. I do, however, believe that the importance of landed influence has been vastly over-rated, more especially, if, as with Moore, 'influence' and 'control' often seem to be used interchangeably. Indeed I would go farther than that and say that of the three factors, landed influence, as such, was the least important. I would certainly not deny the importance of the fact that throughout the period with which this book deals large landowners—and pretty much they alone—provided political leadership in Buckinghamshire. But leadership is different from control. Effective leadership requires that influence flow upwards as well as downwards. There was probably no more successful practitioner of the art in the century and more that this study covers than the Marquis of Chandos, the great boroughmonger who became a 'constitutional reformer,' the owner of 300 slaves who became a moderate abolitionist. Chandos knew when to bend. This was part of the secret of his success. He also had a good nose for a popular issue, as he demonstrated in his opposition to emancipation and his support of the Corn Laws. These qualities, I think, and will attempt to demonstrate more fully in due course, were probably more important to his success than his broad acres and his army of tenants.

To return to the connexion between party, principles, and influence, I shall argue that such lack of party loyalty as existed among electors in the early and mid-Victorian periods can probably be explained in large part by countervailing principles and interests (as distinct from influences). At another level, this would seem to have been true of MPs. Though most historians would probably agree with Moore about the lack of party loyalty at the local level, some have recently demonstrated that there was a high degree of party loyalty in parliament.[14] And of particular interest to those studying politics in the localities are suggestions like those of Professor Aydelotte that when parties did fall apart, as the Conservative party did in the final Corn Law crisis, a large part of the explanation must be sought in constituencies exerting pressures on their MPs.[15] As will be seen, evidence in Bucks bears him out.

This raises a critical question that has never been considered seriously enough. If local pressures were capable of breaking up parties, might not such pressures also have been capable of influencing them and shaping their policies, particularly in an era before the detailed legislative programme, when governments and parties rather tended to respond to issues and pressures as they arose? Peel's Tamworth Manifesto issued before the general election of 1835 was clearly an attempt to bring his new Conservative party into line with what he believed to be electoral realities. The willingness to ease Dissenting disabilities and to embrace municipal reform particularly perhaps demonstrate Peel's political realism, and there can be no doubt that close political associates like Sir Thomas Fremantle at Buckingham felt the benefit in their own constituencies.

The influences that worked on national leaders cannot, of course, for the most part, be studied directly in a work like this one. What a study of local politics can illuminate is the influence of the electorate in shaping the attitudes of its own immediate political leaders, such as members and candidates, particularly towards issues that had not yet become party questions. There were, for example, no party positions on the Corn Laws until the 1840s, and then they changed with bewildering speed. And, while Whigs and Liberals were 'the friends of civil and religious liberty' and generally took a more favourable attitude towards the removal of Dissenting disabilities than the Conservatives, the extent of the national Whig leadership's commitment to religious liberty was often not very precisely defined. Yet, if one had to identify the most important and persistent issues in nineteenth-century Buckinghamshire politics, they would be these.

The question of Dissenting disabilities was of course inextricably connected with the position of the Established Church, and with the issue of Catholicism. I have already suggested the skill with which Chandos turned some of these issues to his own advantage in Bucks—and in the process helped to make them lively issues at the national level. But less distinguished backbenchers may have taken part in a similar process, pressing their leaders towards a position which would meet their own electoral necessities. In any case, there can be no question that it was often a candidate's skill in handling non-party issues that determined the outcome of individual elections.

It is at this point that I come to my main criticisms of the methods that have so far been used in attempts to understand early and mid-Victorian electoral behaviour. Professor Moore has studied county pollbooks in three or four counties. Professor Vincent has studied pollbooks over the the entire country.[16] But, though both have studied *pollbooks*, neither has studied *elections*. Both appear to assume that the party labels of the candidates tell all that needs to be known about issues—which is surely odd in Professor Moore—which means that their studies are based on a highly questionable assumption. Elections may not have turned on party questions, or, again, they may not have turned on the questions that were most agitating the parliamentary parties at that particular time. Professor Vincent is not unaware of the importance of local context, but his ambitious study cannot really take account of it, making his pages of statistics of highly questionable value. And, while Professor Moore studies localities, he manages to miss the most important part of the local contest—the precise issues on which a particular election was fought.

My other major criticism is one I have alluded to earlier in this work; that is that the methods of studying pollbooks that have been used thus far ignore individuals. Professor Vincent studies the voting habits of occupations. Professor Moore studies the voting habits of parishes. But it was electors who cast the votes, and to ignore this obvious fact can be dangerous. Take, for example, the case of some thirty electors in the parliamentary borough of Buckingham who plumped for Chandos in 1831. One might assume from such evidence that they were part of one of Moore's local electoral communities, taking its cue from the dominant local landowner—until one found the very same electors splitting their votes for a candidate the duke violently opposed, or refusing even one vote for his nominee, in the borough election of 1832! Thirty 'deferential' electors vanish before one's eyes.

So, it might be argued (in many cases correctly), do thirty 'Tory' voters, since most of them split for the Whig Verney in 1832. And, in fact, a study of Buckingham electors in the decade after 1832 would indicate few who voted on strict party lines. But there were good reasons for their not doing so—good party reasons. The Liberals in the parliamentary borough of Buckingham, for example, were never given the opportunity to support more than one Liberal candidate in a series of three-cornered contests, or threatened contests. But they used their second votes to make sure that the one Conservative elected would be the one most congenial to their views, the moderate Fremantle; and they used the promise of those second votes, or the threat to withhold them, to prevent Fremantle joining the Grenville schemes to squeeze out Verney and return two Conservatives.

Second votes, or third votes if one was a county elector as well, could have other uses. Some Buckingham electors appear to have believed in 1832 that they could retain the duke's favour by giving him one vote and using the other as they pleased. In this they were wrong; but there are indications that Grenvilles treated a borough voter who also had a county vote, which the marquis of course wanted, with more respect and did not retaliate if he used his borough votes in a way that displeased them. Certainly, this kind of splitting was not uncommon, one and the same elector giving one vote for principle, another for interest, and so on.

Equal opportunities might well bring similar results today; and what is probably more remarkable than the lack of party loyalty in the period is the high degree that in fact existed in the face of the very considerable opportunities for, and inducements to, compromise and cross-voting. As was seen in the last chapter, parties comprised of gentlemen and prominent members of the middling classes undoubtedly existed in the county and in Aylesbury from the 1820s. Much fuller evidence in the 1830s shows that such party loyalty was not confined to a few. About half the Aylesbury borough electorate, 639, appear in both the 1831 and 1835 borough pollbooks, proving that they were alive and voting during the period. Two hundred and thirty-six of these same electors also voted in the 1831 county election. The voting behaviour of these latter, then, can be tested in four elections—one county election and three borough elections, 1831, 1832, and 1845—the rest in the three borough elections. Of the 639, 217 (including eighty-three with county votes) voted only for Liberal candidates. Equally strict reckoning would produce only five Conservative voters! But, if one allows, as one must, split votes for Rickford in borough elections in which there was only one Conservative candidate, the number is 173 (including seventy-six who had county votes). In other words, 61 per cent voted loyally with their party—and this in a time of party transition, as will be seen.

This kind of evidence suggests that we would be unwise to dismiss local parties during the period too quickly from our thoughts. But perhaps I should define more precisely what I mean by a 'party.' For me it is sufficient if men think of themselves as belonging to a party (which usually means giving themselves a label), and, more important, act as if they did—which means acting together. All these requirements are met in Bucks from the 1820s. The aristocrats and country gentlemen who led the two parties called themselves Whigs and Tories. Before 1830 I cannot find that their supporters called themselves anything in particular—which did not, however, prevent their giving consistent support. Whig supporters then began to call themselves Reformers, and after 1832 increasingly Liberals, as did candidates. Tory candidates and their supporters, who were later in assuming a name, began to call themselves Conservatives from about 1835.

I have said nothing about organization, which I do not think a quintessential part of the concept of party. Doubtless effective organization would have made constituency parties more effective. Contemporaries were well aware of this, as a series of abortive attempts between 1832 and 1885 to create party machinery in Bucks constituencies proves. But, however useful, I do not think that organization is essential to a party's existence. In this I agree with Professor Vincent.[17] Where I disagree with him is in his notion that parties were a mid-Victorian creation. There were parties—and there was a Liberal party—long before 1857.

In Bucks all those who had called themselves Reformers before 1832 did not become Liberals after that date. A substantial number became Conservatives, or frequently supported Conservative candidates. Enough did so to create a clear trend towards Conservatism in the years from 1832 to 1846. In this, of course, Bucks was reflecting a tendency general in the nation; and the trend in Bucks can be explained largely in terms of national issues—the great issues of church and state, and the Corn Laws. Indeed there were few great national issues which might be expected to have touched the world of the counties and the small towns that did not touch Bucks. Not surprisingly, movements for factory reform did not; neither did Chartism. The Swing riots of 1830–31 might perhaps be expected to have had more impact than they did; for, so far as I can tell, they had no political impact at all, aside from allowing the *Bucks Gazette* to make sardonic comments on the military gyrations of Lord Chandos and the yeomanry. Perhaps 'Swing' added some impetus to demands for Poor Law reform, but those demands were already strident. And, not surprisingly, the more stringent and economical New Poor Law of 1834 was generally popular with the rate-paying electorate.

The issues that stirred Bucks were those that Peel touched on in the Tamworth Manifesto—municipal reform, church reform, and the further easing of Dissenting disabilities—and the issue that brought the same statesman down in 1846, the Corn Laws. These religious problems influenced and were influenced by the Catholic issue, which was further complicated by its Irish aspect.

Of these issues, the only one that perhaps needs comment at this time is the question of Dissenting disabilities. As has been seen, a militant Dissenting interest had emerged in Bucks in the previous decade. It was to grow more militant in the 1830s; and, as it was to become the backbone of Bucks Liberalism, it is worth pausing over some of its new concerns. It is interesting, and significant of the extent to which Bucks opinion was becoming part of a broader national opinion, that these concerns appear not to have had local origins.

In May of 1833 a new United Committee in London, similar to the one that had directed the repeal campaign, issued a list of grievances for which they sought redress. There were six: (1) the Marriage Act of 1753 which made only Anglican ceremonies legal; (2) Church rates, parochial rates levied from time to time by the vestries to maintain the Church fabric and furnishings;

(3) liability of Dissenting chapels to the poor rate; (4) the absence of civil registration of births, marriages, and deaths, making parish registers the main source of such information; (5) the lack of a clear legal right to burial in parish churchyards; and (6) exclusion from Oxford, Cambridge, and Durham. Of these the first three were declared the most important.

Save for the third grievance which was met fairly quickly by the removal of the liability of both churches and chapels to the poor rates, no progress was made on these demands in 1833. As a consequence, a national agitation began early in the next year. Bucks Dissenters were earlier than most, and apparently forward as well in the radicalism of their resolutions. Professor Gash believed that the earliest mooting of dis-establishment in the campaign came from a meeting of Dissenters at Manchester in March 1834.[18] But a meeting at Aylesbury on 18 February, with the Rev Mr Gunn in the chair, had commenced its proceedings by resolving that the alliance of Church and State was 'unscriptural and ought not to be allowed to continue.' Having stated this 'primary cause' of Dissenting difficulties, the meeting then proceeded to demand the removal of several more limited grievances. These were the same as those identified by the United Committee, with a couple of minor additions; and the same priorities were put upon them, save that a civil register of births and deaths had been moved up to take the place of the poor rate grievance.[19]

It seems likely that the principle of dis-establishment, which the Buckingham Dissenters espoused at just about the same time,[20] also had London origins, particularly as none of the immediate issues seem to have disturbed Bucks Dissenters until very recently. A Church rate—the question that was to persist the longest and be the most crucial—had, for example, been amicably approved by a vestry at Aylesbury as late as 1827—to pay for a loan negotiated by a Dissenting Churchwarden! It was never to happen again. There were other signs of a new rigidity and intransigence. The only notable addition which the Aylesbury meeting made to the list of grievances was a protest against the liability of Dissenters for the office of Churchwarden. This was particularly strange for Aylesbury Dissenters, as in the previous decade they had run their own candidate for the office, fighting hard and successfully for it on several occasions.

Whatever the source of the new demands, Bucks Dissenters adopted them as their own and vigorously advanced them. Both the demands and the vigour opened new and much wider breaches between Church and Dissent. For reasons that will be investigated in subsequent chapters, the new issues tended to become merged in an old and familiar one, the Catholic question. This was to be one of the two dominant issues in Bucks politics in the thirties. The other was one we have also met before, corn. There was a continuity of a sort with the period before 1832—but it was not the sort recent historians have imagined.

Chapter 6 CORN

IT MAY be as well to recall to the reader's mind the main provisions of the Reform Act that has aroused so much controversy. The act abolished some fifty boroughs, mostly nomination (or 'pocket') boroughs, and reduced the representation of thirty more by one member. Two pocket boroughs in Bucks, Amersham and Wendover, were in the former category, completely losing their existence as parliamentary boroughs. The seats vacated were divided up among other constituencies, new and old, throughout the United Kingdom. England got the lion's share, some 120, which were about equally divided between boroughs and counties. Most of the borough seats went to large towns previously without the franchise, and, not surprisingly, Bucks received no additional borough seats under the act. But precisely because Bucks was lacking large centres of commerce and industry, it was one of seven counties to receive a third member, the aim being to assure the agricultural interest of a block of MPs who would give it a clear voice in the House.

The government's stated intention in the redistribution of seats was to assure all interests, old and new, fair representation, without making any interest predominant. (It has yet to be proven I think that this was not more or less the effect, but it is not a question I can answer here.) The announced intention of new provisions for the individual franchise was to make the electors independent. This was to be achieved in several ways. In the boroughs the franchise was to be open to all who occupied premises (a building, or a building and land, but not land alone) of £10 annual value. The meaning of 'annual value' was not defined, which caused great difficulties in the revising barristers' courts set up to supervise the new electoral registers; but by the late 1840s a receipt for rent was taken as final proof for tenants. The occupier must have paid by a certain date in July all rates on the property. He was then eligible for the franchise. In the final analysis, however, it was the individual elector's responsibility to make sure that his claim came before the revising barrister who was empowered to place his name on the electoral register, and this was an annual process. In the counties the 40s freeholder remained eligible for the franchise, with several possible new qualifications added, the most important being that for £50 occupiers (of buildings and or land). Once placed on the electoral register, a county voter remained there unless he was successfully challenged before the revising barrister.

The £50 occupier clause, better known as the Chandos clause, was introduced by the marquis and carried against the strong opposition of the government. The 'farmers' friend' argued that it gave the tenant farmers a vote; the government spokesman claimed that, in effect, this would be more votes for their landlords. Other provisions of the act probably retained voters subject to influence or bribery on the electoral rolls. On the grounds of equity, all holders of the ancient borough franchise who were resident in a borough were to retain the franchise for their lifetimes. Residence was defined as living within seven miles of the borough's boundaries; and, as many boroughs were drastically enlarged, this could include a very large area. The enlargement of boroughs was to be another means of ensuring their independence. According to the government, no borough had been disfranchised where it had been practicable to extend its boundaries sufficiently to produce an electorate of approximately 300 £10 occupiers, which would supposedly be sufficient to the desired end.

The above are the main provisions of the act. Even in my hopefully simplified version, they are fairly complicated; and their complexity almost immediately produced a result that no one had intended. In the final analysis, the qualification to vote was inclusion on the electoral register. It therefore became an important object to politicians to get their friends on the register. This spurred local organisation, and in a couple of years this was followed by the beginnings of national organization with the founding of the great political clubs, the Carlton (Conservative) and the Reform (Whig-Radical). Like everything else connected with the act, the nature, extent, and significance of the new organization is hotly debated.

What were the effects of the act in Bucks? The answer is that it wrought an immense change. But the nature of that change is perhaps best appreciated by a glance at a constituency where in many ways the change was least great, Aylesbury. The borough's boundaries remained the extended ones of the 1804 act. The electorate was not appreciably increased by the addition of the £10 occupiers; in 1831, 1,150 polled; in 1832, the figure was up to 1,268; but in 1835 it had fallen to 1,212. There was, it is true, a change in those who made up these totals. A large number of out-voters (non-residents) were disfranchised. A number of £10 occupiers in the hundreds were given the vote for the first time. The result, especially of the disfranchisement of out-voters, was another blow to a Grenville interest still reeling from its recent defeat in 1831. Independent before 1832, the borough simply became more independent after 1832. Its character, however, was not radically altered. By and large, the same kind of middle-class (as I shall call them henceforward) electors indulged in the same kind of vigorous political activity that had characterized the borough since at least 1818. The great change wrought by the 1832 Reform Act was to create much the same kind of electorate in three other Bucks boroughs, which brought much the same kind of political life, and to eliminate the two where such changes were difficult or impossible.

Professor Seymour thought it strange that Wycombe should have retained its two members, while other boroughs like Amersham and Wendover lost both of theirs; and he believed that Whig party interest was the reason.[1] But this explanation is based on two misconceptions; for Wycombe was neither under Lord Carrington's control, nor was Lord Carrington a Whig, as Seymour assumed. In any case, Wendover, which Carrington did own, was not saved; while Buckingham, on the Tory Duke's doorstep, was. The most likely explanation for the decisions is the one the government advanced; those boroughs that could be reformed were, and those that could not be were disfranchised. Both Wendover and Amersham fall into the category of those that could not be reformed. Not only was Wendover an insignificant town, it lay squarely in the middle of the parliamentary borough of

Aylesbury, so that the requisite wealth and population could not be added by an extension of the borough boundaries. Amersham was in much the same position. Aylesbury's boundaries almost touched the town on the north, the extended boundaries of Wycombe almost reached it from the west, and an enclave of Hertfordshire lay to the south. The only convenient way to extend its boundaries would have been to the north-east, towards the estates of Lord George Cavendish at Chesham and the Duke of Bedford at Chenies—the direction to have gone if party advantage had been the aim!

The other boroughs though they retained their two members were otherwise changed beyond all recognition. Buckingham and Wycombe are both included in Professor Gash's list of 'extra-ordinary cases of enlargement.' Buckingham went from an area of 0.6 square miles before 1832 to one of 28.9 square miles afterwards; Wycombe from 0.2 to 9.8 square miles.[2] Marlow is not included in the list, but having been enlarged from the town itself to include a couple of miles of rural hinterland in every direction save south-east, it probably ought to have been. In short, all three became large rural boroughs.

Nor was the immense increase in physical size the most import-ant change, save perhaps for Marlow; there was an even more momentous change in the size and quality of the electorates. It is true that the £10 occupier franchise hardly produced enormous electorates in any of the boroughs. Buckingham only exceeded by twelve the desired minimum of three hundred electors by the first election under the new franchise.[3] And Wycombe with only 298 registered did not reach it.[4] Comparison with these figures makes Marlow's electorate of 450 look eminently respectable. Yet small though the electorates were, they represented a very marked contrast to what had gone before. The change in the size of the electorate was least in Marlow which had had two to three hundred scot and lot voters before 1832; and, as will be seen, the change in quality was also least there. In Buckingham and Wycombe, however, the difference made by the act can hardly be over-emphasized. Three hundred middle-class electors represented a dramatic change from the forty or fifty aldermen and burgesses who had returned Wycombe's members before 1832, and an even more dramatic change from the corporation of twelve that had returned

Buckingham's. The political consequences were less at Wycombe, where the members of the corporation had always been closer to the town in feeling and opinion, and managed to save much of their influence by a timely concession that restored the burgesses to their rightful place in the corporation. Wycombe remained what it had been before the Reform Act, a Whig town, whose whiggery was graced, from 1832-37, by having the son of Lord Grey as one of its MPs.[5] But the difference at Buckingham was that between night and day. Where once the duke's hand-picked corporation had dutifully registered his every political whim, the new middle-class electorate in 1832 returned the Whig Verney, who had scarcely an acre of land in the constituency, at the head of the poll in the teeth of the duke's violent opposition.[6] The Great Reform Act did not create a new kind of politics in Bucks, but it did generalise a kind of politics previously able to thrive only in the county, and the near-county constituency of Aylesbury. In this sense, the act was a decisive turning point.

Perhaps the best way to grasp the nature of reformed politics in Bucks is to begin by looking at Aylesbury politics in some detail; for not only are these extremely well documented, they were also central to much that went on in the county and other borough constituencies. Political events in the county town were bound to be given more publicity and assume more importance than happenings elsewhere. And Aylesbury's influence in the county was direct as well. The parliamentary borough of Aylesbury accounted for about one-fifth of the total area of the county and about one-fourth of the county electorate; and because of the old freeholder franchise in the hundreds the electorates were not only not dissimilar, but in part identical. The act, it is true, made a county and a borough vote on the same qualification no longer possible. But many voters could, and did, qualify themselves for both. (A farmer, for example, could qualify as a county voter on a cottage he owned, and for the borough on a farm he rented.) Aylesbury politics were critical in county politics; and shortly after the passage of the Reform Act, Aylesbury politics took a critical turn.

In July 1832 Lord Nugent, long in severe financial straits, jumped at the government's offer to make him Lord High Commissioner of the Ionian Islands and prepared to vacate his seat for Aylesbury.[7] But when announcing Nugent's appointment, the

Bucks Gazette also promised that 'the electors may rely on it that
a candidate will be presently in the field, whom Lord Nugent
himself would nominate without hesitation.' This meant a Whig of
a radical stamp. The first candidate mentioned, Denis Le Mar-
chant, Brougham's private secretary as Lord Chancellor, proved
unable to stand. The one finally settled on was T. B. Hobhouse,
the young half-brother of the Radical secretary at war, Sir John
Cam Hobhouse.

The Tories charged that Hobhouse was Nugent's 'nominee';
but, as he quite rightly replied, 'his Lordship's influence, it was
well known, was not the influence of wealth . . .; it was the legitimate influence of persuasion and reason.'[8] That Nugent's influence
did not rest on money had recently been made embarrassingly
clear, when on the occasion of his last election, his canvass through
the town had been accompanied by dunning tradesmen—doubtless urged on by his fond nephew—loudly demanding payment.
That his 'legitimate influence' had been great had been proven
most dramatically perhaps by the fact that almost alone among
Bucks Dissenters and residents generally Nugent's party at Aylesbury had supported Catholic emancipation in 1829. It is doubtful
however, that even Nugent could have led his constituents along the
next path he chose to follow; and Hobhouse certainly could not—
not enough of them at any rate.

In an address to his constituents at the end of July Nugent
announced his opinion that the Corn Laws needed further reforming. As they existed, he said, they benefited only the landlord
by providing an excuse for keeping rents high. The Tories immediately seized upon the issue. The Tory candidate, Col Henry
Hanmer of Stockgrove, Fenny Stratford, proclaimed that
'zealously attached to the Agricultural Interests, I consider the
system of Free Trade, (particularly as applied to the Corn Laws,)
to be prejudicial to the Farmer, and to the best interests of the
Country.'[9] So far as I can determine, Nugent had never actually
used the term 'free trade'—but Hobhouse did.

In an address dated 11 August Hobhouse announced that he
stood at Nugent's suggestion and advocated the same principles,
which he then proceeded to elaborate. Implementation of his
'Reforming principles', he said, would bring: (1) the reduction
of public expenditure; (2) a reform of the Church and an extension

of religious liberty by removing the remaining disabilities for
nonconformists; and (3) the abolition of slavery. On all these
points, he was on fairly safe ground. Religious libertarianism,
humanitarianism, and retrenchment was a formula Nugent had
already proved to be an effective one. Hobhouse's fourth point was
another matter, and what made it even more dangerous was the
fact that he chose to found it on a general principle:

> The propriety of an alteration in the Corn Laws must be felt
> even by the Agriculturist. Free trade in this, as in every other
> branch of industry, must be the ultimate end of our policy.

It is true that having made this categorical pronouncement he then
went on to qualify and to state a more limited objective for the
immediate future:

> Yet interests have grown up, under a mistaken system—interests,
> not only of the rich, but of the poor, which are well entitled to our
> consideration. All, therefore, that, with justice to the farmer, or
> advantage to the community can, for the present be accomplished,
> is to do away with prohibition, and to substitute fixed and moderate
> protecting duties, as, while they ensure employment to the
> agricultural labourers, and protect the farmers from a ruinous
> fluctuation of prices, will leave a more steady, and, perhaps, only
> in nominal amount more moderate income.[10]

The immediate proposal proved quite unpopular enough.
Though the *Bucks Gazette* claimed that Hanmer found little
encouragement for 'his trash about the Corn Laws', the proof that
emerged from its columns was not very convincing. The paper was
able to publish only one letter from 'An Unprejudiced Farmer'—
which suggests that the 'prejudiced' opinion was the usual one—
and he was not an Aylesbury elector, but from the neighbourhood
of Newport Pagnell![11] Judging from the *Gazette's* scanty evidence
and from the play made of the issue in surviving Tory handbills it
would appear that the paper's opinion that the issue was innocuous
was at best wishful thinking.[12]

The 1832 election also saw the beginning of a definitive breach
in the ranks of the former 'Reformers'. This was partly because of
the issue that Nugent and Hobhouse had introduced, but the
quarrel was more complicated than that. It became an open one at

a great dinner at the King's Head on 21 August to celebrate the triumph of reform and to take leave of Lord Nugent. Both Hobhouse and Rickford were present, and Rickford used the occasion to disclaim all connexion with Hobhouse on this his first introduction to the constituency. Rickford had, he said,

> never attached himself to party, and never will do so, or to any individual whatever. (Bravo, and hear) I am anxious to express myself unequivocally on this point, because I am convinced that I shall best study your interests and best study my own independence by continuing the advocate of measures, not men (cheers).

This brought an acid rejoinder from Hobhouse that it was necessary to support men in order to advance measures. John Churchill, the grocer who had chaired the 1830 parliamentary reform meeting, and others sprang to Rickford's defence. A noisy and acrimonious debate ensued in which Hobhouse proclaimed himself the firm supporter of the 'present liberal administration' and Rickford protested that he had always been an 'Independent man'. Though attempts were made to paper over the cracks at the end of the meeting, they were not very successful; and the cold handshake with which Rickford and Hobhouse parted cannot have convinced many that anything was forgotten or forgiven.[13]

Rickford's claim to complete political independence which had started the debate was, of course, one that had long been *de rigueur* with candidates. But it was fast coming to be a convention which, though often receiving the homage of lip service, was increasingly broken in practice. The distinctions between words and deeds are clearly illustrated in advice Nugent had given to G. H. Dashwood, the second Whig candidate for the county, sometime before the unfortunate Aylesbury meeting. Nugent urged that

> a strict understanding of union should be established between you and [John] Smith. I do not mean, of course, an avowed coalition, against which there is always a foolish but very strong cry raised, as if it were dishonourable in two men of the same principles to support their own principles in the persons of each other, and as if it were an attack on the independence of electors to canvass them to vote in such a manner as not to neutralize the representation.

But the prejudice on this subject is so strong that there is no
resisting it. . . . What I mean therefore is a strict understanding
among your *common* friends.[14]

This advice was in fact put into practice (with excellent results, as
we shall see). The candidates, though they strongly denied 'coalition', were served by the same local committees; and only those
who wanted to be can have been fooled.

This sort of harmless deception was one thing, but Rickford
obviously meant something much more serious by his remarks at
the Aylesbury meeting. He had been moving in the direction of a
break for several years. Relations between Nugent and Rickford
had begun to be distinctly strained at the time of the struggle over
Catholic emancipation, and on several occasions Nugent's friends
had felt that Rickford had exceeded the demands of convention in
maintaining his independence. The disagreement over the Catholic
question was one of principle, and one which separated Rickford
from Nugent and the overwhelming majority of the Whigs, and
put him on this matter on common ground with Chandos. The
latter relationship was further cemented by a shared concern for
agriculture, and it was one that soon blossomed and bore fruit. In
the hotly contested 1831 elections Rickford had given Chandos
one vote for the county, and the marquis had returned the compliment for Aylesbury. And Rickford had gone on to desert the Whig
government on the question of the Chandos clause, which he
supported.

The growing alliance was also reflected on the local level. The
Bucks Gazette charged that Rickford had been much tamer 'since
that very party who once oppressed him, as they now do Mr.
Hobhouse, took him into favour and made a magistrate of him . . . ;
soon . . . after that change he built up the dignity of a country
gentleman, as a fresh face to his character of honest politician . . .'
And the *Gazette* went on to denounce 'the well known inconsistent,
tame, aristocratic-leaning character of Mr. Rickford's *local* politics
for the last two or three years.'[15]

But however aristocratic-leaning Rickford's local politics, his
national politics had been those of a good Reformer, the politics of
his middle-class supporters in Aylesbury. And, while Rickford's
own particular 'party' agreed with him on the Catholic question,

and thus agreed with Chandos and disagreed with Nugent on this issue, as good Reformers they continued to support Nugent against Chandos. Rickford may have forgotten, but Aylesbury men like the Dells and John Churchill remembered as clearly as Abraham Wing, the farmer who had often chaired Nugent's committees and who nominated Hobhouse in 1832, that 'in 1818, when two noble families endeavoured to ride over them, they came forward manfully against all the powers of the aristocracy of the county to secure their independence.'[16]

Through 1831 the common memory and the continuing threat had kept Aylesbury Reformers united. Scarcely a year before the ill-fated meeting they had given aristocratic influence another sound trouncing securing Nugent a triumphant return in the face of the marquis and his army of faggot voters. Not only had they dramatically vindicated their independence in 1831, the Reform Act had struck down great numbers of their enemies; it was estimated that the duke lost some 100 pocket votes from non-resident electors. As has been seen, the act defined residence as living within seven miles of a borough's boundaries, which meant that many Bucks voters who lived outside the borough retained their votes; but the duke also had many London and Hampshire men amongst his pocket voters. Both the recent defeat and the still more recent pruning of aristocratic influence doubtless made Wing's appeal for consistency seem irrelevant to some, and made other considerations appear more important. The Reform Act had obviously altered some important balances in Aylesbury politics; and some electors may well have thought that it was wiser to judge the election in terms of the immediate issues rather than to continue to joust with what now might well have seemed aristocratic windmills.

At any rate Hobhouse lost the election, though he was only fifty-five votes behind Hanmer. With such a close result, a number of factors might have been important. But, as will be demonstrated presently, had a number of Reformers, largely farmers and other rural electors, supported both candidates as they had done in 1831, rather than either plumping for Rickford or splitting their votes for Hanmer the result would have been different.

Most Reformers did vote for both Hobhouse and Rickford, and the overwhelming majority of Tory supporters split their votes for

Rickford, the combined effect of which was to give Rickford a commanding lead. For both sides it was only sensible. Rickford had, it is true, offended many liberal Reformers by his refusal to support Hobhouse. But the fact remained that in parliament he had supported all the important questions which they had supported, save for Catholic emancipation. With this exception, he had from the beginning been, as he rightly claimed at the next election, their representative 'on liberal principles, for the support of which he had always voted in the House of Commons . . .'[17] To Liberals (as they were coming to be called), Rickford's flirtation with Chandos and his refusal to support Hobhouse were irritating, but few could bring themselves to cut off their noses to spite their faces by refusing to vote for him. For Conservatives, on the other hand, it would have been foolish indeed not to have voted for a good Protestant churchman and friend of the farmers against a free-trading friend of religious liberty. Many Aylesbury electors may have shown a technical disregard for party, but this did not imply a disregard of principles—quite the contrary.

It is indicative of the close connexion between the politics of the county and the borough, and of the importance of the latter in the former, that the issues in the county largely reflected those in the borough contest. Certainly this was partly coincidence. The new 'Liberal'[18] candidate George Henry Dashwood was the son and heir of Sir John Dashwood King and did not need to be told by an outsider the importance of such questions as economy and retrenchment, church reform, and the abolition of slavery. But, so far as I have been able to find, if he and John Smith had any opinions on the Corn Laws, they kept them to themselves. The charge made in Tory handbills that they were free traders, they would seem to have owed to Hobhouse; and doubtless it was loyalty to him that accounts for the fact that they did not make a great play of a public denial. It is doubtful that John Smith was a free trader—the Carringtons emphatically were not—and though Dashwood may already have accepted the theory, the first indication he gave of his opinions was a quiet vote for the principle of a fixed duty two years later. At any rate, their game appears to have been simply to keep quiet; and, despite the vigorous Tory propaganda, the Bucks electors seem to have been inclined to give a Smith and a Dashwood the benefit of the doubt.

They were aided by the fact that the Marquis of Chandos, always cautious in estimating his own chances of success, chose to shelter behind the convention of independence. In view of the old jealousy of the family influence, a Grenville, it is true, had more reason to honour the convention than most;[19] but the supporters of a second Tory protectionist, Charles Scott Murray of Danesfield, were incredulous, and seem to have remained confident almost to the end that Chandos was not serious. They were sadly mistaken. In the middle of the polling, on 19 December, Sir Thomas Fremantle, the chairman of Chandos' committee, stated the marquis' position unequivocally. Scott Murray had come forward late, after a long search for a second candidate had caused many to promise plumpers to Chandos; and Scott Murray's committee noised it about that Fremantle had indicated Chandos would look favourably on promised plumpers splitting for the second Tory. Fremantle denied this:

> I said that if any Gentleman who desired to split his vote chose to take the responsibility on himself and make such an excuse as the one you mention or any other for so doing neither Lord Chandos nor myself could prevent it; but that his Lordship would not either directly or indirectly release any gentleman from his promise.[20]

Scott Murray's committee also appealed directly to the 'good sense and good feeling of the Farmers of Bucks' complaining that:

> Mr. Scott Murray at the last moment has come forward at great expense to support
> ### YOUR CAUSE
> Mr. Smith the friend of Free Trade, and therefore your enemy, splits his votes with Mr. Dashwood, the friend of Free Trade also.
> [But] the Farmers, who can only exist through Protecting Duties, give plumpers to Lord Chandos, and desert Mr. Scott Murray . . .[21]

The appeal was unsuccessful, or at any rate not sufficiently successful. Chandos finished at the head of the poll, with 2,856 votes; Scott Murray at the bottom, with 1,534. John Smith retained the second seat, with 2,402 votes. And the third seat (the one the Reform Act had given to Bucks) was secured by Dashwood, with 1,646 votes.

Scott Murray's defeat caused considerable discontent among the Tory rank and file. John Newman, the former secretary of the Brunswick Club who was helping with a subscription to pay Chandos' expenses, reported to Fremantle:

> Lucas of Newport . . . told me that he is disappointed in the farmers who have not shewn that disposition to give their pecuniary aid which he expected, which he says is owing to their chagrin at Mr. Murray's defeat.[22]

Chandos' sensitive seismographic self was not one to disregard such tremors. He was not long in turning to political purposes a new organization that would bind up the wounds the election had made and prepare the way for the next one, when three Conservatives would sweep the field.

The organization to accomplish these feats was the Buckinghamshire Agricultural Association, founded hardly a month after the election in January 1833 and, according to the *Bucks Gazette*, 'got up for election purposes by Lord Chandos . . .'[23] In fact, the charge was not entirely accurate. Chandos was not the original mover in forming the association, but Robert Sutton, a gentleman farmer of Cholesbury. And the association was originally bipartisan. Sir Harry Verney was one of its vice-presidents, and its original committee included several prominent Liberal farmers, like the famous grazier Richard Rowland of Creslow. Verney had made the motion that put Chandos in the presidential chair. Nor is there any reason to disbelieve Sutton when he said of the resolution passed at the first meeting against any change in the Corn Laws, that 'it is only a repetition of the wishes and opinions of Farmers who meet at the Market Tables of this county in the last three months.'[24]

But it did not take long for the body to assume a political character. It was founded towards the end of January, and by the beginning of April, Verney was attempting to secure the passage of a declaration that it 'be one of the rules of the Association, that *no political subject shall be proposed or discussed at any of their meetings.*'[25] That Verney should have been the mover of this declaration—which was soundly defeated—was doubly ironic in that not only had he put Chandos at the head of the body; he had also moved the resolution at the first meeting that 'the objects of the Association be the Protection of the Agricultural Interests of the County', and went on to argue that they should exert their united strength, among other things, for protection and a reform of the poor laws, which were certainly political objects. It was soon apparent, however, that there was not a political object of the farmers that did not also swiftly become a political object of Lord Chandos.

This was in a sense true even of the Corn Law question. Chandos, of course, had long ago made clear his devotion to the Corn Laws; and recently, in Bucks and elsewhere, he had been making speeches on the question that have the appearance of trial balloons to test the advisability of emphasizing it again. But he seems not to have made up his mind by the time of the county election. At any rate, there is no record of his having said anything about the Corn Laws at the nomination. He had talked of his famous clause, of his moderation on the question of slavery, and in general terms about his solicitude for agriculture, but had said nothing specific about the Corn Laws. Scott Murray and his supporters had been left to make the running on that issue but it had obviously been a popular question, and Chandos was not one to leave a popular question to someone else. The *Bucks Herald*, a new paper which he was generally believed to subsidize and which was certainly his mouthpiece, gave strong support to the formation of the Agricultural Association as the kind of measure the farmers must take to save the Corn Laws in the face of the threat from the newly-enfranchised manufacturing boroughs and the reformed electorate.[26] And at a great dinner of the association in November Chandos personally spread horror stories. Protection, he said, was the farmers' only salvation. It was in great danger from the unity and purpose of the representatives of the manufacturing districts. The farmers must not be lulled by reliance on their friends in the government; 'I know most certainly, whatever may be the views of the government, that the repeal will be brought forward at the next session, and supported by the strength of its advocates.' And he went on in the same vein, intimating that disaster might well be just around the corner.[27] Chandos may have been unduly alarmist, but there can be no doubt that he was enormously successful in gaining the farmers to his cause. A year later, on the

eve of the general election, there was another great dinner, with
the duke himself in the chair. And we have it on the testimony of
the *Bucks Gazette*, which had begun by deriding the association
and denying that it had any genuine support among the farmers,
that 'upwards of 800 persons sat down to dinner, the great
majority of whom consisted of the farmers of the county.'[28] By this
time Chandos had switched his emphasis to the repeal of the Malt
Tax, which probably had even less direct relevance for the
farmers of Bucks than the Corn Laws. But it made no difference.
By this time, Bucks farmers had confidence in the 'Farmers'
Friend' and were ready to follow his lead. This may have been
irrational, but it was not necessarily 'deferential' in the sense in
which that word has come to be understood. Chandos owed his
position not only to who he was, but to his own not inconsiderable
political skill.

The two issues that figured most importantly in both the county
and the Aylesbury election in 1835 were Dissenting disabilities and
the interests of agriculture. As has been seen, the formation of a
United Committee in London in 1833 to press for the removal of
the remaining Dissenting disabilities had been echoed in Bucks by
a series of meetings in the major towns early in 1834. The Dissenters were fully aroused by the time of the general election a year
later. As John Smith did not stand again and no one emerged to
take his place, Dashwood initially stood alone in the Liberal interest
for the county. He responded warmly to the Dissenting demands,
endorsing especially the abolition of university tests and the entire
abolition of Church rates without substitutes, which were probably
their most controversial demands. Dr John Lee of Hartwell, a last-
minute candidate and a recent convert to the Liberal camp took a
similar position.

But where Dashwood, at any rate, was pressed hardest was on
his opinions on agricultural questions. (Lee was in a different
position, as will be seen presently.) He stoutly defended himself
against the charge of being inimical to the agricultural interest,
declaring that he had and would continue to vote for the repeal of
the Malt tax, though he did not expect wonders from success.
In response to a direct question, he admitted that he had voted for
a revision of the Corn Laws, giving his vote for a fixed duty on 6
March 1834. More questioning revealed that he had been ill on

the occasion of a division for total repeal, and that, though he had
voted with Chandos in the first division on the latter's motion for
an inquiry into agricultural distress, he had not voted with him in
the second division because the result had the motion succeeded
would have been to bring down the government.

It is clear that Dashwood's opponents considered his position
on agricultural questions his Achilles heel—and their strong point.
Chandos doubtless did not suffer from being able to announce that
his devotion to the repeal of the Malt Tax had prevented him from
joining Peel's new Conservative government, which refused to
take up the cause. Sir W. L. Young, a new candidate who had
been a member of Scott Murray's committee, declared his support
for the repeal of the Malt Tax and his belief in the existing Corn
Laws. The third Conservative candidate, J. B. Praed, an old ally
of Chandos from the days of the Brunswick Club, stood on similar
grounds. The Conservatives were pressed mainly on religious
questions, particularly Dissenting disabilities. Chandos pointed
to his support for Lord John Russell's attempt to relieve Dissenters from the necessity of being married in an Anglican service,
but had to admit opposition to most of the other Dissenting demands. Sir W. L. Young invoked the Tamworth Manifesto, with
its promise of easing Dissenting disabilities. And a spokesman for
Praed, who was not present, got round the problem by pleading
ignorance of the candidate's position.[29]

The contest was pretty clearly between the friends of agriculture,
as defined by Chandos and the Agricultural Association, and the
friends of Dissent. The friends of agriculture won. The poll ended
with Chandos having 3,094 votes; Young, 2,349; Praed, 2,179;
Dashwood, 1,671; and Lee, 1,383. The Liberal defeat apparently
caused the Liberals some surprise. Lee, it is true, had only come
forward on the day of nomination, 11 January, resigning his
candidacy for Aylesbury on the same day; so he was hardly a
serious candidate, something which made his not unrespectable
vote even more impressive. Dashwood's defeat, however, had not
been anticipated. For much of the campaign it had appeared that
his seat would not be contested. Though Sir John Chetwode had
stood and then stood down, the third Conservative candidate in
the person of Praed did not arrive on the field until Dr Lee—in
fact, in the literal sense, Praed did not arrive on the field at all,

not even being present at the nomination! Thus the vote he received
was an eloquent proof of Conservative strength and organization. The chairman of Dashwood's committee at Newport Pagnell
wrote after the event:

> It appears to me that the influence of the Marquis of Chandos
> is too great and ought to be diminished but at present it forms a
> formidable barrier to the interest of the County. Whether you can
> meet it with hopes of better success on a future occasion I am not
> competent to state—but I am convinced you have many steady
> friends—and would have more but for the powerful influence of
> party accompanied with the most disgraceful intimidation.[30]

An election never passed without both sides alleging 'most dis-
graceful intimidation'; but however that might have been on this
occasion, there seems little doubt of the 'powerful influence of
party'.

The Aylesbury election went equally badly for the Liberals.
Rickford and Hanmer, the sitting MPs, stood again. So did
Hobhouse. And they were joined by Dr Lee, standing as a Liberal.
Lee's candidacy was a complicating factor in the election. Lee
himself was a highly complex character. He was an anti-clerical
ecclesiastical lawyer, whose own religious opinions were deistic. He
was a gifted amateur astronomer and a noted Egyptologist, and an
ardent opponent of foxhunting and the Game Laws as inter-
ferences with scientific farming. But he was also a large landowner
in several counties, the heir to his uncle, William Lee Antonie, as
well as to his cousin, Sir George Lee, and the bearer of an ancient
name.[31] Perhaps because his own father was a London merchant
named Fiott, of whom the Lees never quite approved, the doctor
was inordinately proud of the name that he had assumed. In any
event, throughout his life an extreme political radicalism was to be
shot through with apparently discordant aristocratic notions. Lee,
in short, was an eccentric, and his eccentricity was apparent soon
after his arrival in the county. He commenced relations with his
fellow country gentlemen by pinning back the ears of the Master
of the Bicester Foxhounds, T. T. Drake, while at the same time
espousing Drake's anti-Catholic and anti-reform political positions.
His reasons were probably not Drake's. The only specific objec-
tion Lee stated to the Reform Bill of 1831, as a measure of parlia-

mentary reform, was that it deprived of the franchise some who already had had it. He also objected to the fact that it increased Catholic influence. Liberal and enlightened himself, Lee found Catholicism neither; and, while he supported emancipation as a measure of religious liberty, he opposed anything tending to increase Catholic influence in the counsels of the nation—a distinction that was not always easy to draw. Thus, though he had started as a supporter of Lord Nugent, he broke with him and gave his support to Kirkwall for the borough and Chandos for the county in 1831. Lee highly approved of the Chandos clause on the radical grounds that it increased the electorate, and he made it clear in the speech in which he nominated Chandos in 1832 that he took seriously the marquis' claim to be a dedicated, if 'moderate', reformer.[32] Lee also had a strong belief in resident representatives and an intense dislike of anything that smacked of party organization, both of which told against Hobhouse in 1832 and caused him to divide his vote between Rickford and Hanmer. But the latter dislike also seems to have told against Chandos in time. As Lee explained to the Aylesbury electors at the nomination on 8 January:

> I have stated in my Circular, that I am a friend to Agricultural Associations; but I will not, as a County gentleman, sit down and see an Agricultural Association perverted into a political machine. ... Until Sir Harry Verney broke up the Tory interest at Buckingham, and threw open the doors of that rotten Borough, the Noble House of Grenville never thought of Agricultural Associations.[33]

As a consequence, Lee became a strong partisan of Sir Harry in the struggles inside the association, and the steadfast opponent in every and all areas of the man whom he dubbed 'that agricultural harlequin, Lord Chandos, Marquis of Malt'.

But, though an opponent of the marquis, Lee remained a friend of agricultural associations and by implication of the Corn Laws. In fact, he had no very strong opinions about the matter one way or the other; but his lack of interest did not become apparent in this election, and his supposed views probably gave him an appeal that other recent Liberal candidates did not possess. The main part of his address, however, was devoted to the need for Church reform, quinquennial parliaments, and the ballot. Most important in terms of appeal to the electorate, he stated that 'I am disposed to deliver the Dissenters from all unjust Restrictions, and to concede to them immediately, a portion of their ... claims'; but, rather than specifying what he meant, he gave a general endorsement to guidelines proposed by the Bishop of Chichester. This was an unfortunate mistake, as the bishop favoured the retention of Church rates, which Lee subsequently stated he was willing to abolish immediately.[34]

It is not possible to judge fully Lee's electoral appeal as he only stood the poll for the first two days, retiring on the morning of the third to contest the county upon the Conservative introduction of Praed. In his address he told the electors that he hoped both actions would 'aid our mutual objects of annihilating local aristocratic tyranny and promoting a Reform representation.'[35] As it was, his candidacy for the county did not save Dashwood, and some thought that he cost Hobhouse the borough by his candidacy there. Rickford, as has been seen, still claimed liberal principles; and, as 'A Dissenter & Freeholder of Bucks' who commented on all the candidates for his fellow Dissenters' benefit remarked, he 'in many cases has voted relative to the Dissenters' will . . .'[36] The commentator was suspicious of Rickford, as were some Aylesbury Liberals, but as yet there was little solid foundation for their suspicions. Thus the Liberal vote was split in three directions. Once again Rickford, who again attracted many Conservatives, and Hanmer were returned. The final vote was Rickford, 855; Hanmer, 587; Hobhouse, 518; and Lee, 268. It was a temptation to argue, as Hobhouse did, that if his votes and Lee's were added together there would have been a Liberal victory over the Tory Hanmer.[37] And so there would have been if all those who voted for Lee could have been assumed to have been possible Hobhouse supporters—but that was a highly unsafe assumption.

Indeed, it was almost certainly a wrong assumption. The existence of pollbooks for all three borough elections between 1831 and 1835[38] enable us to pronounce with some confidence on the important factors in politics during the period. I have used the evidence in the following manner. I simply selected all those names that appear both in the pollbook of 1831 and that of 1835, the aim being to study the voting records of these electors in the hope of finding suggestive trends. The resulting sample of 639 represents some half of those voting in the three elections (56 per cent in 1831, 50 per cent in 1832, and 53 per cent in 1835).

From this sample, it is possible not only to predict the outcome of every election, but also to account for the electors who made the difference. The sample takes account of about half (46 per cent) of Lee's votes. Half of those also voted for Hobhouse. Of the other half, only about a third (36 per cent) were regular Liberal voters, and their voting records suggest that most of the rest would not have voted for Hobhouse under any circumstances, indicating that his rosy predictions for the future were unfounded.

What an elector would do in the future can only be a matter of speculation. But the sample also indicates what a crucial swing vote actually did do in the three elections under consideration. In 1832, in the actual poll, Hobhouse was fifty-five votes behind Hanmer; in 1835, he was sixty-nine votes behind. The sample accounts for seventy electors who had voted for Nugent in 1831 but voted against Hobhouse in 1832, and for eighty-two electors who had voted for Nugent in 1831 but voted against Hobhouse in 1835 (fifty-five of them voted against Hobhouse on both occasions). In other words, the sample accounts for voters who would have given Hobhouse a fifteen vote plurality in 1832 and a thirteen vote plurality in 1832—had they voted for him as they had voted for Nugent in 1831. Why had these electors switched their allegiance?

Residence may give some clue. Of the total of ninety-five, thirty-two came from the town, and twice as many, sixty-five, came from the hundreds. There were, of course, several small towns and large villages in the hundreds—Wendover, Princes Risborough, Great Missenden, and Haddenham (the population of the parishes in which they were located ranged in 1831 from Hadenham's 1,500 to Wendover's 3,100)—so this division of the constituency does not completely coincide with a division between town and country. Occupation would, however, suggest a similar rural bias among these electors. Twenty-nine, about a third of the total number, are identified in the pollbooks as farmers; and analyses of voters in the hundreds in a slightly later period, when there is fuller information available, suggest that a good many more would have done some farming at least. There were seven 'gents' among the total, of the sort we have met before, retired large farmers and tradesmen. And there was only one 'esq', who was, in fact, of the same sort, a Wycombe draper.

What the pollbooks suggest, then, is that a substantial number of middle-class electors swung against a Liberal candidate who espoused a revision of the Corn Laws. Large landed influence can have had little to do with the shift; for the only important shift of landed influence, and it had been a major one, was in the opposite direction, against the Tory influence of the Grenvilles. Doubtless that agricultural harlequin, the Marquis of Malt, had had something to do with the swing of opinion; but, so far as one can judge, it was from the hustings and the chair of the Agricultural Association that he wrought his tricks. 'Corn' had achieved what his battalions of faggot voters could not do—broken the party who called themselves Reformers. 'Catholics' were to finish the job.

Chapter 7 CATHOLICS

'CATHOLICS' IS perhaps a deceptively simple sobriquet for an enormously complicated issue; for what usually went under the guise of anti-Catholicism in Bucks in the thirties comprehended several elements besides the ostensible one. As Sir Harry Verney said in 1836 about proposed Whig legislation for dealing with the problem of the Irish Church, legislation destined to be the centre round which most of the anti-Catholic storms of the decade raged, it had 'much to struggle against, all our English prejudices against the Irish—the feelings of Protestant against Catholic, and the violent and almost ruffianly conduct and language of O'Connell.'[1] The fear and hatred of O'Connell was, of course, more than a purely personal one. He was feared because he threatened to rouse the Irish masses and impose terms on the British government, and hated because he had done it already and because the Whig government of Melbourne seemed once again to be knuckling under as Wellington's Tory government had done in 1829.

Then there was another factor Sir Harry did not mention, the kind of concession the Whigs proposed to make to popular militancy in Ireland; stripping the Protestant Church of Ireland of some of its property, which was then to be put to the uses of a predominantly Catholic people. This gave rise to fears not only of the spread of Catholicism, but of popular dictation—and despoliation. It was to these latter fears that Sir John Chetwode alluded, addressing the electors of Buckingham in 1837, when he declared that he should 'always be the Opposer of Revolutionary measures, by which the Rights of Property are invaded, and the wild Theories of Democracy substituted for our Constitutional Establishment . . .'[2] More obviously, perhaps, the threatened despoilation of the Irish Church aroused fears for the Established

Church of England which many believed to be an essential bulwark of Christianity and thus of civilization in the land. Some, or all, of these elements were present in the minds of the defenders of the Protestant cause in Bucks.

There were some, however, who had been prominent in the cause in the 1820s but were not to be in the 1830s—the Dissenters. This was an important change, creating serious stresses and strains among the former Reformers. Dissenting demands in the 1820s had not been such as to frighten off the large numbers of sincere Churchmen who allied with them in political causes. The abolition of the Test and Corporation Acts only recognized a legal right to offices which many Dissenters held already, certainly in Bucks; for, whatever else they may have left to be desired, exclusion of Dissenters was not a fault of either the Buckingham or the Wycombe corporations. And the majority of Bucks Dissenters demonstrated quite clearly that, so far as they were concerned, there was no desire that the same political rights be extended to Catholics.

The Dissenting demands from 1833 onwards, taken up by meetings of Bucks Dissenters from the beginning of 1834, were very different from those of the previous decade, both in nature and in effect. The new Dissenting demands, particularly the crucial one for the abolition of Church rates, attacked rights that were not merely theoretical but very immediate and practical privileges of the Church. The loss of Church rates would mean an important loss of revenue for parish churches. The Dissenters were attacking Church property—as the Irish Catholics were. Furthermore the two sets of demands began to be pressed on parliament in earnest at just about the same time. Not surprisingly, Catholic and Dissenting demands became entwined in most people's minds, moderating at least the overt anti-Catholicism of Dissent, and stiffening the attitude of churchmen against criticism from whatever source it came.

Buckingham provides an example of the strains these changes could create. Buckingham Dissent had been particularly strong in its anti-Catholicism, and at an 1830 dinner for Chandos, Philip Bartlett acknowledged its exertions in a toast to 'The Protestant Dissenters who nobly came forward to support our common cause.'[3] Prominent Churchmen like the Bartletts and George

Nelson had gone on to fight shoulder to shoulder with Dissenters in causes they shared with them—but not this time with Chandos—such as freedom for the slaves and the independence of Buckingham; and together they had returned Sir Harry Verney in 1832 despite the strenuous efforts of the duke and the marquis to defeat him.

At the beginning of 1834, however, the alliance began to show signs of strain. The issue of the appropriation of Irish Church property to secular purposes like education (commonly known as 'lay appropriation') was being increasingly hotly debated in parliament, and—at the same time—the Dissenting campaign in Bucks was beginning in earnest. On 25 March one of Sir Thomas Fremantle's supporters wrote exultantly:

> I think I have fixed a good shot at old Nelson. A declaration has been drawn up to present to the Archbishop on the subject of the Church. As you know the Dissenters here have been pretty active. This [declaration] was put into my hands to introduce it for Signature. I considered the Bailiff [Nelson] the proper person, and intimated the propriety of calling a meeting for the purpose of suggesting the best mode to obtain Signatures. To this he objected. I evidently [sic] saw that he was afraid to put himself in a way against the Dissenters, and I prevailed upon him instead of assembling, to use his *private* influence amongst his friends. This succeeded, and he has obtained many favourable to it, but poor man at the expense of being bitterly assailed by his Dissenting friends.[4]

Precisely what the declaration said is not recorded, but presumably it was a general statement of attachment to the Church and its privileges, which, in view of their own demands, the Dissenters could not accept. It would have been particularly difficult for Dissenters to have accepted any such declaration in view of the general principle on which they felt called to ground their case. As the Rev David Aston had explained to Fremantle the previous month, 'I must disapprove of an established religion, as making an invidious distinction . . ., and I must disapprove of the other grievances which are now made public, especially in a pamphlet entitled "The Case of Dissenters Addressed to Earl Grey".'

Clearly, Buckingham Dissenters were loyally following the London formulae, though neither they nor most who were responsible for the cry, considered dis-establishment an immediate practical objective. Certainly, the Buckingham Dissenters did not, as Aston attempted to make clear to Fremantle;[5] but that they felt it necessary to enunciate the principle placed obvious limits on discussion, and doubtless did nothing to reassure Churchmen.

As the year 1834 progressed, parliamentary discussion of Church questions became more heated, bringing first the resignation of Lord Stanley from the Whig ministry, and then the resignation of Grey himself. Grey was followed by Melbourne, and he, late in the year, by Peel. Even before the crises of 1834, Buckingham's Whig MP had felt strongly drawn towards the political centre. As Verney had confided to his Buckingham solicitor and parliamentary agent, Thomas Hearn, in September 1833:

> The *most powerful man* in the *House* is without any exception *Peel*. He is almost always right. . . . I am *happy* to *think* that *Peel supported* the *ministers*, on *almost every occasion*. He separates himself very much from the High Tories, who are, doubtless very angry with him: I *live* in *hopes* that the *course* of *political events may draw him* and the *best* of the *present ministers together*; and so *form* a *strong* and *wise government*. . . .[6]

And in December 1834, after Peel had decided on a dissolution, Verney wrote to Stanley for advice about a 'Liberal' candidate 'equally removed from the Radical and Tory views.'[7]

Given Verney's moderation and his high opinion of Peel, it is hardly surprising that after he and Fremantle were given an uncontested return in the general election he joined his colleague in efforts to give the new government a chance. Verney voted for the Conservative candidate for Speaker and against the Whig amendment to the address at the commencement of the new parliament.[8] But he did not go so far as Stanley, who soon crossed over to the Conservative benches. Nor did he go so far as some of his most prominent supporters at Buckingham like Hearn and George Nelson, who, a week after Lord John Russell had successfully moved a lay appropriation motion in the face of government opposition, attended a meeting of the 'Magistrates, Gentry, and Inhabitants of the Town of Buckingham' on 8 April and signed a petition begging Peel that 'notwithstanding the opposition which is arrayed against your Measures and Person, you will not now withdraw your inestimable Services from your King and Country; as upon the continuance of them we believe—the Stability of the Throne, the Integrity of the Empire, and the Safety of the Protestant Religion, mainly depend.'[9] For his part, Verney remained loyal to the Whigs. He had not voted for Russell's motion because he had been on his honeymoon; but he came back to support the Whig legislation based on the principle of lay appropriation, as well as the government's efforts to meet the Dissenting demands on Church rates and other questions.

The Buckingham Dissenters were fully satisfied with their representative. No prominent Dissenter had signed the April petition—despite the fact that, probably by design, it spoke only of 'the Safety of the Protestant Religion' and said nothing about the Church. But others at Buckingham were deeply offended by the line Verney had taken. In June of 1836 the possibility arose that the government might appoint him to a colonial governorship; something which gave rise to angry charges by some of his constituents that he had deserted his principles for personal political gain. Verney wrote a long letter to Hearn defending himself. He reminded him that his decision had been made the year before: 'I differed with Ld. S[tanley] on that which was considered the turning point, and therefore I did not cross over with him.' He went on to justify the Whig policy embodied in the famous Lichfield House Compact earlier in that year in which O'Connell had pledged his support for government in return for favourable legislation for Ireland;

At the present moment the fault found with government is that they are too much influenced by O'Connell. Now I know not what confidence other men have in O'Connell—I have none. But O'Connell has great power with his countrymen; a power conferred on him by the injuries his Catholic countrymen have sustained from England, and especially from what has been called the 'English garrison' in Ireland, the Orange Party. That power O'Connell is now using to do good—to keep his countrymen quiet; it is his interest to shew that when he is friendly to the government of the Country he can keep Ireland quiet, and he does so now, and I believe that at this moment Ireland is in a better and safer state—property more secure, the laws better observed—life less exposed to danger, commerce and agriculture

there more flourishing than it ever was before; and all this simply
and solely because Ireland and the Priests find it to their interest
to keep Ireland quiet.

Now if this be the case, do the government perform their duty
faithfully or the reverse by conciliating O'Connell? that is the
question—and do they in order to obtain his good will, concede
measures to him contrary to their opinion. As yet, I have not seen
that they do so, and I cannot think measures bad for a country
simply because they are supported by 7/8 of its population. Such
is the case with the measures of the present government on Irish
matters. But they have much to struggle against, all our English
prejudices against the Irish—the feelings of Protestant against
Catholic, and the violent and almost ruffianly conduct and language
of O'Connell.

I have no doubt that within a short time there will be a change
of public opinion on the subject of the Irish Church, and that the
present ministerial plan will be considered *at least sufficiently
favorable* to our Protestant Establishment in Ireland.[10]

It seems highly unlikely that Verney's last prediction proved
correct. Certainly, his continued support of the government's
policy put him in a most dangerous position at Buckingham. At
the beginning of March 1837 Hearn, whom Verney had apparently
brought around, felt it necessary to write a pamphlet defending
him from the charges of being an enemy to the Church and to
Protestantism. The main complaints were over his votes for the
Irish Church bill and for a resolution moved by Stephen Lushing-
ton calling for the exclusion of the bishops from the House of
Lords. The latter vote Hearn explained as being dictated by
Verney's conviction that the mixing of the bishops in politics was
not conducive to the cause of religion, and he argued that in fact
Verney was a staunch friend both of Protestantism and of the
Church. He hastened to add, however, that Verney was by no
means exclusive and that he was also a strong friend of the Dissenters. He ended with a plea that the peace of the borough be
maintained. As it was, he said, 'churchmen and dissenters, conservative and liberal (to use the phraseology of the day) meet on
cordial terms . . . *Each* party is *represented*; the conservatives have
their representative, the liberals *theirs*—thus *each* is *content*.'[11]

Verney's colleague, soon to become Conservative chief whip,
was quite content with the situation; but, as Sir William Fre-

mantle, himself a former MP for the borough, wrote to his nephew: 'we are likely to have some little trouble in appeasing the Storm which has been raised in Buckingham by Verney's folly.'[12] They could not. Despite Fremantle's open opposition to a contest in the July general election following the death of William IV, a candidate of High Tory views appeared in the person of Sir John Chetwode. The duke and the marquis backed Chetwode strongly. Fremantle refused to have anything to do with him, doggedly maintaining his neutrality. And when Chetwode was not returned, Chandos complained at the Carlton that it was Fremantle who had defeated him—in what was supposed to be the Grenville borough of Buckingham! The charge was not justified. The suggestion was that Fremantle could have brought Chetwode in by dividing his plumpers for the second Conservative—which was untrue. And the fact was that had Fremantle lifted a finger for Chetwode he himself would almost certainly have been defeated by the loss of the second votes of Dissenting supporters of Verney, who left him in no doubt that their continued support depended on his remaining aloof from the schemes of Sir John and his noble supporters.[13]

As a result of the second votes of Verney supporters, Fremantle headed the poll with 235 votes, Verney came second with 156, and Chetwode came last with 138. Clearly, Verney's return was a close thing. He had lost a score of votes since his first (and only previous) contested return in 1832, and he was only eighteen votes ahead of Chetwode. There can be little doubt that his votes on church questions are an important part of the explanation of his reduced electoral vote. He lost the votes of two of the three clergymen who had supported him in 1832. It seems likely also that the strong Churchmanship of the Bartlett clan, or perhaps it was their ardent anti-Catholicism, cost him the support of his wealthiest and most aggressive local supporters. On the other hand, strong Anglicans like Hearn and Nelson, the latter a former member of the Brunswick Club, remained true to Verney's cause.

It was plainly a time for agonising reappraisals among the old Reformers—some went one way, some the other. And the issues that forced this reappraisal were, ostensibly at any rate, all religious ones. Fremantle and Chetwode emphasised their Churchmanship and their Protestantism and attempted to make the two issues into one by arguing that a strong establishment was the only sure bulwark against Catholicism, and thus in the interests of all good Protestants of all denominations. Verney concentrated on anti-Catholicism, indulging in violent and doubtless sincere— Verney was to be one of the founders of the Evangelical Alliance— abuse of that religion. Probably, as was suggested above, the issues were rather more complicated than they appear. Chetwode's addresses stressed the threat to all private property constituted by the proposal to appropriate the property of the Church, and saw sinister democratic implications in what he felt to be Irish dictation of terms and in the attack on the bishops sitting in the Lords.

Some electors may have been swayed by these arguments, but it seems likely that many more would have been swayed by what Sir Harry had called 'all our English prejudices against the Irish— the feelings of Protestant against Catholic, and the violent and almost ruffianly conduct and language of O'Connell.' And there was a final issue that the Rev Mr Coker in nominating Fremantle managed to roll into most of the others. Equating the cause of Protestantism with that of the Church, he charged that recent attempts by the government to deal with the question of Church rates had been undertaken at the behest of O'Connell and was just one more instance of papist dictation![14] Common sense would suggest that such arguments would have had more appeal for Churchmen than for Dissenters, and this would appear to have been the case. Buckingham Liberalism took on a more—though not exclusively—Dissenting character, while Churchmen tended to gravitate towards the new Buckingham Conservative Association, founded the following autumn, according to the *Aylesbury News*, by 'two or three active busy parsons.'[15]

In Buckingham, then, what would seem primarily to have determined the Liberal/Conservative split—at least for the time being— was an individual's attitude towards the Dissenting demands for a redress of grievances, particularly with regard to the question of Church rates. The Liberal party was made up of those Dissenters who placed great stress on the achievement of Dissenting demands and those Churchmen who refused to see the Dissenting programme as a threat to the Church; while the Conservative party was made up of those who would not contemplate any basic change in the legal position and property rights of the Church of England.

Similar considerations apply to shifts in party allegiance in Aylesbury and in the county, with the added and at least equally significant consideration of differing attitudes on the question of how much—if any—protection should be afforded to agriculture (an issue that was not yet of concern in Buckingham, though it soon would be). The most dramatic confrontation of principles came in Aylesbury. Late in May there was a crucial vote on a government measure to abolish Church rates. Voting for it were Verney of Buckingham, Robert Smith and Charles Grey of Wycombe, and Col William Clayton of Marlow. Voting against it were Chandos, Young, and G. S. Harcourt for the county, Fremantle for Buckingham and Hanmer and Rickford for Aylesbury. It was Rickford's position on this question that caused what was probably the most decisive breach in the ranks of the old Reformers in Aylesbury. In the opinion of the *Aylesbury News*, it removed any possible doubts that might have existed about his principles and made it impossible that any Reformer could support him in the future—though this, of course, ignored the Anglican wing of the coalition that made up the Aylesbury Reformers, making the party there subject to precisely the same stresses as those felt by the party in Buckingham.[16] Two of the Dissenters' three prime demands, a civil register of births, marriages and deaths, and an end of the Anglican monopoly on the marriage ceremony, were met in 1836. In the following year Bucks Dissenters waged a vigorous agitation, with meetings and petitions from every major town in the county, backing the Whig government's efforts to meet the third prime demand, the abolition of Church rates. The government's attempts ended in failure when, at the May division just noticed, the bill passed the Commons by only five votes and was not therefore sent on to meet certain death in the Lords.

The general election came some two months later at the end of July. As had become embarrassingly usual in Liberal politics in Aylesbury, the campaign commenced at the end of June with acrimony and disorganization in the Liberal camp. Dr Lee accused Hobhouse of being a nominee and tool of the Reform Club for having accepted £500 support in his last campaign, and Lee proposed to stand again himself as an 'Independent Liberal.' Well aware of disastrous consequences of division, nine leading Liberals (all but one from the town) decided to invite Lord Nugent to return to the borough, as the candidate who had the best change of success. Nugent had resigned his High Commission at the time of of the last Conservative government and was now seeking a seat, and it was hoped that he could reunite the party and that his great personal prestige would carry the day. The plan was successful in so far as both Hobhouse and Lee at once stepped aside in his favour, but not in its ultimate goal. Contrary to the expectations of Nugent and his supporters, he was defeated. And it was the most decisive defeat the party had yet received. Nugent was 117 votes behind W. M. Praed, the poet, whom the Conservatives had brought down to suceed the retiring Hanmer. As usual, Rickford headed the poll.

Unfortunately, the election which might have revealed most in the decade after the Reform Act, is the only one with no surviving pollbook. But a good deal can be deduced from other evidence. As the *Aylesbury News* predicted, Rickford lost a large block of votes, and the reason suggested by the newspaper, his vote on the Church rates, was almost certainly an important one, Yet despite the fact that Nugent received 226 plumpers (to Hobhouse's 88 in 1835), Rickford who nevertheless remained the main beneficiary of Liberal split votes, not only maintained, but slightly bettered his over-all position (855 votes in 1835; 865 in 1937). Praed had bettered Hanmer's vote in 1835 by seventy (657 as opposed to 587). As for Nugent, he was only twenty-two votes ahead of Hobhouse in in 1835 (540 as opposed to 518).

In the absence of evidence on split voting and on who actually voted, it is clearly impossible to speak with certainty. One cannot, for example, know where Rickford got the 148 votes that more than made up for the loss of the Nugent plumpers. There are a number of possibilities—former Hanmer plumpers, those who had previously split votes for Hanmer and one of the other candidates, new voters, and new converts from the Liberal camp or those who had remained neutral in the previous election. Since, however, there was not much change in the registration since the last election, the electorate was probably much the same.[17] And one assumption seems fairly safe—that not many of the 126 electors who had given a vote for Lee, but not for Hobhouse, in 1835 voted for Nugent in 1837.

There is no reason why anyone should have voted for Nugent in preference to Hobhouse, aside from the former's local connexions, the importance of which would seem to have been over-rated. The objections to Hobhouse were precisely those raised against Nugent. As the *Bucks Herald* put it, Nugent was 'a type of the Ministry, as he is their firm supporter' and the Whig administration was 'inimical to the best interests of the Farmer—[and] dangerous to the dearest immunities of the State.'[18] Nugent would have been personally objectionable as an exponent of Corn Law revision, though it is interesting and significant that after three years of opposing the pet projects of the Agricultural Association, the government had overshadowed Nugent's personal iniquities. Beyond that Nugent supported the government's ecclesiastical policies, both as regards Church rates and Irish Church legislation. And, as at Buckingham, the Conservatives tried to make the several religious issues into one.

Indeed, George Carrington (of Missenden Abbey and no relation to the Smiths) in seconding Praed warned that he was 'fearful that the Protestant Church, as established by law, was placed in imminent danger.' And he warned the Dissenters that they would suffer if the 'Protestant' cause did! Carrington may have carried it a bit far, but the line of argument was a shrewd one; though, in fact, it does not seem to have converted many Dissenters.

The 1837 election in Aylesbury largely completed a process of party realignment that had been going on since 1832. The new Conservative party became the party of the farmers and the Church. The new Liberal party became the party of Dissent. Both drew from the old party of Reformers, the Liberals probably exclusively, but the Conservatives to an important extent—to a degree that swung the balance in the constituency away from a party still largely led by the old leaders of the Reformers, the Liberals, to one largely led by the old Tory leaders, the Conservatives. There is nothing strange or baffling in the split in the ranks of the old Reformers; it was created by new political issues and emphases, and there was nothing inconsistent in an erstwhile Reformer choosing to follow either path.

The situation in the county largely mirrored that in Aylesbury. In the county a by-election caused by the death of J. B. Praed preceded the general election by only six months. The by-election is interesting in showing the considerable strength of the Liberals under what were probably the least favourable circumstances. G. H. Dashwood, defeated for the county in 1835, had had intimations from Col Grey that he would vacate Wycombe. He was anxious to take Grey's place. The borough was strongly Liberal and close to his estate, West Wycombe Park. Dashwood was not therefore interested in a county contest,[19] but, as another candidate was not immediately available, he was persuaded to stand. 'It was,' as the *Aylesbury News* said, 'purely a fight of principle: no carriages were provided, no dinner were given, no "favors" distributed, neither was any music employed, nor any unnecessary expense incurred.' The 'necessary' expenses would seem to have been only the fees for the Under-Sheriff and other unavoidable legal expenses, which never got anyone any votes. And Dashwood did not even appear at the nomination.

The Conservative candidate, G. S. Harcourt of Ankerwycke, in contrast, spared none of the normal expenditure. He was returned easily, with 2,228 votes to Dashwood's 982; but for Dashwood to have secured nearly a thousand votes was, under the circumstances, not unimpressive. The *Aylesbury News* charged that the Dissenters had not done enough, and that by their apathy they had assisted Harcourt's return. Nevertheless, it would appear that what had been done was largely the work of the Dissenters. Chesham, for example, where the agitation against Church rates was particularly vigorous, gave Dashwood ninety-five votes to Harcourt's thirty-nine.[20] In any event, the election demonstrated that though the Liberals were in a minority, it was a sizeable one.

In putting Dashwood forward, J. T. Leader, the Radical MP and a Bucks freeholder, had argued that the Conservative monopoly of the three county seats was unnatural and that the 'liberal portion of the county' ought to be represented.[21] To that end six Whig gentlemen signed a requisition to G. R. Smith, the nephew of Lord Carrington, to stand in the general election. The Conservatives, however, appear to have had a low opinion of minority representation. And they responded with a requisition addressed to Chandos, Young, and Harcourt, which showed not only the powerful backing of the Conservative cause, but also its boldness and confidence. The seventeen initial signers were all resident gentlemen, while the Liberal requisition could boast only three, Verney, Cavendish, and C. S. Ricketts of Dorton, whose wife had fallen heir to part of the Aubrey estates. And the Conservative requisitioners declared their intention:

> to use our utmost exertions to return again to Parliament, Conservative representatives determined to uphold the institutions of the Country in Church and State, and to give effectual support to the just claims of the Agricultural Interest [and requested] that you [the three candidates] will allow us to put you conjointly in nomination at the ensuing Election, as the three Conservative Candidates united in one common cause . . .[22]

Polite fictions of 'independence' were cast to the wind, and with impunity.

Again the Liberals were confident of victory, and again they were disappointed, despite the fact that Smith was a strong candidate. He had the backing of the most powerful Liberal interest in the county and of his family's great wealth. Beyond that, he at least suggested support for the Corn Laws. He said at the nomination that 'the farmers ought to be protected,' though he does not appear to have been very specific about the precise nature and degree of protection that ought to be afforded. No one pressed him. On religious questions he took the only attitude that a Liberal candidate in Bucks could take. He said he had been 'accused of being an enemy to the constitution. His opinion was, that he should best support it by giving a conscientious relief to those who differed from him in religious opinions . . .' And in response to a question about the Irish Church from George Carrington (who believed that Protestantism and the Church were synonymous), Smith replied that 'he was a conscientious supporter of the church, but if by "Protestant Church," "Protestant supremacy" was meant (hear, hear) he thought the time had gone by when that supremacy should be maintained.'[23]

Smith did by no means badly. He received 2,078 votes, with 4,456 electors polling, giving him, as he himself pointed out, votes from almost half the electors who voted. And 1,057 of Smith's votes were plumpers, a sizeable hard-core Liberal vote ('hard-core' being suggested by the fact that it was remarkably close, only sixty-five more, than Dashwood had received in the very different circumstances of the by-election earlier in the year). Yet, though

Smith did well, the Conservatives did better. Young, who was the Conservative lowest in the poll, was some 550 votes ahead of Dashwood, with 2,633. Chandos had 2,993 votes, and Harcourt 2,704.

How does one account for the great Conservative victory? In terms of issues the ones that took up by far the greatest amount of time were the religious ones—the Church, Church rates, and anti-popery. But whether these were the most important issues is questionable. As will be seen, a few years later, in a period for which the evidence is a good deal more complete, there is good reason to believe that, while religious issues were of great importance to the Conservative leadership, they were probably of secondary importance in producing the bulk of the Conservative vote (at least in Aylesbury which approximated to a county constituency).

In the later period, at any rate, many Conservative voters appear to have been more concerned with questions that affected their livelihoods. The same may well have been true in the thirties. It is interesting that in the speeches and exchanges at the nomination in 1837 the Liberals hardly attempted to challenge the Conservative claim to be the farmers' particular friends. And the Conservatives did little more than perfunctorily state the claim—probably because they felt they did not have to justify it in most people's eyes. A remark of Robert Sutton, the founder of the Agricultural Association, is an example of the Conservatives' confident appropriation of the title, as his presence was a living reminder of their claim. In seconding the nomination of Sir W. L. Young, Sutton said that the candidate 'was a man on whom the farmers could rely for support—he was associated with Lord Chandos and with Mr Harcourt . . .'[24] Apparently the statement was considered self-evident and not requiring elaboration.

This was by no means the first occasion on which the Conservatives had claimed exclusive right to the title, and the circumstances on the last notable occasion point to another important Conservative advantage over the Liberals—organization. At a great Conservative dinner in Aylesbury in December 1836 toasts to the Agricultural and Conservative Associations of the county had been mixed in what the Liberals considered very bad taste. By this time, there were three Conservative Associations in existence, one for

North Bucks, one for South Bucks and one for Aylesbury. The
first, the South Bucks Conservative Association, had been founded
at a meeting on 4 June 1835, with G.S. Harcourt in the chair. The
resolutions passed, obviously referring to the religious issues on
which Peel's government had recently been brought down, declared attachment to 'the Constitution of our country in Church
and State, as by law established . . .' The last Conservative
Association founded was to be that at Buckingham in the autumn
of 1837; as we have seen, it was founded by several clergymen.
And the South Bucks association, though a number of 'Messrs' (as
distinct from 'Esqs') were present at its first meeting, had none but
clergymen and country gentlemen on its first committee.[25]

The circumstances of the founding of these associations, and the
people who led them, suggest the concern of upper-class Conservatives with religious questions, and the issues raised by those religious questions—for example, the sanctity of private property.
There is no indication that agricultural concerns played any part
in sparking their foundation. Perhaps this was because the Conservative leadership felt that the Agricultural Associations (besides
the one at Aylesbury, there was a separate one at Salt Hill) were
already looking after their interests in this area—as was certainly
the case. In any event, it did not take long for the Conservative
Associations to remove any doubt of their concern for the farmers.

For their parts, the Liberals, though they clearly recognized the
necessity for organization and were canvassing the possibility of
a county Liberal association at this time, were not successful in
achieving it until 1839 and it does not seem to have outlasted that
year.[26] Aylesbury Liberals had an organization that went back to
1826 and had been in more or less continuous existence since that
time under different names. And whether it called itself the 'Aylesbury Independent Society' (1826) or the 'Independent Union of
Aylesbury and its Hundreds' (October 1831) or the 'Aylesbury
Reform and Registration Society' (or some variant, from 1832), it
generally fulfilled the functions of a local party organization,
generating enthusiasm, raising money for campaigns, and, after
Nugent's retirement, searching for candidates.

Considering that the association was entirely a voluntary
middle-class effort, these functions were fulfilled fairly effectively.
Two or three men, most notably and consistently W. H. Poole, a

Dissenter and an itinerant bookseller, donated their services to superintend registration, for example. But enthusiasm could not make up for lack of money; a lack that was never met despite two extensive reorganizations, one in 1835 and one in 1837.[27] Unpaid amateurs could not possibly devote the time to registration given it by the large body of solicitors hired by the Conservatives. John Parrot, writing to Sir Thomas Fremantle in 1839, said that 'on the subject of the expense of the registration of voters [there was] the policy which has for so long a time existed of keeping up a political Interest in the County by retaining nearly all the most respectable professional men . . .'[28] In any case, the Aylesbury Liberal organization had never attempted to look after the county.

The Conservatives too, however, were to find money a problem. It had never been a primary purpose of the Conservative organization to raise money. The subscriptions for election expenses were ad hoc affairs, organized for each election; and the annual expense for registration, or most of it, was borne by Chandos so long as he was MP for the county. In 1839, however, Chandos succeeded to the dukedom, and had to face alone the increasingly dismal state of the family finances, which his own generosity and extravagance (mainly in things political) had done so much to create. And, without his financial resources, it was not long before the Conservative organisation was plunged into the same chaos that plagued the Liberals. A Bucks Conservative Club, with branches and subscriptions (all who contributed over £5 were to be on the Committee) was hopefully launched in the autumn of 1841 after the general election of that year.[29] It seems never to have amounted to much, and did not long outlast the next general election. The Liberal 'Aylesbury Reform and Registration Society' does not even appear to have survived to the 1841 contest, or if it did, only for a short period. The 1840s saw the end of any enduring political organizations in either the boroughs or the county for at least twenty years, and, so far as the county was concerned, until after 1880 ,the last general election under the 1867 Act.

In 1837, as in every other Liberal defeat during the period, the losers ascribed their failures to what Lord Nugent called 'unconstitutional intimidation' on the part of the Conservatives, especially on the part of Lord Chandos. It was alleged that the Grenville tenants and those on other big estates were driven to the polls to

vote against their wills. This sort of 'influence' will be examined in
due course; it need only be suggested here that, as might be expected from the nature of their source, these charges were probably
exaggerated. What seems much less open to question is the importance not only of Chandos' leadership, but of his—unfortunately all too exhaustible—financial resources in explaining Conservative success in Bucks in the 1830s.

The county Liberals hoped for, and as long as he was their
prospective candidate received, the same kind of financial benefits
from G. R. Smith, a wealthy banker. And the Aylesbury Liberals
after the 1837 defeat began to look for a candidate with similar
qualifications. Previously Liberal candidates had not only not been
wealthy, they had been downright poor, which suggests that such
success as they had enjoyed did not derive from their advantage in
corrupting the electorate (another question that will be considered
in the light of the fuller evidence that exists for the period after
1847). Nugent's 1831 election had been subsidised by £500 from
the 'Patriotic Fund' in London. Hobhouse's 1835 expenses by a
like sum from one of the predecessors of the Reform Club, and
Nugent had had £600 from the Reform Club in 1837. At a July
1839 by-election caused by the death of W. M. Praed, however,
the Aylesbury Liberals, with the aid of Joseph Coppock the Liberal
agent at the Reform Club, secured a more financially promising
candidate, W. G. Cavendish, the son of C. C. Cavendish of Latimer, the former MP for the borough.

There was another reason why Lord Nugent was by-passed. At
the 1837 county election, in which G. R. Smith had been the only
Liberal candidate, Nugent had given one vote to his nephew. He
explained it as a mark of private and family respect in a situation
in which Chandos' seat was not really being contested by the
Liberals. But many of the Liberals could not accept his distinctions.
It was pointed out that it was Chandos' commanding leads which
allowed him to split his votes for other Conservatives, and argued
that it was impossible to distinguish between private and political
respect. As the *Aylesbury News* remarked in a restrained comment
on a letter defending Nugent's actions:

> 'Fair-Play' asks, 'Do you say it was Lord Nugent's duty not to
> vote for any man with whom he does not agree in politics?' We

have never yet said so, because we know that it would be impossible for electors to find candidates who agree entirely with them in political opinions. The impracticability of so doing obliges politicians to form themselves into two distinct parties, and the view with which politicians regarded the late county contest was that of a trial of party strength. . . . [It was a choice] between Toryism and Reform—Conservatism and Liberalism; and the men that gave one vote for each party, did (in our humble opinion) but half their duty.[30]

Because Nugent did not understand these basic political realities, he must be taught them.

On 16 July W. G. Cavendish issued an address in which he proclaimed himself a 'Friend of the Agricultural Interest and an undeviating friend of civil and religious liberty.' The latter quality was essential in a Liberal candidate for Aylesbury; the former, which signified that the Cavendishes were not among those in the party tending towards a fixed duty, would have been a most useful one. But Cavendish's appeal for the electors never came to the test. On the 17th Nugent issued an address asserting that he had the best right to the support of Aylesbury Reformers; and he said at the nomination that he would never give way to the private nominee of any other man, charging that Cavendish was the 'unknowing and unwilling representative of a stranger and an agent'—Coppock. With Liberalism thus divided, Cavendish on the 18th issued an address withdrawing from the contest. Meanwhile, the Conservatives had come forward with a candidate, who had announced himself on the same day as Cavendish. Charles Baillie Hamilton was related to the Scottish nobility and on occasion served on diplomatic missions abroad; but he was also a kind of grand major domo to the notorious Lady Wenman of Thame Park, who owed her peerage to the friendship of William IV, but was possessed in her own right of a considerable estate on the Oxfordshire borders of the constituency. Hamilton argued in his address that the country, and, referring to the debates over the Corn Laws and growing Whig sentiment for a fixed duty, particularly the agricultural interest, needed a Conservative majority in parliament.

Nugent was not at his best in this affair. He made it clear at the nomination that in fact he had only come forward to block Caven-

dish. He was of the opinion that it was a hopeless contest. He
pointed to a great shift of influence. Since Cavendish's father had
last stood in 1818 (actually since the Reform Act) the influence of
the Russells of Chequers, of the Smiths at Wendover, and of Sir
John Dashwood King of Halton had been lost to the Whigs, as had
the Aston Clinton influence of the Lakes, because the estate had
been sold to the Duke of Buckingham since the last election.
Though the shift had undoubtedly occurred, such defeatism on
Nugent's part was no political asset and hardly a reason for not
letting Cavendish have an opportunity to try his luck. Nor was
Nugent's inveighing against Coppock and the Reform Club very
convincing in one who had himself enjoyed their aid and largesse.
And when he said that he would give way to the expressed opinion
of the electorate but not to the private nominee of any man, he was
drawing a foolish and completely unreal distinction. Unfortunately
for him, it was all too easy to demonstrate its foolishmess and
unreality.

At the election on 31 July John Gibbs nominated John Ingram
Lockhart, a member of an Oxfordshire family and a radical of
Nugent's own stamp, who endorsed all of the latter's proposals for
reform—the ballot, shorter parliaments, an extended suffrage, and
a revision of the Corn Laws. It was explicitly stated by Gibbs and
by Lockhart that the point of the candidacy was to teach Nugent a
lesson, to show him that he could not impose himself on the
Liberals of the borough. Nugent had often warned his constituents
of the dangers of aristocratic influence, and some had clearly taken
his warnings to heart. The poll ended after an hour, when both
Liberals withdrew. Hamilton headed the poll with 620 votes,
Lockhart came second with 73, and Lord Nugent had only 3.[31]

The ground now seemed clear for Cavendish at the next election.
A requisition was sent to him in September, which he accepted,
and he duly provided professional assistance at the registration.[32]
But by the time of the general election the following June the
situation had changed completely. The government's 1841 budget
provided for a low fixed duty on corn, as well as on sugar and
timber; and C. C. Cavendish, a member for East Sussex, was one
of fifteen Whig and Liberal MPs who voted against the ministry
on these proposals. As a consequence, relations between the
Cavendishes and other members of their party were temporarily

strained. They were the only prominent Liberals in the Commons connected with Bucks who had opposed the government policy, though Robert Smith, since 1838 Lord Carrington, and successor to the Duke of Buckingham as Lord Lieutenant, was an opponent in the Lords. It was therefore thought inappropriate that the Cavendishes should join with other Liberals and thus confuse the issues in this election. This at any rate was the thinking so far as a county candidacy for C. C. Cavendish was concerned,[33] and it is the most likely explanation of his son's failure to appear in the borough.

In Cavendish's absence, Lord Nugent once again took the field, issuing an address on 8 June. Less than a week later, he withdrew. The ostensible reason was that promised funds had not been provided. A subscription had been got up to which the Duke of Bedford had been the sole contributor. But the lack of funds probably reflected a conviction of the hopelessness of the cause, and it was undoubtedly a well-warranted opinion. Nugent reminded the electors that 'a moderate and well considered fixed Duty on Foreign Corn I always declared in my opinion to be preferable to what has been called a sliding scale . . .' There was good reason to believe that his opinion was not that of the majority of his constituents. Seventy-one electors stated their confidence in Nugent and deplored the necessity for his withdrawal; but most of them were Dissenters and town-dwellers.[34]

There can be little doubt that the dominant issue in the other elections was the same. Though some Liberals would have argued with its conclusion, few would have argued with the *Bucks Herald*'s identification of the issue:

> The great struggle of the General Election will arise from the question, of whether the Agriculturists of the Empire shall or shall not retain that protection which is virtually necessary to their existence as land owners, farmers, and labourers . . .[35]

Most electors would seem to have agreed with the conclusion as well. As has been suggested, this would appear to have been the basic reason behind Nugent's withdrawal at Aylesbury and thus, for the uncontested return of two Conservatives, Hamilton and Rice Richard Clayton, brother of the Whig member for Marlow, who took the seat from which Rickford finally retired. It was also the reason why there was no serious contest in the county, and why Verney retired at Buckingham and thus allowed the uncontested return of two Conservatives there. And it was probably not the least reason why Col Clayton only squeaked into his seat at Marlow by one vote, and that vote bought, resulting in his subsequently being unseated. On the other hand, his support for the existing Corn Laws was also the main reason why Lord Carrington, who was generally thought to have at least one seat at Wycombe firmly in his pocket, saw both his candidates soundly defeated.

The contest in the county was an unusual one, not least because Dr Lee, who was one of the two Liberal candidates, dismissed the Corn Law issue as of secondary importance, and, beyond endorsing the principle of the fixed duty in his address, refused to discuss the matter. But Lee's address was only issued on 2 July, the day before the nomination; and Henry Morgan Vane, a relative of the Duke of Cleveland whom Lee had selected as the second candidate, simply appeared on the day of nomination. Thus the electors had little time to think about the Liberal candidates and ponder their principles.

In contrast, the three Conservative candidates, again running conjointly and served by one committee, had been in the field for almost a month, hammering the Corn Law issue. C. G. Du Pre of Beaconsfield, son of one of the successful candidates in the notorious 1802 Aylesbury election, had succeeded Chandos in an uncontested by-election in 1839. Sir W. L. Young stood yet again, and Charles Scott Murray, the young son of the unsuccessful candidate of 1832, succeeded the retiring Harcourt.

As in the 1837 by-election, the Liberal candidacies were again clearly only aimed at putting up 'a fight of principle'. Lee had been one of those most pressing for the necessity of contesting the election; and when Sir Harry Verney, who seems to have been the only other leading Liberal anxious to put up what all acknowledged to be a hopeless fight, deserted him, he went on alone.[36] A member of the Aylesbury Religious Freedom Society and often its deputy to London meetings,[37] Lee's address and speech at the nomination were mainly concerned with steps towards the Society's ultimate object—the separation of Church and State. And Dissenters were strongly in evidence among the supporters of the radical candidates. John Gibbs seconded Lee's nomination and urged his fellow

Dissenters to support their own principles in Lee. And Vane was nominated by Parnham Philips, a Dissenting baker from Wendover.

The contest was clearly one between the party of Dissent and the party of the Corn Laws, and the party of the Corn Laws won. There was remarkably little splitting of votes between parties. Young led the Conservatives, with 2,578 votes; Du Pre was only five votes behind him, with 2,572; and Scott Murray just twenty-five votes behind that, with 2,547. The party of Dissent failed to match these totals by a long way—Lee had only 495 votes, and Vane 450. The total poll was 3,071, and it is significant that the Liberal vote had been almost exactly halved since the two county elections of 1837 (then the vote had been 982 for Dashwood in the by-election, and 1,057 plumpers for Smith in the general election).[38] The by-election of 1837 and the 1841 election possessed remarkable similarities—in both the Liberal candidacies had been last-minute affairs, with no canvassing, and no money spent on electioneering. The most important difference between the two elections was the prominence of the Corn Law issue, which in 1841 was squarely and unavoidably before the electorate. Another difference lay in the fact that this issue deprived the Liberal candidates of the support of Lord Carrington; but he was the only Liberal grandee who deserted the cause. The others, including the Cavendishes, loyally supported Lee and Vane, and Carrington's influence would certainly not have accounted for the loss of five hundred votes, or anything like that number.

The most likely explanation of the decline of the Liberal vote therefore is the issue. And this would seem to be the interpretation the Liberal leadership accepted. So long as the Corn Laws remained an issue, they did not put forward another candidate, and the Conservatives were allowed to fill two vacancies without a contest, one on the death of Sir W. L. Young in 1842, one on young Scott Murray's resignation following his conversion to Roman Catholicism—a contingency for which he was undoubtedly right in assuming that his constituents had never bargained! But, it if was the decline in the Liberal vote and the issue that caused it that were to be important in the short run, it was the size of the Liberal vote that did turn out, and issues that brought it out, that were to be significant in the long run. The extent to which the Liberal party in Bucks depended on the Dissenters was perhaps never more clearly illustrated than in the 1841 election. The loyalty and enthusiasm of the Dissenters was obviously not enough to return a Liberal candidate, but the lack of it would certainly have been enough to decimate Liberalism, a fact of which Liberal candidates were well aware.

One of the centres of Dissent in Bucks was Wycombe. Dissenters very likely made up a majority of the borough electorate, and undoubtedly the most influential part of it. Quaker families like the Wheelers, the Edmondses, and the Lucases provided the main leadership of the Liberal party, and Independents, Baptists, and Methodists provided its backbone, in a borough that was heavily Liberal. It was in large part because the Smith family were so evidently deserving of the gratitude and support of Dissent that the Hon Robert had been so warmly received in 1831, when he retired from the county, and that his cousin, George Robert, the unsuccessful candidate for the county in 1837, followed him without a contest in 1838. But gratitude for support of popular principles was one thing, and unquestioning obedience quite another—as the new Lord Carrington found to his cost in 1841.

The Wycombe electorate included a minority of poorer voters, some inclined towards bribes, some towards Radicalism, and some probably towards both. The most colourful candidate that Wycombe had seen, or was to see, for a long time, Benjamin Disraeli, had been able to appeal at least to the Radical element—he claimed that it was the non-Radical 'corrupt' element that had defeated him—in both 1832 and 1835. He had also enjoyed the whole-hearted support of the Tories on both occasions. But, though his vote was creditable in both elections, it was not sufficient. In 1832 the totals were Smith 179, Grey 140, and Disraeli 119. In 1835 the candidates were the same, and their votes were 288, 147, and 128 respectively. George Dashwood, who, as he had expected at the time of the county by-election, had duly become a candidate on Grey's retirement at the general election of 1837, described some of the main factors in the political situation in the town in describing his own:

It is evident that I have all the middle classes of the respectable order decidedly with me. There is a lower class of voters

waiting to be bought, which are doubtful, who wd. give me the
preference to a tory or another if left to themselves. Smith has got
hold of many of these by his Abbey feasts [the reference was to
Wycombe Abbey, Lord Carrington's seat]—but the tories combined with the class I mention are not strong enough even with
immense bribery to beat us. . . .[39]

The Conservatives appearently came to the same conclusion.
Though there were several abortive candidacies and a London
banker named Hopkinson actually appeared at the nomination, he
ended by declining a poll. The New Poor Law, which had also
been an issue in 1835, had once again been exploited by local
Conservatives on this occasion. But, although Wycombe was the
only Bucks constituency in which the Poor Law became a major
issue, it did not prove overwhelmingly effective. Samuel Treacher,
one of a well-known family of chairmakers, said that, 'as a radical,'
he seconded Robert Wheeler's nomination of Dashwood.[40] Smith's
and Dashwood's unopposed return suggests, what was certainly
the case, that the Radicalism with the strongest appeal for the
Wycombe electorate was the advanced Liberalism in political and
religious questions of men like Nugent and Dashwood, as opposed
to Radicalism with a strong social reformist element.

The general election of 1841, however, demonstrated the appeal
of a question which, depending on the interpretation put upon it,
could have political, religious, economic, and social implications—
the question of Corn Law Reform. In Wycombe, there were two
elements in the opposition to the existing Corn Laws, one economic, the other anti-aristocratic. There was strong feeling among
all classes in the town of Wycombe, from the bankers and substantial tradesmen and the paper and chair manufacturers (the
last just beginning to make their appearance as a large employer
class) to the very poorest of the poor, who lived in dread of the
New Poor Law, that a greater freeing of trade, particularly a lower
duty on corn, would be to the advantage of all. This feeling was
almost certainly not shared by the farmers in the rural hinterland
that the Reform Act had added to the borough, and it was definitely
not shared by the borough's former representative, the new Lord
Carrington. But the election was to prove that the town held the
balance of electoral power and could triumph over both.

Not only did the bulk of the town feel that the government's proposal of a low fixed duty would be economically beneficial; many felt the issue provided an opportunity, as one of the Liberal seconders said at the nomination, 'to read the Abbey . . . a lesson . . .' The second Lord Carrington had, it will be recalled, become MP for the county in 1820 as the champion of Dissent and Catholic emancipation. He became the champion of parliamentary reform as well. But, while he was never to lose his belief in the most liberal solutions to religious problems, his other reforming views did not long survive the Great Reform Bill. And by the late thirties Liberals like Sir Harry Verney were beginning to have grave reservations about Carrington's Liberalism and Conservatives were exulting that the new Lord Lieutenant was 'not quite so much of a Rad as they wish . . .'[41]

Always proud and aloof, Carrington now began to demonstrate a cynical contempt for public opinion which he made no attempt to hide; and it was not only his growing conservatism, but also his contemptuous high-handedness that caused offence at Wycombe. Dashwood wrote to his wife after election preparations had begun that 'Lucas [Richard Lucas, a Quaker brewer] was here the other day & seems to think the Abbey party have overshot their mark in endeavouring to be quite independent of the better class of electors . . .' Shortly afterwards Dashwood informed Mrs Dashwood that 'a candidate has just started for Wycombe supported by Lord Carrington, a Tory of the name of Freshfield . . .' James Freshfield was Carrington's London solicitor. The next day G. R. Smith, who had differed from his cousin and supported the government on the budget, announced his retirement; and Dashwood reported: 'There is now little doubt that Smith retires to make way for two tory nominees of Lord Carrington. I am glad it has incited extreme disgust . . .' And, he added in a postscript: 'Every person of respectability I have seen is staunch to me.'[42]

It made matters no better that after the government's defeat on the protection issue in the Commons Carrington gave his proxy to Lord Stafford to be used in the government's support. It was doubly insulting that, while he chose personally to parade his Whig loyalty he attempted to impose two Conservatives on Wycombe. As a consequence of Carrington's actions, those who came to call themselves the 'Independent Liberal Party,' or the

'Town,' as opposed to the 'Abbey,' party, brought forward a second Liberal candidate in the person of Ralph Bernal (later Bernal Osborne). It was to be a straight fight between anti-Corn Law 'Town' and the pro-Corn Law 'Abbey'.

In nominating Dashwood, Robert Wheeler recalled the services of another Dashwood, against another noble lord and his flunkeys, half a century before. Addressing himself as well to the non-electors, Wheeler remembered that 'they had of old been of great service to the borough of Wycombe (cheers); for what placed Sir John Dashwood [King], when he came forward to represent the borough, over the oligarchy of the day, which would have destroyed the independence of the town of Wycombe, but the pressure from without?' And Wheeler remembered as well the crowds which had helped to drive Dashwood King from the borough, when he had clashed with the town's sentiments by refusing to support the 1831 Reform Bill, and how he who was now Lord Carrington had been put in his place. The time had come to pay Carrington the same compliment and vindicate the independence of Wycombe once more.

Wheeler also strongly endorsed the ministerial plan for revising the Corn Laws, and the Liberal speakers who followed echoed his sentiments in both respects. Dashwood was seconded by Freeman George Spicer, who declared himself 'a member of the manufacturing interest,' (he was a paper manufacturer). Thomas Edmonds, a wealthy Quaker miller, nominated Bernal as another candidate who would contribute both to the freedom of the borough and the alteration of the Corn Laws. And William Winter seconded the nomination, calling on his fellow electors to teach the Abbey a lesson. The Abbey countered with two of Carrington's local allies, William Parker, a retired draper whose son was to be Carrington's local solicitor, and William Rose who occupied the latter position at the time, who nominated and seconded Freshfield. The second Conservative candidate, Robert Alexander, was nominated and seconded by two local farmers. Aside from the two major issues, both Dashwood and Bernal promised to work for a mitigation of the severities of the New Poor Law, which doubtless increased their popularity—as it was certainly meant to. The popular candidates won handily. Dashwood headed the poll with 189; Bernal Osborne got 159 votes; and Freshfield and Alexander lost with 130 and 86 votes respectively. Aristocratic influence had been beaten once again.[43]

At Buckingham, Sir Harry Verney put the entire blame for his withdrawal, and thus for the uncontested return of two Conservatives, on aristocratic influence. He said in an address to the electors on 12 June:

> I have no reason to believe that your political opinions have changed since you did me the honor to elect me your Representative in 1837; but much property in the Borough has changed hands during the last four years, and the mode in which the influence thus obtained has been used against me hitherto, render it certain that I could not contest the seat with a prospect of success . . .[44]

This interpretation was not however universally accepted. The *Bucks Herald* freely admitted that much property had changed hands:

> but it is equally true that the feeling of the Borough has changed even more than the property, and Sir Harry would have been rejected had the Borough property remained in the same hands as in 1837. In proof of this we could mention Electors of the first respectability in Buckingham whose property has not changed hands—members of Sir Harry's Committee who have declared their intention not to vote for Sir Harry had he come forward . . . Sir Harry who to the last adhered to Government—who sought a last opportunity of expressing his admiration of their tortuous policy and disgraceful conduct—of course must expect that a rural constituency would reject him.

And referring to Sir Harry's previous differences with his constituents over Church legislation, the newspaper's comment concluded:

> If his votes respecting the Church injured him with Churchmen —his votes with an Anti-Corn Law Government must affect him with Electors, whose trade and prosperity depend solely on the Farmers of the neighbourhood or on persons deriving their entire existence from the soil.[45]

The *Bucks Herald* was hardly impartial, of course. But its analysis was also that of one equally partisan in the other direction —Joseph Parkes, the Liberal parliamentary agent, who reckoned in his report to Lord John Russell that the Corn Law question

would lose Buckingham at the election.[46] There was also truth in
the allegation that Verney's position on the Corn Laws cost him
some of his most prominent and influential local supporters. One
example was Humphrey Humphreys, the mayor, who seconded his
nomination in 1837. Another was Philip Box, an auctioneer; and
there can be no doubt of the strength of Box's feeling on the question. In 1852 John Gibbs wrote the then Marquis of Chandos (to
whom what remained of the family estates after the second duke's
financial disasters had been transferred) requesting the use of the
Buckingham town hall for a free trade meeting. Chandos returned
a polite reply that he was quite willing but that the mayor's
approval must be secured. Box was the mayor—and he was not
willing.

> In reply to your note of the 16th Inst. I beg leave to say that
> as Free Trade (so call'd) has now full possession of the Country,
> it certainly cannot be a source of much difficulty for you to find a
> place for discussing its merits, but as long as I am Chief Magistrate
> of Buckingham I shall most respectfully decline granting the Town
> Hall for any such purpose.[47]

It sometimes seems to be assumed—then and since—that auction-
eers and their like had no important opinions without reference to
noble lords and their like; it is an unsafe assumption.

Chapter 8 INFLUENCE, COERCION, AND PRINCIPLE: PART I

DOUBTLESS THERE are those who will suspect that this book has paid too much attention to issues and principles, and too little to the influence of the great and the powerful. I think to the contrary that others have paid too much attention to such influence, and that closer examination of the evidence will reveal that its role in the electoral politics of Victorian England was less crucial than is usually supposed. Bucks politics from the forties to the late fifties provide an excellent opportunity to examine the question of the relative importance of various kinds of influence, on the one hand, and issues and principles, on the other, in determining electoral behaviour.

As has been seen, the thirties and early forties saw a marked trend towards Conservatism, a trend that did not apparently coincide with any marked shift of influence. From the late forties there would be a decided trend away from Conservatism and towards Liberalism. This time the trend coincided with an important shift of influence in the same direction. With the fall of the house of Grenville the Conservative cause waned, as the Liberal cause waxed with the rise of the house of Rothschild, and of other lesser Liberal luminaries. The question is, how, and in what way, were the phenomena connected? For it is certainly not enough simply to point to their coincidence and assume that the explanation is self-evident.

It must be borne in mind, for example, that Chandos in his prime provided the Conservative cause with more than just the votes of the Grenville tenants. He also provided much of the money for fighting elections and looking after the party's interests between elections. Well-disposed persons had to be registered and they had to be got to the polls, which cost a great deal. Chandos paid out a great deal, at a time when the Liberal expenditure on such critical items was sporadic at best; and, while Conservative organizations never declined to the low ebb reached by their Liberal adversaries in the thirties, there can be little question that after Chandos' fall the machinery provided by wealthy Liberal patrons was much better. The factor of organization could be, and often was, equally as important as influence.

Perhaps it will be argued that by providing organization the grandees only further solidified their influence. There were two sides to the coin, however. If it was difficult to win without organization, it was impossible to win without votes; and those who spent lavishly on organization did so with only one end in mind— to win. The size of their investment may well have made them more, rather than less, vulnerable to electoral pressure. There would, of course, have been no difficulty had the grandees also been able to produce the necessary votes to win. It seems likely, however, that their ability to do so has been vastly over-estimated. Certainly in the two Bucks constituencies about which there is fairly complete information great landlords were far from being able to produce majorities.

The great landowner who came closest was the Duke of Buckingham in the borough of Buckingham itself. At the time of the 1841 election it had 392 voters on the electoral register, 116 of whom were the duke's tenants; and the Conservative agents considered all but two or three of the more substantial among them safe votes for their landlord's candidates.[1] Undoubtedly the 30 per cent which the duke's tenants represented was an appreciable proportion of the electorate, and it might be thought that with the co-operation of one or two other large Conservative landowners the duke would have had the borough in his pocket. As it happened, however, there were no other large Conservative landlords. The duke's nearest competitor was a non-resident landlord, W. A. Hammond of Canterbury, with seven tenants at Bourton, all of whom voted Conservative. Then there were half a dozen clergymen, boasting from one to half a dozen tenants, most of whom voted Conservative. This other Conservative 'landed influence' in the borough therefore added perhaps twenty-five votes to those of the duke's tenants, still obviously a long way from a majority. And, of course, until 1841 it was patently obvious that the Con-

servatives did not have a clear majority in the borough, Sir Harry
Verney having been once again returned as a Liberal in the contested 1837 election.

Verney had one tenant in the borough; and the only landed
influence behind him was that of the young Lord Clifden having
six of the seven electors in Lenborough as his tenants. Some of
Verney's other leading supporters—his agent, Thomas Hearn,
George Nelson, the banker, and a couple of large tradesmen—had
a few houses, and Edward Bartlett's widow had a good deal of
property. All had some Liberal tenants, but all also had Conservative tenants; so it is evident that they did not demand political
obedience from those occupying their property. The most important function of these smaller Liberal landlords seems to have
been to provide for those whom the duke ejected for voting contrary to his wishes.

It might perhaps be argued that what a great nobleman like the
duke lacked in tenants he made up for by a judicious distribution
of custom and patronage. There is no doubt that the duke tried
this, giving the most minute attention as to where the Stowe
household spent its money between the contested elections of 1832
and 1837. On 14 July Sir Thomas Fremantle recorded in his
journal:

> The Duke full of anger because poor Louisa [Lady Fremantle]
> went inadvertently to Mr Kirby's shop at Buckm. Tried in vain
> to pacify him but was unable. He is very disagreeable & cross.[2]

Kirby was a Congregational baker and a Liberal. But, though the
duke clearly took infinite pains, even to noticing where Lady
Fremantle bought her buns, he failed in his objective of unseating
Verney in the election.

As has been seen, Verney was not unseated until the first great
crisis over the Corn Laws in the general elecion of 1841. Perhaps,
as Verney claimed, the increase in the duke's influence would have
been enough to defeat him had he stood. Lacking full evidence, it
is impossible to say. But it is virtually certain that had the duke's
influence not defeated him his support of the proposed modifi-
cation of the Corn Laws would have done. In 1837 he had defeated Chetwode by only eighteen votes. It would only have been
necessary therefore for ten electors to have voted differently for the

result to have been different. And there were at least twenty-six electors who voted for Verney in 1837 who declared their intention of not doing so again, or who were highly doubtful in canvasses before the 1841 election. For two of these, there is the explanation that the duke had become their landlord in the interim, but there is no indication that similar factors had weighed with any of the others. For most of them, the most likely explanation is that the Conservative agents gave for one of the doubtfuls, Perridge Langton, a large farmer with two or three tenants of his own in Padbury—'Corn Law Supporter'.

For seven, there was the terse explanation 'has joined Association', referring to the Buckingham Conservative Association formed in the autumn of 1837. By 1841 the association had sixty-nine members. Some may have joined to please their landlords, but there is no indication that any pressure was exerted on them to do so; and membership was more likely an indication of enthusiasm for Conservative causes. Certainly the association was not a mere tool of the Grenvilles. The second duke, or Chandos as he was in 1837, had not been forward in its foundation. It is not clear which of the clergymen in the constituency had been the two or three most active in founding the association; but very soon the dominant figure in it was its secretary, Henry Smith, a large Buckingham solicitor and long to be the leading legal light of Bucks Conservatism.

Smith naturally worked closely with the Grenvilles, but he was by no means their creature. And the duke seems to have taken exception to the association's insistence on—at the very least—giving its stamp of approval to candidates by formally requisitioning them.[3] The association may have done more. It is not clear how Sir John Chetwode had first come forward in 1837, nor who decided that he should stand again, though the association claimed that honour.[4] The duke probably brought down Gen John Hall on Chetwode's death in 1845, and the young marquis took Fremantle's place after the latter had resigned early in 1846 when Peel's government, of which he was a member, was preparing to repeal the Corn Laws. Both might be considered the duke's nominees. But they were also the kind of staunch Protestant and Protectionist candidates the constituency appears to have wanted. Both were returned without opposition in 1852, and Hall again in

1857, long after the duke's financial collapse in 1847, which occasioned the closing of Stowe and the sale of much of his Buckingham property. One may at least wonder whether the constituency's loyalty was not more to the duke's principles than to his person.

The duke may have thought that he could nominate a member for Buckingham, and in the sense that no candidate could have secured the one fairly safe Conservative seat without his support he would have been right. This was certainly not the same kind of right of nomination the Grenvilles had enjoyed before 1832, and whether 'nomination' or 'pocket borough' are very useful terms to describe the situation after that date seems highly questionable. In any event, whatever he may have thought about his powers at Buckingham, the duke never imagined that he could nominate a member for Aylesbury after the Reform Act. His role there he described to J. C. Herries in 1842 as merely that of one who had 'always taken an active part in protecting this Borough from the Whigs.' He suggested to Herries that if he seriously considered becoming a candidate he should come down to Wotton, meet others with political influence in the borough, and generally 'sense everything connected with the place and the Constituency . . .'[5] Herries' candidacy never materialised, since Hamilton did not die as the duke expected; but the complexities of the borough's politics that the duke hinted at soon became apparent.

The most serious complications began in 1842 when Peel modified the sliding scale as part of his sweeping fiscal reforms and the two members for Aylesbury, Hamilton and Rice Clayton, supported him. The duke was furious and at the annual meeting of the Agricultural Society he announced that as a consequence of their voting for an alteration of the Corn Laws he could no longer support them. Hamilton was abroad in 1847 and so did not stand again in the general election. Clayton, however, did, after having clashed with the duke further because of his support for Peel's increased grant to the Catholic college at Maynooth in 1845. True to his threat, the duke refused his support. He first tried to bring down the Recorder of Buckingham, Serjeant John Byles, but found insufficient support for him. The duke had then given his sole support to a large local landowner, John Peter Deering of the Lee, near Great Missenden. Lord Nugent also came forward again, the major issue that had divided him from many of his constituents having been removed by the repeal of the Corn Laws in the previous year.

Perhaps fearing that the absence of the issue would greatly strengthen Nugent's postion, perhaps out of pique because the duke would not support their candidate, some leading Conservatives, mainly in the town, refused to support the duke's candidates. The angry rector of Horsenden wrote to Mrs Disraeli:

> We shall . . . have Deering for the Borough. . . . What a set those Aylesbury Borough [ie town] electors are. They actually supposed we were going to hand over the Representation to 'milk & water Clayton' merely because they were fearful that a third man coming forward against Nugent & Clayton might jeopardize the chance of the latter. And so forsooth they turn a cold shoulder upon Mr Byles and say they cannot promise him their individual support!—as though the Town of Aylesbury with its army of petty-fogging [sic] Attorneys and Cheesemongers constituted the whole constituency. So now we intend to prove to these deluded people that it is the Hundreds & not the Borough that can return the member they choose. They have also behaved very shabbily to the Duke, just at the very moment when in his sad difficulties they should have supported him to the very death; but such is the gratitude of the multitude.[6]

It seems doubtful that the duke's 'sad difficulties' had anything to do with the town Conservatives' intransigence. In fact, he was in his financial death throes. At almost this very time, in May 1847, control of the family estates was being transferred to the young Marquis of Chandos in an attempt to save something from the wreck. But there had long been rumours of financial difficulties, and it was to be some time before the world knew the full extent of the disaster. Perhaps the duke's troubles made his Aylesbury agent Humphrey Bull somewhat bolder. In any event, Bull led what different reports put at between some thirty to sixty of the Grenville tenants to poll for Nugent and Deering, and both the duke and the marquis swore that they had nothing to do with the former vote. They would appear to have been speaking in good faith; for all the evidence suggests that the strategy was one concerted between Bull and two electioneering clergymen, the Rev Edward Owen, Rector of the St Leonards and son-in-law of the founder of the Agricultural Association (Robert Sutton) and his son, who could not forgive Clayton for his vote for the May-nooth grant. [7]

Be that as it may, the votes of the Grenville tenants would have made up a substantial part of the seventy odd that put Nugent ahead of Clayton and divided the representation between him and Deering. The duke was generally blamed for this, and for the fact that the third Conservative candidate for the county, Christopher Tower, stood down and gave C. C. Cavendish an uncontested return. Sir William Fremantle reported that 'every one . . . whom I have heard speak on the subject considers the D. of Buckm. to have acted with inconsistency and folly not to be understood. He has introduced a member for the Co. over whom he has no control [Disraeli], also a Whig, and a Radical for Aylesbury.'[8]

There can be little doubt that the main explanation of the duke's actions was his attachment to the protectionist cause. This explains his ardent support for Disraeli, the real leader of the party in the Commons, for the county seat. His suspicion of Clayton's solidity on the question was the reason he gave him for refusing support. And Tower's failure to appear at the county meetings protesting against repeal had led to suspicion of him as well. The suspicion of both was probably quite justified. Clayton had already demonstrated his moderation on the question in 1842, and his father-in-law Sir George Nugent and brother-in-law Sir Thomas Fremantle were strong Peelites. As for Tower, he was more than willing to let the Corn Law question drop, and by 1857 was being proposed as a Liberal candidate for the county. [9] It seems likely that both these MPs were among those who voted against Peel on the question out of deference to the opinions of their constituents.

The protectionists did not enjoy their victory at Aylesbury for very long. Clayton and his supporters were bitter over their defeat, and one of the most prominent, Acton Tindal, an Aylesbury solicitor and Clerk of the Peace for the county, petitioned against Deering's return on the grounds that his supporters had indulged in treating so extensive that it amounted to bribery. This was proved to the satisfaction of a parliamentary election committee, Deering was unseated, and in 1848 a by-election was held to fill the vacant seat.

Initially, the two Conservative factions once again each put a candidate in the field. One Liberal came forward, John Houghton of Broom Hall, Sunninghill, Berks and Upton Farm, Dinton, a large land agent and grazier. Houghton stood as the representative of 'Free Trade and Liberal opinions' and made a great deal of the fact that he was a tenant farmer, and, if elected, would be the first one to sit in the Commons. Fear that a division in Conservative ranks would give the game to Houghton, or that the Liberals would advance an even more formidable candidate, finally brought about at least a papering over of Conservative quarrels.[10] Clayton's former supporters withdrew their candidate and left Quentin Dick, a protectionist and the choice of the Deering party, as the Conservative candidate, though Tindal and his father, the County Treasurer, remained neutral in the ensuing election. Dick won easily.

At the time of the 1848 election the Grenville estates were still intact. But later in the year the duke's financial disasters set in train events which were to throw all the patterns of influence in the constituency into violent dislocation. The Grenville estates in the town and hundreds had to be sold to satisfy the duke's creditors, and there were those ready, willing, and able to seize the opportunities thus afforded.

The Rothschild brothers were already well known in the area. Their staghounds had hunted the Vale since 1839 and Baron Meyer had acquired property at Mentmore and was High Sheriff of the county in 1847. At the sales of the Grenville property, Sir Anthony bought the great bulk of the Aston Clinton estate and Baron Lionel bought varous properties in Aylesbury, Bierton, and Hulcott. In addition, in 1849 Baron Lionel increased his holdings at the expense of another old family in the constituency, acquiring the Halton estate on the death of Sir John Dashwood King. This was just the beginning. In the years that followed most of the Grenville property which had initially gone to a number of smaller individual buyers, and a great deal more, was gradually bought up by the Rothschilds' ever-watchful Aylesbury agent, James James. Others profited to an important, though lesser, degree. Lord Carrington whose property at Bledlow and elsewhere already gave him considerable influence in the constituency bought more, mainly in the town. And Acton Tindal acquired the Lordship of the Manor of Aylesbury and other bits and pieces.

Thus when Lord Nugent died in November 1850 the contest for

his vacant seat took place under much altered circumstances. Not only had there been a change in those possessing influence, influence had also changed its direction. Others besides the Rothschilds were involved. Acton Tindal had never recovered from his bitterness over the 1847 election. His family were Peelites—Peel had made his uncle Lord Chief Justice—and by 1850 he was firmly convinced that the Conservative attachment to protection was not only misguided, but dangerous to the continued tranquillity of the country. As Clerk of the Peace, he was naturally closely associated with Lord Carrington, the Lord Lieutenant, and marriage to the daughter of the Rev John Harrison, the Liberal vicar of Dinton, increased his Liberal sympathies and brought him even more closely into Carrington's orbit. For a variety of reasons, then, by 1850 Tindal was ready to shift his party allegiance.

The result was to complicate even further the party situation in Aylesbury. The Liberals were now comprised of three roughly defined groups. There was the 'old' Liberal party, largely Dissenters, many of whom had fought together every liberal battle from repeal of the Test and Corporation Acts and Catholic emancipation through parliamentary reform and free trade. Their political position tended to be extreme-Liberal to Radical. Then there were the newcomers. The Rothschilds were generally loyal to 'the party'—that is, the parliamentary party leadership—but not unnaturally, they took a firm and uncompromising attitude on the rights of religious nonconformists, which gave them a bond with the 'old' Liberals. Finally, there were those who chose to call themselves 'the old Whig party'.[11] This consisted of a rather unusual alliance between Tindal, his father-in-law the Rev Mr Harrison, Lord Carrington, and last, but by no means least, the former agent of the Duke of Buckingham, Humphrey Bull.

There was not the inequality between these partners that the difference in their social positions might suggest. As the Conservative counsel at a later election inquiry, after Bull had made another political migration, was to admit:

Mr. H. Bull was a land-agent, and had considerable influence at Aylesbury. He had an opportunity of being of service to small farmers in many ways in regard to loans, mortgages etc., and by merely lifting up his finger and saying for whom he could vote, he would probably carry between thirty and forty voters with him.[12]

In addition to considerable influence, Bull knew the constituency inside out. As the duke's former agent, through his own extensive business activities, and as the relieving officer of the Aylesbury Union since its inception, he had acquired that intimate knowledge of voters which was invaluable in an election agent.

Lord Carrington's contribution of influence and landed interest to the alliance is obvious. Harrison's was largely monetary. With large property in three or four other counties (he had no extensive property in Bucks), he was a wealthy man, and willing to use his wealth. Tindal too, besides influence, provided money. Together, he and Harrison secured Bull's services as their political agent to look after registration and election matters generally. It was a complicated transaction which involved a cash payment of £300, a salary of £150 per annum, and Bull becoming Harrison's land agent.

It was a formidable combination, and its object at least as far as three of its members were concerned—Bull was a complete opportunist—was to build up a powerful centre party which could both hold the line against the protectionists and check the Radical-ism of the 'old' Liberals.[13] To this end, with the assistance of Coppock and the Reform Club, the 'old Whigs' produced Frederick Calvert as their candidate for the vacancy caused by Nugent's death late in 1850.

Calvert had many advantages as a candidate. As the brother of Sir Harry Verney (who had been born Calvert but took the name of the family whose estates he inherited), he benefited from his brother's popularity. As the brother-in-law of Abel Smith, he attracted important support from the Smiths' former pocket borough of Wendover. But, unfortunately for the success of this undoubtedly clever scheme, Calvert's candidacy was announced without prior consultation with the 'old' Liberals. This aroused deep suspicion and the old cry of nomination. Calvert was also equivocal about the total abolition of Church rates, a question that had been particularly acute since 1847 when prosecutions for non-payment had commenced before the Aylesbury magistrates. And some of the 'old' Liberals, led by that doughty opponent of both nominees and Church rates, John Gibbs, persuaded Houghton to come forward once more.

Meanwhile, the protectionists had once more produced Serjeant Byles. As was to become the usual practice hereafter, Byles had apparently been decided upon by a few of the leading gentlemen of the constituency meeting at the Carlton, and with their blessing he came down to Aylesbury and began his canvass. But either the gentlemen at the Carlton had not inquired closely enough into Byles' opinions, or had been unconcerned by them. Others, however, were not only concerned, but horrified, when it was disclosed that Byles was a Unitarian (though he proclaimed his support of the Established Church). The Rev Edward Owen, who had played so important a part in Deering's campaign, indignantly withdrew his support, and Byles beat a hasty retreat,[14] leaving the Conservatives without a candidate.

Houghton, who had temporarily withdrawn to close the free trade ranks, now reappeared, and thus the 1850 contest was between two Liberals. Houghton had spent little money in 1848, and he spend none at all in 1850. Neither did he have any of the grandees of the party behind him. Calvert won easily.

But Calvert was not to enjoy his seat for long. Tindal's petition against Deering's return had set an unfortunate precedent, and Calvert had hardly been elected when, not Houghton's supporters, but the Conservatives lodged a petition against his return. This seems to have been planned in advance of the election, and the ground prepared by issuing treating tickets in Calvert's name.[15] Calvert was unseated and a new election ordered, which took place in April of 1851.

The Conservatives were ready with their candidate, the ultra-tory protectionist W. B. Ferrand. The Liberals countered with Richard Bethell, already famed as a Chancery lawyer and subsequently, as Lord Westbury, Lord Chancellor. Bethell was a friend of Calvert, which recommended him to Tindal. The Rothschilds endorsed him as the candidate from 'headquarters.' The 'old' Liberal party were at first distinctly cool. Bethell, like Tindal, was a converted Peelite and, also like Tindal, still a member of the Conservative Club (though both were soon to be ejected). But this time the candidate was more tactfully introduced. Before he began his canvass a meeting was held at the Liberal head-

quarters, the Bell Inn, where Bethell explained his principles and
answered questions. His principles were not only Liberal, but,
with prodding from Gibbs, Houghton and others, seemed to grow
more Liberal as the contest progressed. By the day of nomination
he had come to believe not only in free trade, but also in a further
extension of the franchise, a redistribution of seats, and a total
abolition of Church rates. But the great issue in the election
remained protection versus free trade. In a hard-fought battle
Bethell edged in with a majority of twenty-six in a poll of 1,062
electors.[16]

During the course of the year that followed before the general
election called by the new Conservative government of Lord
Derby in 1852, there was real danger that the victory won with
such effort would be sacrificed because of internal squabbles in the
Liberal camp. Bethell and Tindal fell out over a difference of
opinion on election bills, and the quarrel soon became transformed
into a struggle for power between the 'old Whigs' and the Rothschilds. The former declared they would never support Bethell
again under any circumstances. The Rothschilds not only continued to support Bethell, but, according to Lord Carrington, were
looking for another candidate to run with him.[17] The 'old Whigs'
countered by seeking their own candidate. After an unsuccessful
attempt to persuade Calvert to run again, they settled on Austen
Henry Layard, a young diplomat already famous for his exca-
vations at Nineveh.

The 'old' Liberal party were in a dilemma. Bethell had become
very popular with them, especially since he had recently developed
an enthusiasm for the ballot, and a meeting of Liberal electors late
in March enthusiastically endorsed him as a candidate. This was
before the breach between Bethell and Tindal became an open
one; and Houghton had called the meeting with the aim of dis-
cussing a second Liberal candidate—himself. But John Gunn, son
of the late Independent minister and a large grocer, argued that the
battle should be fought by men 'who really had a chance of being
elected,' and others agreed with him. It was decided to postpone
any decision on a second candidate until a subsequent meeting.
That took place on 14 April and passed a vote of no-confidence in
Houghton.[18] In the meantime, however, there had been a meeting
between Tindal and some twenty of the 'old' Liberals at the Bell

two days before, where Tindal had fully explained his differences with Bethell. Pragmatists like Gunn constituted a majority of those present and the meeting regretfully recommended that, as the dispute made his return seem doubtful, Bethell should stand down. At the same time Layard was endorsed as a candidate.[19] The larger meeting two days later was divided on the question and came to no conclusion whatever, once again postponing a decision and adjourning to a later date.

Meanwhile, the Conservatives had found two candidates, J. Temple West and Dr Augustus Bayford. So as matters stood at the end of April, there were two Conservative candidates working in tandem and two Liberal candidates working at cross purposes, with Houghton still threatening to come forward and make a third. The Reform Club was frantic. Sir William Hayter, the Liberal whip, begged in vain that Tindal reconsider. Joseph Parkes was equally unsuccessful.[20]

The way in which the quarrel began to move towards settlement is most enlightening as to the balance of power in the Liberal party at Aylesbury. The adjourned meeting of the Liberal electors met on 28 April and resolved to adjourn once more until two days later when Layard would be present. The meeting duly occurred on Friday, 30 April. Layard, introduced by John Gunn, declared that he did not wish to divide the Liberal interest and left it up to the meeting to decide whether he should remain a candidate. He was then asked to state his opinions. He proclaimed himself a free trader, an advocate of an extended suffrage, and, if it was the will of his constituency, of the ballot. Frederick Payne, a chemist and a member of the prominent Independent family, then moved that Layard was a fit candidate. This was seconded by John Hamilton, later the editor of the *Morning Star* and at this time of the Gibbs' *Bucks Advertiser*, but only after he had received a firm assurance from Layard that he would vote for the ballot. The motion was carried unanimously. Tindal then expressed the hope that his personal differences with Bethell would not influence anyone else's vote. This was followed by Joseph Jones, an Aylesbury solicitor and self-avowed former London Chartist, moving that Bethell was a fit candidate, which was seconded by John Gibbs' son, Robert and carried with enthusiasm.[21]

What makes all this of particular significance is that it was in

direct contravention of the advice of Layard's especial patron, Lord
Carrington. Carrington was in favour of complete separation from
Bethell and the Rothschilds. More important, in mid-April when
Tindal was beginning his overtures to the 'old' Liberals, Carrington
warned him against accepting the authority of meetings and
promising support for 'extreme measures.' He cautioned Tindal
that 'too great concession to the radicals never answers, and tho' I
quite adopt, and thoroughly approve of what you are reported to
have said, still we must not bid too highly for the democrats.'[22]

Layard's promise to vote for the ballot, subsequently incor-
porated in his address 'in deference to an unanimous expression of
opinion in its favour on the part of a large majority of the Liberal
electors of this Borough,' shows how far Carrington's advice was
followed.[23] Someone at the Wycombe nomination expressed
surprise that, while in that town his cousin and nominee Martin
Tucker Smith strongly opposed the ballot, in Aylesbury Carrington
supported a candidate in favour of the ballot.[24] But it was not
really strange—it was simply political realism. Though the 'old'
Liberals could not guarantee the success of a candidate, they could
guarantee his failure; for they provided the votes, or a good many
of them, at any rate. Tindal early accepted the implications of this
fact. Carrington had to come to accept them. The 'old Whigs' had
to choose between holding the line against Radicalism on the one
hand, and political success, on the other. They chose the latter.
They produced and paid for the candidates, but the 'old' Liberals
could largely shape the candidates' programmes.

Continued pressure from the 'old' Liberals and pleading from
'the Party' in London, added to the candidates' own instincts for
self-preservation, gradually brought about at least a papering over
of the differences between the two Liberals and their supporters.
Though they maintained separate organizations, there was grud-
ging co-operation between their agents, and finally on 17 June the
two candidates appeared on the same platform and endorsed the
same principles. At the same meeting, after satisfying himself of
Layard's soundness on parliamentary reform, the abolition of
Church rates, and one or two other questions, Houghton declared
his own candidacy at an end.[25] At last, the Liberals were reunited.

The two Conservatives talked mainly in their addresses about
two issues—protection and anti-popery—but they were highly

equivocal on both. They were apparently even more equivocal in private conversation. The gentlemen at the Carlton had learned some of the same lessons about the wisdom of wider consultation as had their Liberal counterparts; and William Lowndes of Chesham, who had to some extent assumed the Duke of Buckingham's place as the presiding genius of Aylesbury Conservatism, took the precaution of trying the candidates on certain of the more formidable Aylesbury Conservatives before they went down to begin their canvass. The Rev Edward Owen jr reported to Tindal that when he and his father pressed them on what Lord Derby's government would do about the repeal of the Maynooth grant and protection, the only reply they got was, 'Can't say—see how the wind blows.'[26] The Owens, who had long hankered to use their electioneering talents on a winning side once more, used this wishy-washiness as an excuse to throw in their lot, and become the final element in, the motley alliance that went by the name 'old Whig.'

The result of the contest between two Liberals and two wavering protectionists was an impressive victory for the Liberals. Layard, who headed the poll, was 111 and Bethell 78 votes ahead of Bayford, the leading Conservative.

Different problems and issues governed the 1857 election. There was once again a breach in the Liberal ranks, but this time it began as a clash between the two sitting members over policy. Layard's Radicalism, which had budded so uncertainly in Aylesbury, blossomed forth in the House of Commons. An ardent advocate of the Crimean War, he was no less ardent in espousing the Radical demands for the military and administrative reform it aroused. His support for parliamentary reform and the ballot had grown from political concession into political conviction. And he had also become highly critical of Palmerston's blustering foreign policy—so critical that he joined in the vote against the government on the coercion of China after the Arrow incident, the question on which Palmerston dissolved.

Bethell, the darling of the Radicals, had also undergone a certain transformation. He had gained a knighthood and had been made first Solicitor General in the Aberdeen Coalition and then Attorney General in the Palmerston government. As a member of the government, he was, not surprisingly, extremely critical of those who had turned it out. Never the soul of tact and moderation, he vented his spleen, indirectly but no less obviously, on Layard at a Liberal meeting in Aylesbury.[27]

The Conservatives, for their part, put up only one candidate, Thomas Tyringham Bernard of Winchendon Priory, son of the former member for Aylesbury. Not only was Bernard a very popular local resident, but styling himself a 'Liberal Conservative,' he also made a very moderate and uncontroversial appeal. Protection, he said, was a dead issue, and he was very glad of it. On the question of Church rates, he was most conciliatory, hoping for a just settlement that would be accepted by all parties. In short, he made every effort to offend no one.

The result of the three-cornered contest was that Bethell and Bernard were returned and Layard squeezed out. The 'old Whigs' had suffered a humiliating defeat. It was no less humiliating because one of their own number had contributed to it. Humphrey Bull had become Harrison's land agent as part of the arrangement by which he entered the alliance. Harrison came to believe, with good reason, that Bull was feathering his nest at his employer's expense. As a consequence, Bull was dismissed, not only as the land but as the political agent. His reprisal was to support Bethell in the 1857 election and throw all his influence against Layard.

All this was not forgotten in 1859. Unknown to Bethell, Tindal arranged for another Liberal candidate to stand, Thomas Vernon Wentworth, a son-in-law of Lord Clanricarde. Perhaps suffering from a guilty conscience, Bethell believed that the object was to squeeze him out. This would appear to have been unjustified, as Wentworth was secured through Sir William Hayter and at his urging. In any case, after unsuccessful efforts to get Wentworth withdrawn, Bethell himself thought it prudent to withdraw to a safer haven at Wolverhampton.[28]

The Rothschilds were furious. According to one source, Baron Lionel swore to turn out any tenant of his who voted for Wentworth. Certainly James, the Rothschild agent, made their sentiments known at a meeting of the tenants.[29] Once more, it appeared that the party in Aylesbury was irrevocably split. But the Rothschilds came around. Wentworth's agent later remarked: 'It is not Aylesbury that they regard but the great liberal party with which they are identified and by whose means, they are getting into the highest circles in town—If they were not politicians, they would be nothing.[30] The judgement is too harsh, but the Rothschilds did show great loyalty to their party. Two days after his first instructions to the tenants, James called another meeting and reversed them. Liberal influence was again intact—except, of course, for Bull. So deep was his hatred of Tindal and Harrison, that even the Rothschilds, who were also his landlords, could not entice him, and he backed the two Conservative candidates.

Bernard stood once again, and he was joined by Samuel George Smith, a cousin of the Lord of the Manor of Wendover. Indeed it was Philip Abel Smith's decision to put his cousin into the field that prompted Hayter to think that a second Liberal candidate was also necessary. Both candidates expressed their firm support of Derby's second Conservative government, with especial reference to the parliamentary reform bill that had occasioned the dissolution.

Wentworth was away on his honeymoon when his address was written. In any event, he left questions of political principle to his agent, Henry Darvill of Windsor, and Tindal; and now, as subsequently, they concocted an address that they thought would go down well. This suggested a desire for a more extensive reform than the Conservatives envisaged, and support for the ballot. Most important, however, was an unequivocal statement of support for the total abolition of Church rates. Both Conservatives opposed this; and, though the government had dissolved on the parliamentary reform question after the defeat of its own bill, both parties in Aylesbury would have accepted the *Bucks Herald's* opinion that 'this is a contest between Church and Dissent . . .'[31]

The total poll was 1,053 and only ninety-six electors failed to cast their votes. Bernard received 552 votes and Smith and Wentworth tied with 535 votes each. Three members were returned, and the House of Commons was left to decide between Wentworth and Smith. The evidence before the election committee revealed that there had been extensive treating for both Conservatives. It left no doubt that Humphrey Bull particularly had bribed and coerced voters. But the committee did not consider agency proven for either treating or coercion. The committee also established what Darvill, the Liberal agent, was perfectly willing to admit, that a number of farmers had been approached about hiring their farm carts to transport electors to the poll. The hire was to be two guineas. Darvill made out a very convincing case for the necessity of this measure—that the Conservatives had monopolized the normal sources of transportation—and the reasonableness of the price. In any event, the scheme was never brought into effect because the necessary licences could not be secured. The question was whether Wentworth's agents had made a vote a condition in the negotiations. The committee decided to its own satisfaction that one of them had, and Wentworth was unseated—not, it should be noted, for bribery consummated, but for bribery attempted.[32] So ended the complex—and sometimes bizarre— history of Aylesbury politics in the fourth and fifth decades of the nineteenth century. The next chapter will probe more deeply into the causes of the events here described.

Chapter 9 INFLUENCE, COERCION, AND PRINCIPLE: PART II

SOME OF the important factors in the politics of mid-Victorian Aylesbury have been suggested in the last chapter. But the existence of particularly rich and varied evidence for the years 1847 to 1859 enables one to probe more deeply into this period than is usually possible. A pollbook exists for all seven elections, and in such a relatively short time one can follow the voting habits of a substantial number of individual electors. A county ratebook identifies the landlords, if any, of most of these voters and gives some notion of their wealth. The birth and baptismal records of several Dissenting chapels and Methodist circuit records reveal the religious affiliations of some of them. Combined, and used in conjunction with other evidence, this information makes it possible to draw some not uninformed conclusions about the relative importance of influence, coercion, and principle in Aylesbury politics during the period.

As at Buckingham, the influence of great landowners was far from predominant. Of the 570 electors who are on the electoral register throughout the decade (producing a sample of about forty-five per cent of the electorate at any given election[1]) only about a hundred (18%) were the tenants of great aristocratic landowners, squires, and clergymen. In the town there was no major landlord, and it is clear from the votes of their tenants that the numerous landlords who owned one to a half a dozen houses did not make their own political opinions a condition of tenancy. But even in the hundreds, which accounted for 70 per cent of the electorate, only 26 per cent were tenants of these sorts of landowner (which, of course, is to give a wide definition to 'great landowners').

Other evidence confirms that of the sample. At a by-election at the end of 1852 caused by Bethell's appointment to office in the Aberdeen Coalition, Tindal advised that Lord Carrington had 'numerous tenants in the Borough who are electors; it would therefore be important to secure his Lordship's Interest.' A rough draft of the letter shows that 'numerous' meant 'at least 30 Electors.'[2] Thirty electors could, of course, be very important, sometimes crucial; but they did not constitute a very large proportion of a total electorate that ranged from twelve to thirteen hundred during the period. And Carrington was one of the largest landowners in the constituency.

Probably only the Abel Smiths at Wendover and, by the end of the period, the Rothschilds, would have had more tenants among the electors, between forty and fifty. The ratebook gives precise information, of course, but it is not always very meaningful. Retired generals and naval captains may technically have been tenants, but they are not likely to have been under influence. A couple of men rented of both Abel Smith and Rothschild, and I have not counted them twice. Several rented tiny bits of property and their major landlord was someone else; I have not counted them at all. With these provisos, I would reckon that Dr Lee had about as many tenants as Carrington. They would have been followed by another half dozen landlords with about half as many tenants. And bringing up the rear would have been a couple of non-residents and a few squires and clergymen, with one to half a dozen tenants.

These are the landlords who might have exerted influence. But the crucial questions are: did they in fact attempt to, in what way, and how effective were they? The answer to all is that it depended on the landlord, on the tenant, and on the election.

Lord Carrington maintained a degree of political obedience similar to that imposed by the Duke of Buckingham, and with the same sanction—eviction. Of his ten tenants appearing in the sample, seven gave him complete obedience, plumping for Nugent in 1847, when many Liberals split their votes, and for Layard in 1852 and 1857, when Carrington refused support of any kind for Bethell. Three tenants, however, showed independence. One split for Clayton in 1847 and gave a vote to both Liberal candidates in 1852 and 1857. Two more voted for both Liberals in 1852. The first mentioned and one of the second were large farmers and among the most prominent leaders of local Methodism, influential men in their own rights, with whose votes Carrington probably thought it unwise to interfere.

Influence, particularly influence exerted in Carrington's way, was anathema to Dr Lee. Indeed Lee was so fearful of influencing the political opinions of his tenants that he sometimes went so far as to keep his own preferences a carefully guarded secret until the day of nomination. Other landlords in the constituency shared his scruples, though they might not have gone so far as he did in keeping their own opinons secret.[3] So far as Dr Lee's tenants were concerned, they would have been hard put to follow their landlord's erratic course, and not one appearing in the sample seems to have made any effort to do so.

Falling halfway between the practices of Carrington and Lee were those of Abel Smith. He was not above letting his preferences be known, but he had a horror of coercion and never dreamt of interfering with strongly held convictions. In 1852, when he was suspected of putting pressure on his Wendover tenants to vote for the two Conservative candidates, he protested to his Liberal brother-in-law Frederick Calvert:

> I am not aware of having done any thing wrong at Wendover. I was placed in a political difficulty by having supported you [in 1850] & wished to interfere as little as possible, but I have been very much pressed by the Conservatives & I have written to about a dozen of my tenants to ask the *favor* of them to vote for West and Bayford. This is all I have done & as far as I can judge, Hewlett [his Wendover agent] has been very lukewarm. I cannot therefore conceive what anyone has got to say against me in this matter. Gadsden wrote to me & as I know he is a Whig, I did not even ask him for his vote.[4]

Of his eight tenants represented in the sample,[5] three voted for both Conservatives, three voted for both Liberals, one split his vote between one Liberal and one Conservative, and one did not vote at all. This sort of pattern was not unusual in the Wendover tenantry, though in 1859 they all gave a vote to their landlord's cousin S. G. Smith, the three Liberals splitting their vote between him and Wentworth.

Of the other prominent Aylesbury landlords, William Rickford had always claimed that he never asked for more than a vote for himself and left his friends free to give their other vote as they pleased. It is not clear what his practice was after he ceased to be a candidate. In 1847 Rickford plumped for Deering. Three of his six tenants in the sample voted for both Conservatives, and three voted for Deering and Nugent. Thereafter, under Rickford and his son-in-law Sir Astley Cooper, five voted Conservative and one voted Liberal.

Three large landlords appear to have been politically neutral. Earl Howe and Sir Robert Frankland Russell were both Peelites. Howe was neutral at least through 1852, and there is no record of his stirring himself until 1859 when he talked of his son's standing in the Conservative interest. His five tenants represented in the sample, however, never ceased to support Conservative candidates. One of the four Frankland Russell tenants appearing consistently gave Liberal votes throughout the period. The other three generally voted Conservative. Like the Peelite landlords, T. T. Drake also withdrew from politics, but for the opposite reason: he had become disgusted with Peel early in the forties and refused to have anything to do with politics thereafter. As a consequence, he did not exercise his franchise in Aylesbury during this period. But his three tenants continued to exercise theirs for Conservatives, though not always the same one. In 1847, for example, one plumped for Deering, one for Clayton, and one voted for both.

The direction of influence on the Earl of Buckinghamshire's estates was somewhat uncertain. The earl was a Conservative, but his agent was a leading Liberal, whom the Conservatives accused of seducing the tenantry. In 1847 the five tenants in the sample gave every possible vote and combination of votes, save a plumper for Deering. In 1848 two voted Conservative, one voted Liberal, and two did not vote. In 1849 the earl died and Hampden House and part of his estates went to his son-in-law Donald Cameron. Cameron was a keen Conservative and worked hard for the party's candidates, personally canvassing his tenants. But he was not a wealthy man, the estate was heavily mortgaged, and as a consequence he was unable to follow the practice general with larger landlords of remitting a substantial proportion of his rents in the bad years in the late forties and early fifties. This was advanced as the reason for his alleged difficulty in controlling his tenants.[6] Of the five in the sample, four voted Conservative and one voted Liberal. Even the Liberal, however, remained neutral in 1851 when protection was the central issue, suggesting that the fact they were chalkland farmers might have had as much to do with their votes as their landlord.

The Rothschilds were also keen politicians. They certainly had no financial difficulties and were generous landlords, remitting as much as 50 per cent of their tenants' rent in bad years. From all reports, they, or at any rate their agent, also exercised fairly rigorous discipline. The greater part of their tenantry, mostly former tenants of the Duke of Buckingham, undoubtedly changed their political allegiance with their landlord. But not all. Of the ten Rothschild tenants appearing in the sample two followed an independent line. One was the formidable Humphrey Bull, of whom it was reported that the Rothschilds were more frightened than he was of them. The other was simply a large farmer who remained true to his Conservative convictions.

The above survey covers the most important landowners in the constituency, and the behaviour of their tenants is typical. All that one can say is that, for the most part, tenants of larger landowners followed the general political line of their landlord, though not always his specific preferences with respect to candidates, or the degree to which they should be supported. The latter considerations were not, of course, unimportant ones in close elections, particularly three-cornered ones, where the way in which votes were split could be critical.

In any case, whatever the importance of large landowners in determining the votes of their tenants, it must be emphasized again that most Aylesbury electors were not the tenants of such landlords. Some were the tenants of corporate landlords—an Oxford College, the Mercers Company, several local charities, and Dissenting meeting houses. But most were the tenants of small individual landowners, often of two or three—professional men, large tradesmen, widows, spinsters, and doubtless a few orphans. Where landlords can be identified, their political opinions had no obvious effect on those of their tenants. But the majority of Aylesbury landlords cannot be identified. All that can be said of them is that they were clearly not people of great consequence. The ratebook is a good deal more free with the title 'esquire' than

even the pollbooks—and they are free enough—but most Aylesbury landlords are conceded no more than a 'Mr', if indeed they
are given any title at all. A remark of Frederick Calvert's probably
suggests the priorities of small landlords less wealthy and distinguished:

> Other things being equal, I prefer a good politician to a bad
> one as a tenant. But other things never are equal. So I always take
> the best farmer. [7]

It seems very likely that the majority of Aylesbury landlords
would have taken a similar attitude to the politics of their tenants—
if they took any attitude at all. Both the corporate and the small
landowner would appear to have been seeking an economic, not a
political, return from their property. And the two ends were
probably not compatible. As is generally agreed, and as Cameron's
case suggests, political obedience was a return for a service
rendered, the provision of a shield against bad times. If one did not
wish to provide the shield, one could not expect the obedience.
Political influence was expensive, and the great majority of Aylesbury landlords probably could not have afforded it.

To turn to the question of party affiliation, mid-Victorian
Aylesbury demonstrates a classic two-party pattern, with 167
faithful Liberal voters, 210 Conservatives, and a large floating vote
holding the balance between the two parties. [8] Comparison of the
three groups with respect to residence, occupation, wealth, landlords, and religious affiliation, [9] yielded the following results.
There was a strong Conservative bias towards the countryside, and
a somewhat less marked Liberal bias towards the town. While
sixty-five of the Liberals (38%) were drawn from the town, only
forty-nine of the Conservatives (23%) were; and eighty-eight of
the Conservatives (42%) were farmers compared to only forty-two
(26%) of the Liberals. As is suggested by the lists opposite, even
the Conservative townsmen tended to look towards the countryside. There was some truth in a derisive comment by the *Bucks
Gazette* about the 'hired lawyers, county goal turnkeys, county
brickmakers, county carpenters, [and] county ironmongers' who, it
was alleged, made up the body of Conservative support in the
town. [10]

THE PARTIES IN THE TOWN, INDICATING PROPERTY AND RELIGIOUS AFFILIATION

Liberals	Conservatives
£100 *and over*	
Esquire (grazier) £405	Banker £244
Gentleman (farmer) £126	Solicitor £133
Gentleman (cabinetmaker) £101,	Solicitor £114
Independent	Veterinary Surgeon £115
Land Agent £124	Brewer (and farmer) £818
Auctioneer £218, *Independent*	Brewer (and farmer) £229
Chemist £136, *Independent*	Innkeeper (and farmer) £534
Draper £296, *Independent*	Draper £138
Tobacconist £101	Coachmaker £174,
Grocer £158	*Methodist*
Grocer £147, *Independent*	Builder £116
Printer £153, *Independent*	Grazier £264
Cabinetmaker £100, *Independent*	
Currier £101, *Independent*	
Grazier £106	
£50 *to* £100	
Solicitor £60	Surgeon £83
Brewer (and baker) £73,	Innkeeper £93
Methodist	Grocer £50
Innkeeper £77	Baker (and corn dealer) £87
Chemist £97, *Independent*	Builder £90
Coal Merchant £78, *Independent*	Builder £79
Confectioner £69, *Methodist*	Milkman (cowkeeper) £55
Butcher (and grazier) £68	
Coachmaker (and wheelwright) £50	
Brickmaker £89, *Independent*	
Watchmaker £58	
Basketmaker £52, *Independent*	
Grazier £65, *Dissenter*	
Market Gardener £50	
£40 *to* £50	
Gentleman (carpenter), *Baptist*	
Draper, *Independent*	
Corn Dealer	
Shoemaker	
£30 *to* £40	
Solicitor	Butcher
Bookseller, *Independent*	Fishmonger and game dealer
Baker	Whitesmith and bell hanger
Broker	Coachmaker
Hairdresser, *Independent*	Saddler

Liberals	*Conservatives*
Milkman (cowkeeper)	Bricklayer
	Carpenter
	2 Victuallers

£20 *to* £30

Minister, *Independent*	Printer
Printer	Coal Merchant
Grocer, *Primitive Methodist*	2 Butchers
Confectioner, *Methodist*	Cabinetmaker
Broker	Victualler
Harnessmaker	Seedsman
2 Tailors	
Victualler	

£10 *to* £20

Corn Dealer, *Methodist*	2 Bakers
2 Hairdressers, 1 *Methodist*	Tailor
Pattern Designer	Painter and glazier
Umbrellamaker	
3 Shoemakers, 1 *Methodist*	
Plumber	
Beershop-keeper	
Labourer and Beershop-keeper,	
Methodist	
Basketmaker	
Marine-store Dealer, *Methodist*	

Under £10

Carrier	Saddler, *Independent?*
Tailor	Shoemaker
Plumber	Labourer (bricklayer)
	Labourer

Unknown

Gentleman	2 Esquires (non-resident)
2 Bakers, 1 *Independent*	Coal Merchant (non-resident)
	Tailor
	Shoemaker, *Independent?*
	Labourer
	Farmer (non-resident)

Note: The sums indicated above are the annual value of property owned and/or occupied. A return stitched into the 1857 rate-book makes it evident that annual value corresponded to rent. Where only 'Dissenter' appears, this means that the individual identified himself or was identified by someone else as a Dissenter, but his denomination is not known.

While the Liberals had a broad sprinkling of all the professions, trades, and crafts that one would expect to have found in a bustling market town of 6,000, the Conservatives showed a tendency to cluster in those in which there would have been particularly close association with the gentry and farmers. As the *Gazette* suggests, the building trades were well represented. The victualling trade, especially the houses where the farmer's ordinaries met, were also well represented. And there were two coachmakers, two saddlers, and others who would have been on particularly close terms with the squires and farmers.

There were no country gentlemen among the Liberals, while the Conservatives boasted six; and the Conservatives had five clergymen to the Liberal's one. As these two contrasts suggest, the loyal Liberal vote owed little to landed influence: Carrington's ten tenants, and possibly two of the non-resident Lord Dormer, yield a grand total of 7 per cent. A larger proportion of the Conservatives were tenants of large Conservative landowners, though still only 24 per cent of the total.

In the hundreds, where landlord influence was sometimes important (unlike the town), 29 per cent of the Liberals and 20 per cent of the Conservatives—not a very significant contrast—owned all or most of the land or premises they occupied. (A much higher proportion, 56 per cent of the Liberals, 48 per cent of the Conservatives, would have qualified as forty-shilling freeholders). Deducting the tenants of large landowners, this leaves 20 per cent of the Conservatives and 58 per cent of the Liberals in the hundreds tenants of corporate or small landlords—that is, of the kind of landlords who did not usually interfere with the votes of their tenants.

The fact that most Liberals were either owner-occupiers or tenants of non-pressurising landlords suggests that, by and large, Liberal electors and large landowners, who were mostly Conservatives, did not find one another congenial (although six Liberals were tenants of such landlords). This may be of even greater interest in light of the most marked contrast of all between the party faithfuls, the religious one. The evidence is far from complete; for the 'old' Dissenters, only partial information about half a dozen out of thirty-odd parishes, for the Methodists, circuit records which identify only those who held some office. But, though hardly exhaustive, such evidence as there is points over-whelmingly in one direction. Nineteen Independents, eight Baptists, four Dissenters whose denomination is unknown, seventeen Methodists, and one Primitive Methodist gave the Liberals a total of forty-nine nonconformists. The Conservatives, in contrast, had two Methodists, two Baptists, and two Independents, a total of six; and it seems very unlikely in the cases of all but the Methodists that the individuals involved retained the faith into which they had been born. In any case, the contrast is striking enough. The Liberals were the party of Dissent.

The extent to which the Conservatives were the party of the Church is a question more easily discussed in light of the evidence of specific elections. But, before turning to this, it is necessary to say something about the nature of the floating vote. In fact, not all of the 193 individuals in the sample who do not fall among the party faithfuls were floating voters. Some swung permanently from one party allegiance to the other.

Thirty-six changed from Conservative to Liberal voting between the 1848 and the 1850 election, that is, coincidentally with the major shift of influence following the sale of the Grenville estates; and for at least fourteen of them there is good reason to suppose that 'old Whig' or Rothschild influence was the important factor in the change. Ten, all voters in the hundreds, shifted to Liberalism after the 1851 election, the last one in which Conservatism and protection were clearly identified, suggesting perhaps that it was that issue alone that attached them to the party. Fourteen more followed remarkably closely the shifts and turns of Humphrey Bull, and for nine of them at least there is reason to think that this was no coincidence, all of them being his neighbours and the sort of small farmer and tradesman over whom his particular kind of influence might have been effective. Then, there were a number of special cases. Seven electors never voted or voted only once or twice, too infrequently to establish a pattern. Twenty-five more gave one eccentric vote, or shifted their party after 1852, usually because of influence.

This leaves 101 who constitute the true floating vote. These electors all demonstrated a marked willingness to vote for candidates of both parties, in some cases at the same election, splitting their votes across party lines. It is evident that they did not think

in party terms, on the one hand, and that they were under no
consistent influence, on the other. What factors might have
influenced their votes?

A comparison with the party faithfuls is in most respects not
very revealing. The floaters, too, for example, had substantial men
among them. So far as I can determine, £40 was roughly the
annual rent for one of the better shops around the Market Square
or in Temple Square; and only two or three of the wealthiest men
in the town owned or occupied property of over £100 annual
value. Of the total of twenty-one floating voters in the town—
excluding those in the drink trade, who are a special case—six
occupied property with an annual value between these two figures.
Only eight occupied property of less than £20 annual value. In the
hundreds, again excluding the drink trade, of the total of sixty-four
floating voters about half were substantial tradesmen, or medium-
sized to large farmers occupying property of from £100 to £400
annual value. The remaining thirty-one were small tradesmen,
farmers, and labourers.

The floating voters were like the Liberals in that not many of
them, only eight, were tenants of large landowners. They were
unlike the Liberals in that there were only three nonconformists,
two Baptists and a Methodist, among them. The most interesting
difference between party faithfuls, on the one hand, and the
floating voters, on the other, is that the latter led in the number of
innkeepers, victuallers, publicans, and beershop keepers. There
were sixteen among the floating voters, fourteen among the
Conservatives, and seven among the Liberals.

The relatively large number of those connected with the drink
trade among the floaters is probably no coincidence. Every Aylesbury election petition during the period alleged treating. One of
the cases of alleged bribery, as distinct from treating, was that of
publicans in Calvert's election in 1850. The other case in 1859
involved transportation of electors, which was most often provided
by innkeepers and victuallers. Even if expenditure was perfectly
legal, the entertainment of committees, canvassers, and the hiring
of transportation could be most lucrative; and it was accepted
practice for an innkeeper or publican to vote for the party that
patronized his establishment at the election. Even so keen a
Conservative politician as J. K. Fowler of the 'White Hart' at least

remained neutral in the 1851 election when Bethell used the inn as his headquarters. Since those engaged in the drink trade constituted the second largest occupational group in the constituency, coming after farmers and numbering forty-nine in the sample, money wisely spent with them could obviously have been important. And the peculiar election ethics that were openly acknowledged in their case make them a group to be watched with particular interest in the survey of the elections to which we shall now turn.

In the brief survey of Aylesbury elections between 1847 and 1859 that follows I have been especially concerned with two main questions. The first is the question of what issues and principles were most important in dividing the two parties in Aylesbury in the middle years of the century, a period when our knowledge of party politics in the nation as a whole is perhaps particularly hazy and confused. The second main question that I have set myself is the one suggested in the title of this chapter, the relative importance of influence, coercion, and principle in determining the outcome of elections. The 570 electors who voted throughout the period will be followed with particular interest, especially the party faithfuls and the floating voters; the former because they will throw light on what parties were about, the latter because they represented a group who held the balance of power in elections. The roughly 45 per cent sample is a reliable one, so far as I can determine. It would be possible to predict from it the placing of every candidate in every election, save in the very close 1851 election and in the case of the tie between Smith and Wentworth in 1859. The evidence it gives will also be checked against other information. With this introduction, we can plunge into the elections themselves.

Even the staunchly Liberal *Aylesbury News* would later admit that without the feud between the two Conservative factions Lord Nugent would never have won in 1847. The feud involved two questions. One was suspicion of Clayton's devotion to the protectionist cause; the other was his vote for the increased Maynooth grant in 1845, and it was this latter issue that was most talked about. The Maynooth question itself involved two distinct issues. One was anti-Catholicism, and the other was the issue of state aid to education. It is generally believed that by the mid-forties

Dissenting opinion was strongly voluntaryist, and there is no doubt that the recent government action offering increased grants to voluntary societies in return for more state control had roused violent protests from Dissenters, including those in Bucks.[11]

Lord Nugent, who was fond of reminding his audiences that Protestantism itself had been spawned in Catholic seminaries, left no doubt of his stand on the Maynooth grant. On the broader question of state aid to education he was equally unequivocal. For him, the great object was to extend education, by every possible means, and in almost any way that would render it palatable to the recipients. Nugent was generally regarded as an Anti-State-Church candidate, and he was a strong supporter of the abolition of Church rates; but his Anti-State-Church principles did not imply rigidity on the education question. This would not appear to have disturbed Aylesbury Liberals. Of the 167 in the sample, 105 plumped for Nugent, 23 split with the other pro-Maynooth candidate, and only 39 split for Deering. But 33 of the latter were from the hundreds, and it may have been Deering's protectionist ideas that particularly appealed to them.

The evidence which this election gives of the tolerance and lack of dogmatism of Aylesbury Liberalism is confirmed by other evidence. Apparently unmoved by Maynooth, it greeted the so-called 'Papal Aggression' issue of 1850–51 with scorn and derision. It was unconcerned about the reintroduction of a Catholic hierarchy into Britain, and opposed to the Ecclesiastical Titles bill of 1851, intended to prohibit it. The Gibbses' *Bucks Advertiser* was indignant, Bethell was sarcastic, and only fourteen people appeared at a meeting called in the County Hall to send a loyal address to the queen. As in 1829, Aylesbury was alone among the Bucks towns as the others were greatly aroused on the matter.[12] On the education issue, the trustees of the British School at Aylesbury were joined by their counterparts at Wycombe in accepting the increased government grant, while the rest of Bucks Dissent seems to have been strongly voluntaryist.

The evidence the 1847 election gives of Conservative opinion is less clear-cut. Clayton was heavily favoured by Conservatives in the town, Deering by Conservatives in the hundreds. Deering's supporters charged that the Aylesbury town Conservatives were

'Puseyites,' implying a tenderness for the Oxford Movement and Catholicism. It is quite safe to exonerate them of this charge. Leading town Conservatives like (at this time) Tindal, Thomas Wheeler, a large grocer, and the Green family, carpenters and builders, were pillars of a Church militantly low, as was the case throughout the county. But, as events would prove, some, like Tindal and Wheeler, were far from being militantly protectionist.

Both sides gave Nugent votes. In the sample, fifteen of Clayton's supporters and thirty-nine of Deering's supported him. (Something under half of the regular Conservative voters, 91 out of 210, voted for both candidates, and the rest plumped for one or the other.) As has been seen, the votes that finally tipped the balance in Nugent's favour were those of the Deering supporters led by Bull and Owen, which means that Clayton was defeated by a combination of influence and anti-Catholicism, though in what proportions it is difficult to say.

There can be no doubt at all that what defeated Houghton in 1848 and 1850 was money and influence, which were almost all on the side of his adversaries Dick and Calvert. In 1848 Houghton got only four out of the sixteen floating votes possessed by the suppliers of drink and transportation. It was probably the latter lack, rather than his free trade views, which accounts for the fact that almost a third of the Liberal voters in the hundreds did not vote; for only four farmers, who could transport themselves to the polls, were among the abstainers.

In the poll in 1848, Dick beat Houghton by almost two to one, 614 to 345. Calvert beat him by better than two to one, 499 to 197, in 1850. In this election, Houghton did not spend a penny, while Calvert spent in excess of two thousand pounds; this is reflected by the fact that only one publican, a neighbour in Dinton, gave Houghton a vote. But more interesting than the votes Houghton did not receive were those that he did. The sample takes account of ninety-two of Houghton's supporters, and of these the largest single group was made up of thirty-five Conservatives from the hundreds (he was not popular with the town Conservatives, getting only four votes from them). An analysis of the whole 197 done by one of the Liberal agents after the 1851 election also suggests a rural Conservative fondness for Houghton. One hundred and five voted for the Conservative candidate in 1851 as opposed to sixty-nine for the Liberal candidate.[13] Why would so many Conservative exponents of protection have bothered to take themselves to the polls to vote for a Liberal free trader?

The answer must lie in his other principles. James Oliffe, a substantial Dissenting farmer who had nominated Houghton in 1848, had said of him that he was

> one of the people, and one who felt an interest in their prosperity . . . a farmer, one who lived amongst them, a practical worker, a politician for the people, and a friend to the reduction of taxation, not a spendthrift who expected the country to keep him.[14]

The record on which this eulogium was based included a leading part in the protest against Church rates, and Houghton was an avowed Anti-State-Church candidate. He also stressed the fact that he was a tenant farmer, and as 'plain tenant-farmer Houghton' he had been a bitter critic of the game laws. In the same capacity, he demanded legislation to protect tenants' rights, a single local rate for the poor, highways etc assessed on all forms of property, and, finally, a repeal of the malt tax.

Houghton's Conservative support was not only relatively large, but represented a broad cross-section of the Conservative rank and file in the hundreds, of those who owned their own farms, of tenants of landowners big and small, of big farmers and small farmers, and of tradesmen. The fact that he received such support probably suggests something about the priorities of the ordinary Conservative voter. In view of the lack of Dissenters in the Conservative ranks, it is safe to assume that Houghton's Anti-State-Church principles would not have been the attraction—what is significant is that they did not repel ordinary Conservatives. It must therefore have been the ideas of the 'plain tenant farmer' that attracted them, concern about the Game Laws, tenant rights, and the burden of rates and taxes. In 1852, when the Conservatives were in office, George Boug, a large and influential Conservative farmer in Great Missenden, told the Liberal agent that 'if he were convinced the present Ministry would not restore Protection, he would vote for a Radical.'[15] Boug was one of those who voted for Houghton in 1850, and possibly he was not untypical.

It is interesting that a sizeable number of Conservative voters should have voted for an opponent of the Established Church, suggesting that they did not always put the stress on religious questions that the leadership of the party (both in the town and the hundreds) undoubtedly did. It is also interesting, however, that the Anti-State-Church candidate did not get especially strong support from among his own party. The regular Liberal voters in the sample voted three to one for Calvert; with those identifiable as Dissenters dividing in about the same proportion; this, despite the fact that Calvert's soundness on the Church-rate question was suspect. It is true that Calvert called Church rates 'a great disadvantage to the Church of England';[16] but his view that their abolition must be accompanied by the provision of a substitute was known and bitterly resented by some of the more rigid exponents of Anti-State-Church views.[17] These latter, however, were not in a majority among Aylesbury Dissenters. An Anti-State-Church meeting which took place during the campaign, with the secretary of the national association, Carvel Williams, present, was lightly attended; and it was noted that only one person in Aylesbury subscribed to the funds of the association and no delegate attended its meetings in London.[18]

Lack of support for the Anti-State-Church Associaton was not for lack of concern about specific issues. Indeed Calvert's most prominent Dissenting supporters—Philip Payne, grandson of one of the founders of the Independent congregation, Samuel Gibbs, John's brother and a large cabinet-maker and upholsterer, and Rowland Dickens, a chemist who would long be a leader in local Liberal affairs—had been among the eight summoned before the Aylesbury justices in May 1847 for refusal to pay their Church rates.

This was at the beginning of a long controversy that had more recently led to a case which gained national notoriety, that of an unfortunate farmer named Simonds, whom the magistrates clapped in gaol for refusal to pay his rates. Another of the eight was John Gunn, who was to be the leader of the moderates in 1852. Now, as then, Gunn urged the necessity for Liberal unity behind a strong candidate, and the others, who would also be prominent among the moderates in 1852, took the same line.[19] When efforts at reconciliation and compromise failed in 1850 Gunn withdrew from the controversy and abstained from voting, as did about half the other Dissenters in the sample. There were those who had been pointing out of Bucks Liberalism almost from its inception that one of its greatest weaknesses was that Liberals were too independent and apt to fly in all different directions at times when concert and unity were most necessary.[20] A number of Aylesbury Dissenters appear to have accepted this stricture; and, whatever may have been the case in the rest of the country, to have come to the conclusion that Dissent's best interests dictated that it be part of a strong Liberal party pursuing realistic goals.[21]

Calvert was the candidate who best met these latter require-ments, and the realistic goal that the moderates rallied around was free trade. This was to be the issue that dominated the next two elections, particularly that of 1851. As has been seen, free trade versus protection does not seem to have been the dominant issue either in 1847 or 1848. But since then there had been bad years for farmers. They had been plagued with extraordinarily wet weather, which was bad for crops, and, as Calvert had remarked at the nomination in December, the prices obtainable for meat that Christmas were bitterly disappointing.[22] Calvert argued that pro-tection was no answer, but Aylesbury farmers appear not to have been so sure.

Conservative farmers definitely held the opposite opinion, and the result was a coercion of voters, the organization and intensity of which were unexampled in the constituency's history. As a Con-servative witness admitted when asked about intimidation at a parliamentary enquiry after the election:

> Why . . . we should lose on that head, because the clergymen and the farmers intimidated parties very much, for they went round in bodies to the tradespeople; but the other party never intimidated any person.[23]

The witness was a Conservative saddler, long one of the main organizers of corruption for his party, who on this occasion had himself been bribed to disclaim a petition against Bethell's return lodged in his name. He was telling the truth in the latter instance; the petition had been concocted at the Carlton and no one had bothered to consult him about the use of his name. There is also ample evidence to substantiate his testimony about intimidation. Meetings of Ferrand's supporters all over the constituency resolved not to trade or traffic with anyone who voted for Bethell, and deputations bore the threat to every corner.[24] Doubtless the assertion that the Liberals never intimidated anyone was going a bit far, but there is no evidence of the kind of organized, systematic coercion in which the Conservatives indulged at this election.

This is a classic case of what is often thought to have been one of the major factors in Victorian elections. But the result here at any rate was a dismal failure. The town voted overwhelmingly for the free trade candidate, with the floating voters in the sample giving him twenty-two votes as opposed to only two for the protectionist. Not surprisingly, Bethell did less well among the floating voters in the hundreds, but he did better than might have been expected, with twenty-one votes as opposed to thirty-four for Ferrand. Significantly, however, all but five of Bethell's votes came from the small town of Wendover and the larger villages of Great Missenden and Haddenham, places where the farmers shopped. Clearly the threat to withdraw custom was not very effective, and there were those who argued that the coercion campaign's main effect had been to produce a reaction in favour of Bethell.[25]

One would expect the Conservative farmers to have turned out strongly for Ferrand and they did. More interesting and significant is the fact that a large number of Liberal farmers did not turn out at all. A total of thirty of the Liberal voters represented in the sample abstained in this election, and eighteen of them were farmers and graziers. It is unlikely that very many of the farmers who voted for Bethell did so because of his free trade opinions. William Dover, a large Cuddington farmer, was pressed into service to second his nomination; and Dover, who had demonstrated himself a Corn Law supporter by his votes in the thirties, was not even lukewarm so far as free trade was concerned. Bethell, he said, had not been in parliament when the free trade measures had been passed, and therefore he ought not be be blamed for them (though Bethell, of course, was more than willing to accept the responsibility). Free trade was now an accomplished fact, a return to protection an idle dream. Farmers must make the best of the situation and unite to right wrongs that could be righted—the unfair relationship between landlord and tenant, high rates, and oppressive taxation. Dover's attitude on free trade appears to have been typical of the opinions of many Liberal farmers, and was certainly typical of all those who are recorded as expressing an opinion on the subject,[26] save for Houghton. (But Houghton was also a professional land agent, all half dozen of whom in the constituency, interestingly enough, were free traders.) It would appear that most Liberal farmers adhered to the party for other reasons. They might be realistic about free trade, but they were not enthusiastic about it.

Realism on this question, however, seems to have been unpopular with most Aylesbury farmers; and coming from a most unexpected source, the Conservative Chancellor of the Exchequer, it appears to have been an important factor in the severe Conservative defeat in the general election of the following year. Disraeli did not, in fact, make his famous pronouncement about the repeal of the Corn Laws being a fait accompli until a speech at Newport Pagnell on 10 July, three days after the Aylesbury election; but, as has been seen, there had been strong suspicions of the government's equivocation on the question throughout the Aylesbury canvass. And many would probably have shared the feelings of J. T. Senior, the large Broughton grazier who nominated Dr Lee for the county. Senior said that had Disraeli stuck to his colours he would not have occupied the position which he then did, but 'Mr Disraeli had betrayed the views he proposed for relieving the landed interest' and now came forward as a free trader to bamboozle them.[27] As has been seen, even staunch Conservatives like George Boug gave indications of similar feelings.

While the Conservatives, suspicious of betrayal, were dispirited, the Liberals, after their own differences were sorted out, demonstrated a remarkable unity and enthusiasm—at any rate, the rank and file did. Town moderates like Samuel Gibbs urged unity to return two free traders. His brother, John, called upon ministers of all denominations and Christians generally to support the great cause on moral grounds.[28] And when Bethell and the 'old Whigs' finally patched up an alliance, even the Liberal farmers were ready to support the two free traders. In the previous year, Bethell had defeated Ferrand by only twenty-six votes in a poll of 1,062. In the 1852 election, with a total poll of 1,001, Layard was 111 votes, Bethell 78 votes, ahead of the leading Conservative.

The sample tends to confirm these views of the election. The number of Liberal abstainers was cut in half; and, as was noted earlier, a group of ten electors switched their allegiance from Conservative to Liberal in this election. The number of Conservatives not voting was not markedly higher, twenty-one as opposed to seventeen, but half a dozen otherwise loyal Conservative voters gave one vote to Layard in this election. The floating voters also showed a tendency to split in a manner that favoured the Liberals; of 177 voting in this election all but thirty-three gave at least one Liberal vote. The final factor that favoured the Liberals would appear to have been a decreased registration. As will be noted, the total polled (ie in the actual poll) had decreased by sixty-one from 1851. Those on the register had decreased from 1,292 to 1,211 in the same period. In the sample, nine who had voted Conservative in the previous election were not registered, compared to four who had voted Liberal. This is probably a reflection of the fact that the previous September the Liberals had waged their first serious registration campaign in over a decade. Humphrey Bull, recently employed by the 'old Whigs', had managed matters for the Liberals, and he had been assisted by five solicitors. They would appear to have done their job well.[29]

There can be little doubt that money spent to look after the registration, a legitimate and necessary expense the Liberals had previously been unable to afford, played a part in producing their improved fortunes. What of money spent to corrupt? Among the Tindal Papers, tied in pink ribbons as Tindal himself left them, I found the election bills and vouchers for the three elections that he personally supervised—1850, 1851, and 1852. The evidence appears to be complete, and there is a good deal of frank comment and correspondence about it. As Tindal told Joseph Parkes during the height of the dispute with Bethell: 'I am aware that it may be customary to "cook" up Electioneering accounts to save the consciences of Candidates, but this has not been my practice.'[30] Tindal was no ordinary election agent—a point Bethell never grasped—his services were gratuitous, and, as his remark to Parkes suggests, it was almost a point of honour with him to inflict the sordid details on those for whom he acted. There were, however, few sordid details after 1850.

Calvert and his supporters spent about £2,300 on the 1850 election. Of this about £550 went towards items which usually included some corrupt expenditure. About £200 was spent on stavesmen, messengers, and chairmen. These services usually carried a remuneration of 5s a day for a couple of days and went to the relatives of electors. The remainder, £350, was spent on refreshments. Of the legitimate expenses, the largest items were some £860 on agency—almost always the largest item on election bills—and almost £600 on conveyances.

Bethell in 1851 spent a total of only £1,300. Unfortunately, no summary bill exists, but it is possible to infer a good deal from bundles of individual bills submitted for payment and from other evidence. Calvert's £860 went to six major agents. Bethell employed seven, and several agents apologised that the pressure exerted by the Conservatives had made their bills higher by forcing them to do more work. Bethell may have economised some on transportation, but in a constituency the size of Aylesbury he would have been foolish to have economised too much. This would have left little, if anything, for the usual means of corruption. Tindal claimed that no money had been spent on corruption, and he explained that where there were bills for refreshments they were for necessary items. The bills largely bear him out. Almost all of them come from the hundreds and almost all were for very modest breakfasts provided for voters before they were transported to the polls.

Even less was spent on Layard's striking victory in 1852, a (by Aylesbury standards) modest £1,160. Careful analysis of the bills reveals nothing but perfectly legitimate expenditure. The only ones who might have profited by corrupt spending were those who came lower on the poll. Tindal hinted several years later, in indignantly rejecting a proposal to entertain the electors even out of election time, that James, the Rothschild agent, had indulged in some questionable spending at this election.[31] No bills exist for any Conservative during the period, except a few for Quentin Dick. But the Conservatives seem never to have been short of money, or reluctant to use it. They were always well supplied with agents, and the evidence before election committees reveals that, while the Liberals largely abandoned it after 1850, treating continued to be an important part of Conservative electioneering. It seems safe to say therefore that it was issues, rather than coercion or corruption, that gave the Liberals their victories in 1851 and 1852.

One cannot speak with much confidence about the important factors in the 1857 election. Layard attributed his defeat to two causes, Conservative fondness for Lord Palmerston which told in split votes for the Attorney General, and the influence of Humphrey Bull.[32] The *Nonconformist* later advanced a different explanation, with which some important Aylesbury Liberals seem to have agreed:

> In the election of 1857 Mr Layard was rejected and a Conservative returned in his place, because Mr Layard was believed to be unsound on the Sunday question. He lost his seat by the opposition and the absence of some Liberal Churchmen and many Liberal Nonconformists.[33]

Other available evidence seems to point towards Layard's explanation. The electors divided as follows:

Split Votes		*Plumpers*	
Bethell and Layard	356	Layard	40
Bethell and Bernard	130	Bethell	15
Layard and Bernard	40	Bernard	376

It is evident that what put Bethell ahead of Layard were the votes of the large number of electors who split for the former and Bernard. The question, of course, is what kind of elector gave these votes? Of the forty-nine in the sample who split their votes in this fashion, twenty-three were Conservatives, twenty were floaters, and only six were Liberals. One of the latter was a Methodist local preacher, but he is balanced by the Baptist minister in Cuddington, who split his vote in favour of Layard. Neither is it evident from the sample that Liberal abstentions were important. The number was about as usual, fifteen out of 167. Nor do nonconformists make up a larger part of the abstainers than usual. Five abstained in this election, as opposed to four in 1852. All this would appear to argue against the explanation advanced by the *Nonconformist*. Bernard undoubtedly made a great deal of his oppositon to the Sunday opening of museums, art galleries, and other such places of 'public amusement' (as contemporaries called them), which was a hot issue with some prominent Aylesbury nonconformists. None of those known to oppose Sunday opening, however, opposed Layard; and what was certainly a somewhat lower poll than usual, 957 out of 1,266 on the register, would seem to have been from other causes.

The main reason probably was that there was no burning issue in the election. Bernard proclaimed himself heartily thankful that the protection issue was a dead one, and called himself a Liberal Conservative, stating his support for the removal of Jewish disabilities and his anxious wish for a settlement of the Church-rate question.

The most heated debate was between the two Liberals, over the question of Palmerston's China policy which had caused the dissolution. There is little evidence, however, that many other people were much concerned with the issue. Dr Lee, a prominent member of the Peace Society, was, and a few nonconformists who plumped for Layard may have been. But most Liberals appear to have wished well both to Palmerston's friend and Palmerston's enemy, and John Gibbs and others who took a leading part in the election all pressed for unity and the return of both Liberal candidates. The Conservatives who split for Bethell may have been concerned with the issue. It is difficult to say. Bernard certainly had little or nothing to say about it, but some Conservatives may have split for the Attorney General out of admiration for his chief. Then again they may have acted out of hatred for the renegade Tindal. There can be no doubt that hatred of Tindal and Harrison was what motivated Humphrey Bull. Nor can there be any doubt that Layard was right to stress the importance of his opposition. The sample reveals at least seventeen votes that can almost certainly be traced to Bull's influence.

As has been seen, the 1859 election is another instance in which the national issue that caused the election appears to have had little local relevance. The parliamentary reform question was hardly mentioned, and the battle was fought over Church rates. At any rate, this was the question on the Liberal side, and the result was a Liberal unity and purpose remarkable even to the Liberal leadership. In a three-cornered election, with Wentworth the sole Liberal candidate, 457 electors resisted the temptation to split and plumped for him. As has been seen, the election ended with Wentworth tied with S. G. Smith, and the issue had to be decided by the House of Commons. As has also been seen, Wentworth was unseated on a technicality, since the farmers' carts which were alleged to have provided the excuse for bribery were never employed.

The election had proved a surprise to everyone. The Liberals
had expected to lose, and the Conservatives had expected to win
easily.[34] When the latter recovered from their surprise and coolly
surveyed the situation, they came to the conclusion that they would
not have done even as well as they did without the accession to
their cause of Humphrey Bull, who was duly lauded, fêted and
presented with a handsome gift of plate. They were almost certainly right.[35]

This election delineates a most important feature of elections
throughout the period—the uncertainties that hung around them.
No one knew whether an election would turn on influence, on
coercive pressures of one sort or another, or on principles. As a
consequence, politicians ignored none of these factors. Historians,
who tend to emphasize the former at the expense of the latter, will
probably have to learn the same lesson.

There are principles and principles, however—and those that
figure most importantly in Aylesbury politics during this period
are not necessarily the ones that one would predict from the course
of party conflict at Westminster. Historians usually attribute the
chaos that reigned there to the independence of MPs, their independence of both party leaders and of voters. In a sense, this
explanation would seem to fit the Bucks experience during the
period. A large part of the difficulty, however, would seem to have
been that the leadership had little idea where it wanted to lead, and
that the electorate could not agree on which issues it wanted to
press.

At a county by-election in 1857 John Gibbs took the Whig
candidate W. G. Cavendish to task for vagueness. Cavendish had
said that he would support Lord Palmerston's government, and so
would Gibbs 'in nine cases out of ten.' He then proceeded to
question Cavendish about the abolition of Church rates, the adop-
tion of the £5 franchise for the boroughs and the £10 franchise for
the counties, and the ballot, all of which measures Gibbs supported.[36] The tenth cases would seem to have been rather important ones.

Most of the 'old' Liberals would probably have supported the
same measures, but not all at the same time and with the same
emphasis. In 1847 and 1848 the abolition of Church rates was
probably uppermost in their minds. But in 1850, 1851, and 1852

many would have put the first priority on free trade—which others certainly would not have done. In 1857 the party had two candidates who agreed with them on every important point, but unfortunately not with each other on foreign policy (about which their party seems not to have cared at all). In 1859 they were again united behind Church rate abolition, and willing to tolerate vagueness on most other questions. The same was more or less true in 1865, though N. M. de Rothschild also supported a reform of parliament. Calvert, whom Tindal brought forward once more, refused to give an unequivocal pledge on the total abolition of Church rates, with the consequence that the 'old' Liberals refused their support and Calvert was forced to retire. Thus Rothschild, who willingly gave the required pledge, and S. G. Smith were returned unopposed.[37] Lord Palmerston was as irrelevant to the 1865 result as Disraeli's reform bill had been to the 1859 contest.

The Conservatives were no better off than the Liberals, with consequences which will be traced in the next chapter. If Bucks was in any way typical, it is perhaps not surprising that the period seemed to lack decisive political divisions.

Chapter 10 THE SECOND REFORM ACT AND ITS CONSEQUENCES

As AFTER 1832, so after the second Reform Act recent historians have stressed the essential continuity of political life and attitudes, particularly that attitude of 'deference which had the effect of prolonging the privileges of the aristocracy and the landed gentry.'[1] Once again the history of Buckinghamshire politics does not sustain such an interpretation. Continuity of a sort, there certainly was. Politics had been chaotic and uncertain before 1867; they remained chaotic and uncertain after 1867. As for deference, if it was one of the more important political attitudes of the period—which it seems to have been—its importance was largely new.

So far as the county constituency was concerned, however, deference is not the attitude that most strikes one either in the years immediately preceding or in those following 1867; indeed there can be no doubt that the traditional leaders of county politics led with increasing difficulty. The Liberal rank and file had never been noted for its docility, and after the mid-forties the Conservatives likewise began to show signs of obstreperousness. The most important reason for this was that the protection issue, which before the mid-forties had given the party unity and enthusiasm, was vastly reduced in importance and no other issue ever took its place. As a consequence, divisive issues assumed greater prominence than they had heretofore. For a while protection itself was one of these.

In 1852 the leaders of both parties had their difficulties. The reason was that, while the generals had decided not to fight, some of their troops were eager for the fray. The three sitting members —Disraeli and Du Pre, the Conservatives, and C. C. Cavendish, the Liberal—and their main supporters had agreed that there should be no contest. The problem was to make others honour the bargain. Dr Lee refused to, putting himself up as a radical free trader; and Houghton also stood, on similar principles, until called away to contest Northampton. The Conservative leadership decided not to take these new Liberal candidacies as voiding the bargain, perhaps because they were none too sure of their ability to keep their own side in line. Lord Carrington wrote to Tindal that one of their own erstwhile allies, a Fenny Stratford coal merchant:

> is anxious to bring forward if the gentlemen will not stir Mr Young the great Protectionist . . .
> Our only chance is the refusal of the chief Tories to join in this, but the violent smaller men will I fear succeed in their wishes.[2]

They did not succeed in 1852; but they would appear to have done at an 1857 by-election, caused by Cavendish's elevation to the peerage as Lord Chesham. The two Conservative MPs and most of the other leading Conservatives in the county were conspicuous by their absence at the election, when C. B. Hamilton, the former MP for Aylesbury, stood against Chesham's eldest son, W. G. Cavendish. According to the *Bucks Herald*, Hamilton stood in response to a requisition by 'FOUR HUNDRED TENANT FARMERS OF BUCKINGHAMSHIRE.' Hamilton himself, though claiming the support of Lord Chandos, T. T. Drake, and one or two other leading Conservatives, said that 'the tenant-farmers of this county are a body who have a perfect right to have their own candidate, and their candidate I am.' He would have preferred to have had 'some Resident Gentleman of Property and Influence' stand, but none came forward, so he acceded to the pressing entreaties of the requisitioners.[3]

Though the gentlemen of property and influence do not appear to have stirred themselves much for Hamilton, they probably did not expect his defeat (by 163 votes, 1,617 to 1,454); and 1858 saw a strenuous effort to revise the register in the Conservative interest, a task that had long been neglected. The Conservatives did not, however, contest the third seat at the next general election in 1859. William Powell, the main Conservative agent, was probably rightly cautious, advising that 'a contest in a county returning 3 Members is always an uncertainty.'[4] Besides that, a contest was very expensive; and neither Disraeli, who had also had to assume the costs of the registration, or Du Pre were anxious to spend several thousands on an election.

In 1863, on the death of the first Lord Chesham, the Conservatives gained the third seat without a serious contest, but they would seem to have done so largely by default. Though Powell had earlier advised that he believed that 'there is a feeling abroad that should the Seat held by Mr Cavendish become vacant before a general election there would be an attempt made to wrest it from the Liberals,'[5] the leaders were apparently willing to leave it to the Liberals. The difficulty was that the Liberals could find no candidate willing to stand. All parties would have been satisfied with Lord Carrington's eldest son, Charles; but, despite his father's enthusiasm, he seems to have refused.[6] No one else was found; and Dr Lee, who waged another campaign of principle, was soundly defeated by Sir Robert Bateson Harvey, brother-in-law of the new Duke of Buckingham. The three Conservatives were again returned without a contest in 1865, but again this would seem to have been mainly because the Liberals could find no candidate, with the eligible men like Sir Harry Verney and Charles Carrington (as that branch of the Smiths became in 1839) in borough seats they did not wish to relinquish.

The most important change between the 1865 general election and the next one in 1868 was the appearance of a Liberal who was willing to stand, Nathaniel Grace Lambert of Denham Court, heir to a colliery fortune and himself a large gentleman farmer. The Reform Act does not appear to have made much difference. The famous minority clause, giving electors in three-member constituencies only two votes, simply made the Conservatives more cautious still. Powell now feared for two Conservative seats—instead of one—if the party put up a third candidate, pointing out that the electors in a large county constituency could not be organized like those in a borough. Harvey agreed with him and retired.[7] But the effect was simply to concede the Liberals a seat they had already been conceded before 1867.

The £12 occupier franchise, though it added a large number to the county electorate, similarly made little change in the political balance of the county. Powell had predicted in June 1868:

The new voters are a body subject to influence much the same as the small freeholders. In the Towns they are chiefly Shopkeepers, Butchers and Publicans, and in the Villages Small Farmers, Wheelwrights, Publicans & Blacksmiths. Whether the preponderating influence is Conservative or Liberal the majority of the New Voters will follow that influence. [8]

Professor Hanham takes Powell to mean by 'influence' that of the owners of large estates. I think, in fact, he used the term much more loosely, meaning little more than that some places tended to be Conservative and some tended to be Liberal. [9] In any case, it is only in this latter sense that his remarks have much meaning.

What the £12 occupier franchise meant was that the county franchise was enjoyed by very much the same kind of people who had voted in the boroughs of Aylesbury and Buckingham on the £10 franchise before 1867. As has been seen, in neither case was anything like a majority of the electors made up of tenants on large estates, or very evidently under the influence of large landowners. The same was probably true of the new county electorate, and it was certainly to prove itself almost equally unpredictable.

The new electors would not, however, have much opportunity to prove themselves for almost two decades. In 1874 there was only a token contest, a Slough solicitor named Talley putting up as a 'Progressive Conservative'—a term which he never really explained—and receiving a mere 151 votes. The only other notable thing about the election was that Disraeli's election expenses of £1,500 were paid in full by a county subscription, whereas usually the expenses were borne mainly by the candidates themselves. [10]

The by-election that followed Disreali's removal to the Lords in August 1876 was an entirely different matter, both as regarded the intensity of the struggle and the burden of expense to the unfortunate Conservative who squeaked through to victory. The election serves as an excellent example of the risks and uncertainties of county electioneering.

The campaign commenced as the agitation over the murder of some thousands of Bulgarian Christians by Turkish mercenaries began to gather real momentum. But, though the Bulgarian atrocities were to be the main issue in the election and to focus national attention upon it, neither side seems to have sensed the importance of the question at the beginning. The whole proceeding began in a most leisurely fashion. Disraeli sent advance word of his impending elevation to the Hon Thomas Fremantle, the son of the former MP for Buckingham, in order, as Charles Fremantle told their father, 'that Tom may have the start of everybody, as he considers Tom the proper person to succeed him.' Lord Cottesloe (as the elder Fremantle had become) replied that the news gave him 'much annoyance.' He feared great expense, which he thought particularly senseless in view of his own advanced age, and 'there is also the question of the claims of other Conservative gentlemen, specially those of Mr Du Pre who gave up his seat to Sir R. B. Harvey [in 1874] in order to avoid a split in the party.'[11]

There was, of course, no party organization to give a candidate the official stamp of approval; so the only thing to do was to wait and see if anyone else proposed himself. No one did. A week after Fremantle's candidacy was first mooted, Edward Baynes, Clerk of the Peace and a veteran of many Conservative campaigns, summed up the then state of affairs for Lord Cottesloe:

> He is now safely placed as *the Conservative* candidate; & we do not anticipate any *real* opposition. Mr Drake saw Lord Chesham upon the matter, & from what passed at that interview, it is not the least likely that any candidate supported by the *heads* of the *Liberal Party* in the County will be started. . . . Of course such an opposition as *Mr Talley* caused upon the last occasion may *possibly* occur, but I don't think it *likely*. . . . I was glad to hear from your Son this morning that he had received a friendly letter from Mr Purefoy FitzGerald promising to support to his utmost; for we were rather afraid that he might have been got hold of by the *Farmers* & started as *their Candidate.* As it is possible you may not have seen your son's address, I enclose it. I think it a very *safe* one, & hear it well spoken of. I have ventured to advise your Son, to be *decided* & *clear* upon the *principles* of important *questions* & measures, but not to tie himself down by pledges, upon the *details* of them.[12]

The address was simply an endorsement of the government's record in both domestic and foreign affairs, stated in very general terms and with no mention of specific issues like the Bulgarian atrocities.

As for the government, Disraeli was still in no hurry. The queen was in Scotland, and he did not press her to confirm the peerage, with the consequence that the date of the election remained in the indefinite future. The delay proved most unfortunate. Fremantle's address appeared on the 16th. On the 22nd at the annual meeting of the Wycombe Liberal Association the young Lord Carrington announced that his brother, Rupert, was posting home from Dresden to contest the county in the Liberal interest.[13]

As Baynes had suggested, the other 'heads of the Liberal Party' in the county had no desire for a contest. The heads of the party in London, however, did want a contest, particularly Lord Granville, and the candidacy was concocted with his advice and encouragement. And Carrington's address, in which Granville had a hand, attacked the government's policy on the Bulgarian atrocities.[14] But Carrington himself did not begin by emphasizing the question when he commenced his Bucks campaign. Rather he usually commenced his speeches, as at Newport Pagnell, with an attack on 'Lord Sandon's Education Act, which he characterized as being against the wishes of the Nonconformist body and of the great Liberal party (cheers).' Another favourite issue was the Conservative Agricultural Holdings Act (supposedly giving protection to tenants' rights), which he denounced as a sham. So far as I can determine, the first mention of the atrocities was at the Newport Pagnell farmers' ordinary (ordinaries often provided the occasion for the candidates' speeches) at the Anchor on the 30th. There he denounced them in the strongest terms and said that 'it was a disgrace to civilization to give them the least countenance . . .'[15]

The allusion to the atrocities received the same enthusiastic response as that to Sandon's education act, the 1876 act which made attendance compulsory at schools which under the provisions of the 1870 education act might well be Anglican. The two issues probably appealed to the same constituency. R. Littleboy, the Quaker banker who chaired the ordinary, elsewhere denounced the recent act because 'the children of Dissenters may be driven . . . into schools, some of which are under the influence of clergymen of advanced Ritualistic tendencies.'[16] Dissenters were likewise roused to the atrocities question; and the following day in Chesham, another Dissenting stronghold, Carrington devoted most of his speech to the atrocities. He did not eschew the purple phrase:

> Let us take care that the screams of those outraged women,
> the blood of those children and patriarchs are not imputed to us;
> that we are not involved in one condemnation with the prepetrators
> of these abominable crimes.[17]

Such arguments might go down well with Dissenting audiences.
They were also beloved by Gladstone. But they were anathema to
Disraeli, who saw the question in the broader context of the
weakening Turkey vis-à-vis Russia, whose role as protector of the
Balkan Christians had always had strong expansionist implications. Disraeli's approach appealed to most of the leading Bucks
Liberals, like Chesham and Lambert. The Rothschilds had an
added reason for favouring the pro-Turkish policy, Russian anti-
semitism. These other Liberal leaders in the county therefore
began by proclaiming their neutrality in the contest, and though
all seem to have come round to giving lukewarm personal support
to Carrington, they certainly did not exert themselves for him.
The only leading Liberal besides his brother to work hard for
Carrington was Sir Harry Verney, who, as his brother-in-law the
Dean of Ripon remarked, 'was in the agonies of the Bulgarian
fever . . .'[18] As an influential Evangelical—he was president of the
Evangelical Alliance—Verney was an exception to what appears to
have been the general rule that Evangelicals favoured the Turks;
and his support for Carrington was probably important in Low
Church Bucks.

The Conservatives, however, were not unduly concerned. Fremantle wrote to his father on 5 September that the Liberals were
'working the Bulgarian business hard and it may reduce the
majority.'[19] But they were confident that they had a princely
majority to reduce. On 16 September, six days before the election
finally took place, T. T. Drake reported to Disraeli that Powell
'makes out that we have 3225 promises and he knows of 1547
positive refusals. This leaves a wide margin for our side.'[20] J. K.
Fowler, the landlord of the 'White Hart', lovingly trilling off the
great estates in the Conservative interest, was even more re-
assuring.[21] They were in for a rude surprise. Fremantle beat
Carrington by only 186 votes (2,725 to 2,539). The Conservatives
were 180 below 1874, heretofore their lowest poll since the Reform
Act, and the Liberals were up 800. T. T. Drake told Sir William

Hart Dyke that without a concerted attack on the register 'the Conservative party are *certain* to go to the wall at the next Election.'[22]

The issue is the only possible explanation of what was close to an upset victory for the Liberals. There had been rumours of bribery, which proved to be ridiculous.[23] Carrington had undoubtedly spent heavily on organization, but so had the Conservatives. Fremantle's bill was £6,500 (of which he had to meet all but about £1,500).[24] Influence was overwhelmingly on the Conservative side. The only things clearly in the Liberals' favour was 'the Bulgarian fever' and some agricultural grievances.

Besides Dissenting grievances, a predictable part of any Liberal candidate's programme in Bucks, the most significant additional issue pressed by Carrington in 1876 was that of farmers' grievances. He pressed it harder in the 1880 election, endorsing a large part of the programme of the Farmers' Alliance, including tenants' compensation for unexhausted improvements, reform of the laws affecting the ownership and transfer of land, compensation for damage done by winged game, and representation of ratepayers in county government.[25] The other issues he stressed in this election were the Dissenters' right to be buried by their own ministers in parish churchyards, the assimilation of county and borough franchise (which he had also advocated in 1876), and the protection of railway servants in the performance of their duties. The last issue was undoubtedly aimed at the Liberal stronghold at Wolverton, home of a growing railway works. The rest were either orthodox Liberalism, or, in the case of the first four mentioned, aimed at attracting the farmers.

Another candidate catered for the farmers. Frederick Charsley, the coroner for Bucks, a former Conservative candidate for Wycombe, and himself farming 800 acres, came forward as 'the farmers' candidate' in this election. Among other things he advocated a graduated income tax and a shifting of other burdens, both public and private, to the landlords' shoulders.

Lambert, whose Liberalism had grown increasingly weaker, particularly in foreign affairs, did not stand again. The Conservatives put up only two candidates, Fremantle and Harvey. It was another close election. Harvey headed the poll with 2,956. Carrington and Fremantle tied with 2,790 votes each. And Charsley came in a poor—but not insignificant—third with 796 votes. It was also the last election under the old franchise, and, appropriately enough, it was fought with the old, largely ad hoc, organization. A county Conservative Association was a year away and would never see an election, being outmoded before the general election of 1885. The Liberals never had a county association, though in 1880 they benefited from a recent surge of local organizations, most of the twenty Liberal Associations in the county having been formed since the fillip given by the near victory in 1876. Parties in Buckinghamshire before the Third Reform Act, however, remained largely voluntary alliances. Like all voluntary alliances, they had their ups and downs, but perhaps little or no more than their more highly organised successors. What they lacked in organization, they made up for in large part by a combination of shared sentiments and an ultimate willingness to compromise. It was these qualities that sustained 'the great Liberal party' in Victorian Buckinghamshire.

Particularly baffling and frustrating to the Liberals was the bond of sentiment that bound the farmers to 'the good old cause.' Henry Darvill, the Liberal agent from Windsor, expressed their bafflement in January 1858, just after the close race between Cavendish and Hamilton, the tenant farmers' candidate. He pointed to the absence from the fray of the chiefs of the Conservative party, Disraeli, Du Pre, Harvey, and Lowndes of Chesham. Yet the tenant farmers still turned out in large numbers to give Hamilton their vote, saying, according to Darvill: 'the Conservatives stick to the farmers, and we will stick by them.'

Darvill argued strongly against the good sense of this belief that made the farmers better Conservatives than their leaders, but he freely admitted its existence.[26] And, though the elections of 1876 and 1880 suggest that it may have been weakening with some farmers, it was a belief that persisted. Save for Charsley, who solicited and may have got split votes from Liberals, the so-called 'farmers' candidates' were simply Conservatives by another name, without any distinctive programme to separate them from other Conservatives. It was just that the farmers believed that they were more zealous than orthodox Conservatives—even the prime minister himself!

Probably one of the safest rules of thumb in Bucks politics, then, was that a farmer was likely to be a Conservative—unless he had some other good reason not to be: because he was a Dissenter, for example. But there were other voters besides farmers, who did not always have the same interests; and the Reform Act, by establishing the householder franchise in the boroughs, gave the vote to a class of men who might be expected to have had very different interests than the farmers—the labourers. There can be little doubt that they did have different interests, but elections give little evidence of it.

There is no better example of the lack of any distinctive 'working-class' vote than that provided by the indifferent fortunes of George Howell at Aylesbury. The secretary of the Reform League came down to Aylesbury in 1868 proclaiming that, as he told an audience of working men in a malt house in Aston Clinton, 'it is impossible that the interests of the working and trading classes of this country can be properly cared for as long as the whole of our legislation is in the hands of capitalists and large landed proprietors.'[27] But it was not agricultural parishes like Aston Clinton that were forward in supporting Howell—indeed in Aston Clinton he got only nine split votes out of a total of 129 votes recorded. Rather, it was the towns and large villages that were most enthusiastic for the working man's candidate. Howell received 942 votes, 255 of them plumpers. Of the latter—the clearest proof of enthusiasm—some 83 per cent came from the towns of Aylesbury and Princes Risborough and the large villages of Haddenham and Great Missenden. The rest were scattered over the constituency, with only one relatively large clump of ten, out of eighty-one votes recorded, in the agricultural parish of Dinton.

It is evident that the working man's candidate did not get very strong support from the agricultural labourers—and it is by no means evident that most of those who voted for him did so because he was a working man. The behaviour of those electors who had also voted in the last contested election in 1859 probably gives a fair indication of the attitudes of the old 'middle-class' electors. There were 565 of them, of whom 124 (22%) gave Howell one vote; 15 (3%) gave him plumpers. The behaviour of the whole 2,945 electors who registered a vote in 1868 does not provide very striking contrasts: 32 per cent gave Howell one vote; 9 per cent gave him a plumper. Since I have not checked the 1867 register against the 1868 one, I cannot say how all those registered under the new franchise voted as compared with all those who had been registered under the old. But the figures I have just quoted suggest that, as might be expected, Howell had slightly stronger support among the new electors—not, however, enough to make a great deal of it.

The reason appears to be that Howell's main appeal was not as a working man, but as a Liberal. And, indeed, it was primarily as a Liberal, with the endorsement of the leaders of the party, that he came down from London to contest Aylesbury. He made this clear in his address. He came down, he said, to 'unlock' the borough. In 1865, as has been seen, N. M. de Rothschild and S. G. Smith had been returned without a contest, and the Liberal Rothschild and the Conservative Smith had made a pact to continue the arrangement. Howell protested against this neutralization of the borough's voice. He went on to propose a number of improvements in the Reform Act: the repeal of the clause which required personal payment of rates, the equalization of the county and borough franchise, a thorough redistribution of seats, and the ballot. He gave his 'uncompromising support to Mr Gladstone in his efforts to dis-establish and dis-endow' the Irish Church, and called for a reform of the land laws in favour of the Irish tenants. He gave his 'hearty adhesion to the broadest scheme of National Unsectarian Education, and for opening our Universities to all classes without reference to creed.' He called for economy in national expenditure and a reduction of the heavy burden of taxation. He endorsed equalization of the poor rates, a better administration of charitable endowments, the establishment of county financial boards, an improved tenant right bill for English farmers, and the abolition of the existing game laws.

Finally, he said that as 'the question of Capital and labour must necessarily come before the new Parliament . . . to deal fairly with the subject, labour should be represented as well as capital.' But the closest he came to a specific proposal was in suggesting 'a just scheme for preventing Trade's disputes, for promoting Courts of Conciliation and Boards of Arbitration and such other measures as may tend to the mutual harmony between employers and employed.' He ended with an 'appeal to the whole liberal party who, ever since 1832 have tried to secure a triumph for their principles to give me their hearty co-operation and support.'[28]

Rowland Dickens, the Dissenting chemist and long-time leader of Aylesbury Liberalism, said in nominating Rothschild that he regretted that he was not also able to support Howell. But, though he entirely agreed with the principles stated in his address, he feared that two Liberals could not win. Robert Gibbs' *Bucks Advertiser* took much the same line.[29] But Howell's leading supporters were much the same kind of people—J. W. Reader, the Temple Street auctioneer who proposed him as a Liberal candidate, A. P. Scrivener, the large Congregationalist farmer from Weston Turville who nominated him, and Joseph Jones, the ex-Chartist solicitor who chaired some of his meetings. More often than not his meetings in the hundreds were chaired by the local Dissenting minister, and the clusters of votes outside the towns supporting both Liberal candidates were usually in areas where Dissent was especially strong. Like Howell himself, all his leading supporters also supported Rothschild; they only regretted that the latter was not a good enough Liberal to support Howell.

Rothschild gave the following explanation:

> In answer to your enquiries I beg to inform you that on being asked why I did not coalesce with you at Aylesbury I stated that some of my supporters there informed me that they would withdraw their support from me if I joined you.
>
> They added that in consequence of the warm contest in the Borough an ill feeling had sprung up between the labourers and their Employers.[30]

Rothschild was almost certainly speaking the truth. Though there is little indication of ill-feeling on the part of the labourers, there is a good deal of evidence to suggest that Howell's candidacy frightened and angered farmers and other employers. The *Bucks Advertiser* reported a large meeting of his in the county hall being broken up by a group in which farmers were a leading element.[31] Howell himself listed his opponents in the following order: 'I had to fight against the Farmers, Employers, "Gentleman" Parsons and a large number of "shops" *Tradespeople*!!!'[32] He claimed to have a good deal of evidence of intimidation, and in thanking a Chesham supporter who had been working to collect it he confided:

Rothschild will not go against me next time. I think he is disgusted.[33]

Rothschild did not, however, support Howell at the next election, despite Gladstone's personal endorsement of him. His reason was probably the same in 1874 as it had been in 1868, his supporters' opposition to Howell. The strength of the opposition varied. The *Bucks Advertiser* went so far as to give Howell a half-hearted endorsement, arguing that, while it opposed representation of any particular class or interest, Howell would be swamped in his capacity as a working man's MP and on all other questions would add to the Liberal vote.[34] Such arguments may have told with some middle-class Liberals, and the ballot, adopted in 1872, may also have worked in Howell's favour. In 1868 the poll had given Rothschild 1,722, Smith 1,468, and Howell 942. In this election it was Rothschild 1,761, Smith 1,624, and Howell 1,144. But though Howell gained, his gain was about matched by the Conservatives, even with the ballot.

Howell did not stand again in 1880, and the Liberal candidate who took his place presented a marked contrast, save in one respect —Rothschild refused to support him. G. W. E. Russell was a grandson of the sixth Duke of Bedford, so there was hardly the social argument against him that there had been against Howell; but, whereas Russell denounced Disraeli as 'Jingo, Juggler, and Jew,' Rothschild, though proclaiming himself a good Liberal in all other respects, stoutly defended the Conservative prime minister's foreign policy. All the leading Liberals supported both candidates, though some stated their disagreement with Rothschild's views on foreign policy and deplored his refusal to coalesce with Russell. Similar criticisms were advanced, sometimes hotly, at Liberal meetings around the hundreds; and it was almost certainly Conservative votes that put Rothschild again at the head of the poll. The votes were divided as follows:

Plumpers		*Split Votes*	
Russell	858	Russell & Rothschild	977
Smith	705	Russell & Smith	84
Rothschild	412	Smith & Rothschild	722

According to Russell, when Smith had been unable to get a vote, he had asked for a plumper for Rothschild, and the above figures suggest a strong Conservative preference for the latter, and not surprizingly. As the figures also show, the Conservatives were unable to elect Smith, Rothschild with 2,111 and Russell with 1,919 both being comfortably ahead of Smith's 1,511 votes.[35]

Clearly the Second Reform Act had greatly improved the Liberal position in the borough—provided the Liberals had the right sort of candidate. It is not difficult to see why Howell was not the right sort. The most important question probably is why Rothschild continued to be an acceptable candidate for many Liberal voters? Robert Gibbs gave part of the answer at a Princes Risborough meeting celebrating the return of the other Liberal candidate: 'Every true reformer must regard the name of Russell; every Nonconformist must bear that name in the greatest respect (cheers).' But they had not sent Russell to parliament merely because he was the bearer of a great name:

> We sent him there as the exponent of Liberal principles; because we believe that Liberal principles are those by which this country should be governed (cheers). We also sent him there as he represents our opinions upon civil and religious matters. We are entitled to civil liberties—civil liberties are our birthright. We are also entitled to religious liberties, and what we want is religious equality pure and simple.[36]

It will perhaps be wondered whether Gibbs' current concerns were, in fact, any more relevant than his historical memories—or, indeed, very different. But the meeting, purportedly made up mainly of labouring men, seems to have found them so. And, whatever else he may have left to be desired, there was no doubt whatever that 'Rothschild and Religious Liberty' coupled as well even as Russell. If anyone had ever doubted it, it had been made evident from the first time Nathaniel de Rothschild stepped upon an Aylesbury hustings in 1865 advocating the total abolition of Church rates.

Another factor, though it did not apply only to Liberals, was the Rothschilds' well-deserved reputation for benevolence and generosity. Men of all political parties commented upon and extolled it, and it gave rise to arguments like the following. How, the

rhetorical question went, were working men to be benefited? The
answer was always the same:

> The proper course was to leave the matter in the hands of men
> of influence and position like Mr Rothschild, who could do
> something substantial for the elevation of the working classes.[37]

The words were those of a Dissenting minister, but the basic
argument was one repeated, with variations, by men in all walks of
life in all three elections between 1868 and 1880 (and of Smith as
well as of Rothschild). It was a genuinely deferential argument, and
many working men would appear to have accepted it.

Similar considerations may have been in the minds of some of
the new electors at Buckingham. In 1857 Buckingham had re-
verted to its old situation of being shared by the two parties. Sir
Harry Verney came forward once more. Chandos retired, but Gen
Hall was joined by Philip Box, the auctioneer and former mayor
who took such a dim view of free trade, and the Hon Richard
Cavendish of Thornton joined Verney. Cavendish's candidacy was
launched without the knowledge of Verney and his main supporters, and they refused to have anything to do with it. The
result was that Verney headed the poll with 193. Hall secured the
second seat with 151, though Cavendish was only seventeen votes
behind with 134. Box was a poor fourth with eighty-two votes.[38]

The close result suggests that had the two Liberals worked
together they would probably have won. But it would have been a
chancy thing, and they decided not to take the risk in 1859. Verney
stood alone as the Liberal candidate. The Conservatives, however,
were deeply divided. J. G. Hubburd, a large Russia merchant who
lived at Addington, stood as a Liberal Conservative. Hubburd had
been a staunch opponent of protection, which had long stood in the
way of his ambitions within his own party. But it was another
element in his liberalism which was important on this occasion.
Hubburd was a High Churchman, with ritualist tendencies, which
might be expected to have made him anathema to Low Church
and Dissenting Buckingham. But it was perhaps his High Churchmanship that led him to take a position which the Dissenting
element in Buckingham, at any rate, found a redeeming virtue.
Hubburd in his address proclaimed that 'I should gladly assist in
such a settlement of the [Church rate] question as would confine to

Churchmen the obligation of raising money, and of controlling its expenditure for the support of their Churches.' The second Tory candidate was the Hon G. W. Barrington, brother of the Hon Percy Barrington of Westbury Manor and 'an exponent of the principles of the old Tory school,' particularly on religious questions. The Hon Percy repudiated his brother for dividing the party, but local Conservatives like Box strongly supported him. Needless to say, the Liberals did not, and some forty or fifty of them divided their votes with Hubburd to ensure his election.[39]

Verney and Hubburd were given an uncontested return in 1865. But this was impossible in 1868, as the Reform Act had reduced Buckingham to one seat. A report to the Reform League in September gives what appears to be a very complete description of the situation in the borough:

> Sir Harry Verney is the favorite candidate with the constituency, and if the voting was by Ballot, undoubtedly would be returned by a considerable majority. But as this is not the case, other influences will be brought to bear against Sir Harry, or any other liberals who may offer themselves:—Firstly, Mr J. G. Hubburd deals with many of the Tradespeople in Buckingham, and to a greater extent than his opponent:—Next, Mr Hubburd's numerous charities, and the Buildings for his workpeople, for which Mr H asked £7 per year, as rent; but the men told him that considering their earnings, they could only afford as rent £4 per annum,—Mr Hubburd very readily agreed to that sum. At the present time Mr Hubburd has his election managed by the Duke of Buckingham's Agent; this is considered by many as the 'screw' being put on those electors who rent property from the Duke of Buckingham, and your reporter found considerable 'shyness' on the part of those persons who reside on the Ducal property. They say at the last election Mr Hubburd's agent was not connected with the Duke's man, and now that he is it will make it bad for all who vote for Sir Harry. This, and the fact that Mr Hubburd is a great favorite with many who dissent from him in politics, will, in the opinion of many make it a very close contest.[40]

In fact, it was not a very close contest. Verney won easily, 463 to 338, giving him a comfortable majority of 125. He achieved this with little reference to working-class concerns. Indeed his only reference to them was in regard to repealing the ratepaying clause of the act. He desired this, he said, because he wished 'that the Reform Act should be a truth and should enable all the working classes to take part in the election of Members of Parliament and so in the Government of the country.' But what he apparently thought should be of concern to the working classes were issues like the dis-establishment of the Irish Church. And what he and his supporters hammered hardest of all was Hubburd's Ritualism:

> I say that if you are Protestants you will not return a Ritualist . . . I say that is the question of the day.

So said Sir Harry, and his sentiments were echoed by supporters like the Rev R. Widdowson, a Primitive Methodist.[41]

Primitive Methodism was fairly strong among the agricultural labourers in the area, and such arguments may have appealed to them. But, in any case, working men would probably not have been in a majority in the constituency. Unlike Aylesbury, whose electorate had been tripled by the Reform Act, Buckingham's was not quite doubled. There were 407 registered electors in 1865, and it was reckoned that the act would add about 300, about ninety in the town and the rest in the outlying villages. Not all of the latter, of course, would have been labourers. In any event, being 'working class' was largely a state of mind, and not one that was very strong in Buckingham. According to the Reform League's emissary:

> The working class element is of no very great weight, as there are no associations worth mentioning, with the exception perhaps of the Odd Fellows and Foresters, and these, for all political purposes, are of little or no use.—The working man and his friends in Buckingham have no confidence or reliance in themselves, and I was very much struck with the implicit trust and confidence of the people I came in contact with, regarding the power and influence of Sir Harry's Election Agents, Messrs Hearn & Nelson, who, according to them, have the key of the position in their own hands.

The friends of the working man were more evident in radical politics in the borough than the working man himself. Buckingham had a branch of the Reform League—sharing that distinction with Chesham and Wycombe—but its most active members were a draper and a baker. The latter called himself a 'working man,' but he kept a small shop and prided himself on having pulled himself up to the £10 franchise. The league's other sympathizers included the postmaster, another draper, a cabinet-maker, a shoe manufacturer, a shoemaker, a glazier, and the British schoolmaster. They were not very different from the men who had first returned Sir Harry in 1832.

It is probably significant that as the electorate increased the influence of such men would appear to have decreased, which perhaps suggests that the other influences mentioned by the Reform League's emissary in 1868 grew in importance. In 1874 in a poll of 980 (compared to 801 in the previous election), Verney was defeated by 198 votes. And in 1880 in a poll of 1,048 he barely scraped though to victory finishing only eight votes ahead of Egerton Hubburd, who had also been his opponent on the previous occasion. Issues may have had something to do with the results. According to one of Sir Harry's close friends and staunch political supporters, the Liberals were not very enthusiastic in 1874. The Liberal Government's education act, which allowed a Board School only if sectarian schools were inadequate, aroused great controversy in Buckingham, which by 1873 had only National (ie Anglican) schools.[42] This did not prevent most of Verney's more prominent Dissenting supporters, mostly Congregationalists, from supporting him in 1874, but some of the more radical, like the Primitive Methodist Widdowson did not appear with him on that occasion. In 1880 the Liberals were reunited—if they had ever really been actively divided—behind Gladstone and a policy of peace, retrenchment, and reform. On neither occasion does there seem to have been any evident reason, in terms of issues, why the new electors should have supported Hubburd, which they clearly did in large numbers.

A 'deferential' vote might be expected in Buckingham, whose lagging economy was only slightly bolstered by some new industry like the small shoe factory. It might not, however, be expected in Wycombe, which was already a thriving industrial centre. Its paper mills had long been fair-sized employers of labour; and between 1830 and the 1850s these were joined by a number of chair factories and workshops, there being about fifty, large and small by 1885.[43] By 1862, according to the *Bucks Advertiser*, 'from the growth of local manufacture, the balance of electoral power is in the hands of the working classes . . .'[44] In the eyes of the *Advertiser*, such a state of affairs made a Conservative candidate 'an impertinence.' Experience certainly showed that a Conservative candidacy was hopeless. But it also showed that the constituency would tolerate Liberals of very different degrees of Liberalism.

Lord Carrington had suffered a humiliating defeat in 1841 when he backed two Tory protectionists. He did not make the same mistake again. In 1847 he put forward his cousin, Martin Tucker Smith, a Liberal free trader. Under the circumstances, Bernal Osborne decided to withdraw. The contest, he said, 'would depend more on the solidity of the purse than the purity of the principle . . .' The electors, he continued,

> by their bold and uncompromising conduct in the election of June, 1841, . . . insured the triumph of liberal principles in their Borough, since the same influence which was then so unscrupulously exerted for the election of two High Tory candidates is now transferred to a gentleman professing totally opposite views in politics, and which are so much in accordance with my own, I entertain less regret in resigning the trust so honourably confided to me.[45]

So Smith and G. H. Dashwood were returned without a contest.

In 1852, 'the Town' decided to challenge 'the Abbey' once again. And Dashwood's party brought down W. Simpson, a retired Hammersmith surgeon, for the purpose. Dashwood himself remained as neutral as possible. Besides the independence of the borough, the only other issue dividing 'the Town' from 'the Abbey' was the ballot. An insufficient number of electors found the principles of the former enough to outweigh the power and wealth of the latter; and, though Dashwood headed the poll with 262 votes, Smith secured the second seat with 208, and Simpson was a poor third with 116.[46]

Thereafter, there was compromise. In 1857 and 1859 'the Town' returned Dashwood, an advanced Liberal, and 'the Abbey' returned Smith, a very moderate Palmerstonian, without a contest. When Dashwood died in 1862, Carrington refrained from putting forward a candidate, allowing Dashwood's former party to bring down a Londoner, John Remington Mills, a retired Congregationalist silk manufacturer and prominent Dissenting politician, as the

Liberal candidate. The local Conservatives, who usually supported 'the Abbey' candidate, put up Dondlad Cameron of Hampden House as an 'independent and liberal Conservative' to oppose this 'representative of extreme sectarianism.' But, though Cameron was a very liberal Conservative candidate, pledging himself to both parliamentary and Church-rate reform, the electors favoured Mills by 220 to 158.[47] In 1865 Mills was again returned, together with Charles Carrington, the heir to the title, again without a contest.

The younger Carrington was carefully tutored by his aging father, who advised in the middle of the crisis over the Liberal reform bill in March 1866:

> Pray continue to vote on the oaths bill tonight as these votes set you free in doing what you think best with respect to the reform bill which I take it for granted you do not think desirable . . .[48]

Lord Carrington was referring to what became the Offices and Oaths Act of 1867, which removed further legal annoyances to Dissenters and was warmly supported by them. What he seems to have been suggesting was that if Dissenting interests were looked after the Wycombe electorate would tolerate a good deal of difference of opinion on other matters; it was a policy he and his candidates had long followed, and, for the most part, with great success.

In any case, Lord Carrington did not believe that the town, save for 'some chair-making roughs,' supported reform. There may have been good reason for the lack of enthusiasm. For, though the Carringtons had been Adullamites in 1866, Lord Carrington was convinced that the 1867 Act improved their position at Wycombe. As he told his son in January 1868:

> You are returned by our own strength & the property of the Town. The ultra party must be & are against you, but the reform bill has very much weakened their power.[49]

He was dead before the November election bore him out, his son, William, beating Mills for Wycombe's one remaining set by 701 to 500.

In 1868 there was little to choose between Carrington and Mills in terms of principles. But the same could not be said of the contest in 1874, when Carrington was opposed by Henry Broadhurst, secretary of the Labour Representation League. Working-class Wycombe had a working-class candidate the most impeccable credentials. He did not do very well. Carrington received 953 votes to Broadhurst's 415, with Charsley, the Conservative, getting a mere nineteen.[50] Carrington was unopposed in 1880. The working men of Wycombe clearly liked their neighbour, a Liberal in politics, who, as one of the family supporters had said in 1868, would also be liberal to the town. There was no doubt that the Carringtons were that. The young Lord Carrington's style was very different from that of his father—as he demonstrated by immediately turning the gardens of the dreaded Abbey into allotments![51]—and it was even more effective.

Marlow had always preferred a rich neighbour. Unlike the other Bucks boroughs the town lacked a strong and independent middle-class, at least one sufficiently strong to give it a really independent political life. It had a large Dissenting population, and the failure to abolish Church rates in the thirties had led the *Aylesbury News* to predict that Sir William Clayton would soon be joined by another Liberal member. But just the reverse happened. In 1835 Clayton was at the head of the poll, with 233 votes to T. P. Williams' 185. In 1841, the next contested election, Clayton's vote fell to 170. Williams was at the head of the poll with 233, and Renn Hampden, a Conservative relative of the controversial theologian, was only one vote behind Clayton with 169.[52]

Issues almost certainly played a part in the Liberal decline. As elsewhere, religious and agricultural issues deprived the Liberals of support, and Clayton was deserted by some leading tradesmen of the Church party and some of the farmers. Nor was he to keep the seat he had so narrowly won for long. He was unseated on a petition. The evidence before the election committee revealed that Clayton's bailiff had bribed an insolvent butcher, to whom he had previously refused credit, by supplying him with some of the famous Harleyford southdowns. But it revealed more than that. It showed that the Williams family let their houses at uneconomic, and in some cases almost certainly fictitious, rents to qualify voters. The influence of the Williamses, the largest landlords in the constituency, was backed by that of Wethereds, the brewers, and far and away the town's largest employers. Indeed, had it not been for the Wethereds, who took over the costs from a financially exhausted Hampden, the petition would never have been pressed to a successful conclusion.[53] And most of the other influence in the town was in the same direction. A number of prominent and wealthy families had found Marlow a convenient and comfortable retreat from Town even before the coming of the railway and many more would afterwards.

The consequence of all these factors was that after 1841 not even a wealthy Liberal had a chance in Marlow. In 1847, Williams, 'assisted by the brewers', introduced his cousin, Col Brownlow Knox, as the second Conservative candidate. Clayton stood again, but was beaten by Knox, 179 to 161.[54] In 1852 the Conservative cousins beat another Liberal candidate even more decisively. Williams took his usual place at the head of the poll with 242, Knox came second with 198, and Jacob Bell, who had previously been involved in a notorious bribery case at St Albans, got only ninety-nine votes.[55] There was no contest in 1857. In 1859 there was a candidate from the Reform Club, J. W. Probyn, but he trailed Knox 120 to 175.[56] In 1865 the cousins again came in without a contest. It is evident that the Conservatives had little to fear from the opposition. But they took no chances. On the one issue that stirred public opinion in Marlow at all deeply during the period—Church rates—Williams and Knox were careful to be most conciliatory.[57]

Marlow had begun to assume the appearance of a pocket borough of the Williams family. It was not exactly that, as became evident in the first election after the 1867 Act. The Reform League was active in Marlow, holding several meetings; and its activities evoked a response, particularly among Dissenters. As a result, Edmund Hope Verney was brought down to contest the borough's one remaining seat. A Verney was well calculated to appeal to Dissenting opinion; and the Conservatives were concerned, so concerned that Williams was politely pushed to one side by T. O. Wethered, who was believed to be more popular and perhaps more influential with the new electorate. The result of the contest was much closer than Marlow had become used to. An electorate roughly doubled by the Reform Act placed Verney only thirty-one behind Wethered, 345 to 314.[58] But the Liberals were not sufficiently encouraged to try again in 1874, when Wethered was returned unopposed. The 1880 contest would seem to justify the Liberal pessimism; then Col Owen Williams beat J. O. Griffits, the Liberal Recorder of Reading, by 505 to 365.[59]

If one were seeking examples of political continuity, Marlow would clearly be the place to find one. Influences similar to those that had dominated its political life in the mid-eighteenth century continued to dominate it well into the third quarter of the nineteenth century, though its growing suburban character probably became increasingly important as time went on. Even Marlow saw changes, and there was a period in the 1820s and 1830s when it seemed that a Whig-Dissenting middle-class alliance would give Marlow the kind of politics similar to those in other Bucks boroughs.

But then the balance tilted in the other direction—illustrating how delicate such balances were. Marlow, however, was unique in Bucks. And in the other Bucks constituencies, it would be difficult to argue that continuity after 1867 was the most evident characteristic, particularly the continuity of aristocratic and gentry influence. In the county such influence became increasingly insecure. In Aylesbury, old means continued to be used, but on a new scale and by different—mainly middle-class—people. Perhaps in Buckingham, certainly in Wycombe, aristocratic influence remained important—more important than it had been before 1867. Change after 1867 is more marked than continuity, though it was not always change in a democratic direction.

Conclusion

IN 1760 the Claytons held a seat at Marlow by giving favourable rents to their tenants; Earl Verney, two at Wendover by holding the threat of eviction over the heads of his. In 1880 the Hon Egerton Hubburd barely lost a seat at Buckingham which he had gained at the last election, in part, at any rate, because his father, Lord Addington, gave favourable rents to his tenants; and Sir Nathaniel de Rothschild was returned to a seat that in the not too distant past had been defended by bribery and coercion. It might seem that very little had changed in a century and a quarter.

But there had been change, and the continuity is more apparent than real. When George Howell reported the means used against him to Walter Morrison, one of several Liberal MPs who gave him strong moral and financial support, Morrison was sceptical:

> No doubt unfair means were used more or less, but I have fought three contested elections, and I find that *coercion* is often alleged by men who really want to vote against you but have not the manliness to say so . . . and that I often hear rumours of bribery but seldom can substantiate them on investigation.[1]

Since this was in 1868, the first election after the Second Reform Act, Morrison was clearly speaking mainly from experience under the 1832 franchise; and his assessment of the importance of bribery and coercion would generally accord with impressions gained from a study of Bucks politics between 1832 and 1867.

Howell replied that there had undoubtedly been coercion. It is significant, however, that he did not blame S. G. Smith or Rothschild. Rather he blamed the 'Farmers, Employers, "Gentlemen" Parsons and a large number of . . . *Tradespeople*!!!' In other words, Howell blamed his defeat primarily on the opposition not of aristo-

221

crats or landed gentlemen, but of the middle-classes. Rothschild explained his refusal to coalesce with Howell in precisely the same way, that is, because of the threat of his supporters to desert him if he backed Howell. This would hardly seem to be an example of the perpetuation of the influence of the aristocracy and landed gentry. The methods may have been old, but they were being used by different people—an important difference.

It is not easy to assess the importance of bribery and coercion after 1867. As has been seen, the new electors voted pretty much as the old had done, but there were several possible reasons. They might simply have shared similar interests. They might have voted Liberal because they were Dissenters, for example. It is hard to think of any very good reason why labourers would have voted Conservative—except one—and that would seem to have applied to some Liberal voters as well. In 1868 Joseph DeFraine, a newly-enfranchised elector, served notice that he and his kind would not vote at the command of their landlords or employers; the days of landlordism and influence were over. Twelve years later this same Joseph DeFraine warmly endorsed Rothschild. Sir Nathaniel, he said, 'had been connected with all Liberal principles, and everything for the good of working men.' He cited, as an example, the numerous letters Rothschild wrote to find situations for poor men's sons.[2] A genuinely deferential vote could have arisen from such attitudes, and I think it is likely that such a vote did arise. Again, however, it was largely a new phenomenon.

Generally speaking, then, it seems that the new working class electors in Bucks boroughs voted as their employers voted; either from fear, cupidity, or genuine deference. There would have been every reason for them to have done so, and little reason for them not to have done. George Howell—at any rate, George Howell as a 'working-class candidate'—would probably not have seemed any more relevant to their needs and desires than John Wilkes would have seemed to their predecessors a century and more before had he talked about the elder Pitt's foreign policy. The consequence was the same: men voted according to where immediate advantage seemed to lie. Doubtless it would have been a different story had the labourers around Winslow and Swanbourne, where the Agricultural Labourers Union took firm root in the seventies, had the vote. The Duke of Buckingham believed that they played an

important part in Edmund Hope Verney's triumphal return for the
new North Bucks constituency in 1885:

> The agricultural labourers seem to me to have been generally
> influenced by the desire not to lose a chance of the 3 acres &
> cow—and by the nod of the ALU.[3]

But these were the politics of the future.

Much of this book has been about 'middle-class' politics. They
are not, of course, the politics of the 'urban' middle-class; and
doubtless not everyone would recognize all the participants as
'middle-class.' But as E. P. Thompson has reminded us, *The Book
of English Trades*, published in 1818, lists the apothecary, attorney,
optician and statutory alongside the carpenter, currier, tailor and
potter. The latter considered themselves as 'good' as the former.[4]
So it was in the market towns of Bucks throughout the period with
which this book is concerned. At the beginning of the period, all
would have called themselves of the 'middling classes.' By the mid-
nineteenth century, they would have been calling themselves
'middle-class.' The more radical would have thought of themselves as 'of the People,' but very few indeed would have thought
of themselves as 'working class.' Such people may not fit the
stereotypes of the historian or the sociologist, but they and people
like them were probably the single most important factor in mid-
Victorian electoral politics. This book has been about the growth
and operation of their kind of politics.

The middle-classes of Bucks did not, of course, hold the same
opinions on all political questions. Most of them, however, shared
an ideal that has figured in this book from the beginning—independence. The 'Pawnbroking Interest' (the reference was to John
Gibbs) that supported Liberal candidates in the thirties might be
polls apart on most questions from the 'army of pettyfogging
Attorneys and Cheesemongers' that defied the duke and backed
Rice Clayton in 1847, but both groups would have prided themselves on their independence.

It may perhaps be thought that the farmers have been forgotten
in all this, that they, at any rate, would have been 'deferential.' As
has been seen, it was not necessarily so. In 1868 a large Princes
Risborough farmer testified at a Howell meeting:

He himself rented under a Conservative landlord, and it was
expected that he would give one vote for his landlord if he gave
one for himself. But he declared that he would not do this, and
at the rent dinner very lately the agent, in the most gentlemanly
manner, said it was very nice to have them voting on the same
side as himself, but he coerced nobody.[5]

It is interesting that he had only ever been expected to give one
vote to his landlord—which was apparently not uncommon, as has
been seen. As for coercion, the evidence suggests that by mid-
century few, if any, Bucks landlords would have forced a man
against his strongly held convictions. Not all farmers had strong
opinions, particularly if they had a generous landlord. Many, however, did; and the party of the landlords was the last to take them
for granted, as the continuing Conservative concern about tenant-
farmer candidates after 1850 illustrates.

Apart from the growing independence of tenant farmers, it must
be borne in mind that other besides tenant farmers made up
county as well as borough electorates, particularly others besides
the tenants of large landowners. The studies of Buckingham and
Aylesbury illustrate this. In 1868 Rothschild argued that only one
Liberal stood any chance of winning because 'there are 77,000
acres in the Borough of Aylesbury of which more than 65,000
belong to Conservative landlords.' (If one accepts the reasoning of
most recent historians, it would be difficult to see how any Liberal
could have won!) Leno, Howell's agent from the Reform League,
attacked Rothschild's reasoning. He pointed out that the town of
Aylesbury produced more voters than the grass farms for four
miles around, and that Haddenham was a Liberal stronghold
despite the fact that three-quarters of the land was in the possession of Tories.[6]

The electoral history of nineteenth-century Britain cannot be
deduced from Bateman's *Great Landowners*. Great landowners had
enormous property. But it took only a relatively little to attain the
franchise, with the result, as the Duke of Wellington had remarked
some time after 1832, that there was 'everywhere a formidably
active party against the aristocratic influence of the Landed
Gentry.'[7]

Why, then, it may be asked (and historians have been asking for
some time) do landed gentlemen and their relations continue to

make up most of the membership of the House of Commons during the period covered by this book? The answer, I think, is a fairly simple one. But it requires that we rid our minds of the obviously false, but remarkably tenacious notion that there was a monolithic 'middle-class' opposing a monolithic 'landed interest.' Politics was still an enormously expensive avocation; and the middle-classes of the small towns and the countryside would have produced few capable of affording it. There would not have been many Rickfords and Wethereds. They could, of course, have found good 'middle-class' candidates north of Birmingham. But it is not really surprizing that they did not—no more surprizing than that many Bucks labourers seem to have had little in common with a London trade unionist. Sociological and organizational factors ruled that these things were so.

Under the circumstances, political leaders continued to be supplied by the landed classes—which is not necessarily synonomous with 'landed interest.' Contemporaries sometimes used the two terms interchangeably, but sometimes they meant something much broader and looser like the 'agricultural interest.' In any case, this landed interest stood for no inflexible set of political opinions. If Chandos was a representative of it, so was Sir Harry Verney. If Col Hanmer spoke for it, so did Lord Nugent. It would, of course, have been possible to get much further apart politically than these individuals were. But it is unlikely that many of their constituents would have desired a much wider range of choice. By and large, they represented the opposing points of view in the political world of their own localities.

They were hard-working politicians. Shortly after his triumphant return to Buckingham in 1857, Sir Harry Verney wrote to his son:

> Just concluded a fatiguing week of returning thanks to my constituents, who elected me without the usual close canvass. I have been particularly anxious to see them all, & I believe there are few individuals whom I have omitted.
>
> I consider the practice an excellent one, quite independently of its advantage with reference to a future Election. It is advantageous that any man in the position of a member of Parliament shd have a good reason & an excuse, to go & sit down in the house of each of 500 or 600 Constituents & that they shd have the opportunity of saying anything they desire & making any observa-

tions respecting any public or private affair that may affect them. It leads to setting right many a mistake & misrepresentation & it enables MPs to obtain information valuable to themselves & the country, which they cd get, perhaps, in no other way.[8]

Sir Harry was not unique. Chandos assiduously attended the farmers' ordinaries to canvass their opinions. Lord Nugent never missed an opportunity to debate political questions before, and with, his constituents. Are we to believe that all this was mere ritual, an elaborate ceremonial played out whilst influence followed its inexorable course? I think not.

Of course, these men possessed influence. But, as Hobhouse said of Nugent's, it was mainly 'the legitimate influence of persuasion and reason.' (Was this a use of the term 'legitimate influence' peculiar to Hobhouse, or did other Whigs mean the same thing, when they are thought to have meant something quite different?) At any rate, it was primarily the influence of political leaders over their followers, as distinct from that of superiors over inferiors. Successful political leaders have rarely been mere rubber-stamps for popular opinion. They anticipate it, articulate vaguely held notions, and shape the public mind. These aristocratic politicians were no exception.

Nugent left an indelible imprint on the 'old' Liberal party in Aylesbury. It was his notions of religious liberty that they championed throughout the century, particularly with regard to Catholicism. It was he who had convinced his party of the justice of Catholic emancipation. And he could have had no better memorial than the fact that, shortly after his death, Aylesbury remained calm, while Buckingham and Wycombe and Marlow petitioned against 'papal aggression.' Nugent had also helped to teach his party to 'abhor aristocratic influence.' They needed little instruction, but what enthusiastic pupils they had been he was to learn to his own cost in 1839. Nugent is but one example. Chandos, Dashwood King, and Verney are other prime examples of popular and influential MPs who left a strong mark on their constituencies. And Dashwood King brings to mind another example of constituents who probably learned at least one lesson too well; they remained true to reform in 1831, while he forsook it. In none of these cases, of course, were the aristocratic leaders the only influence at work; but that they were important influences is undeniable. It is often said that the English aristocaracy retained political influence by judicious concession, as in 1832 and 1846. It is probably at least as true that they retained their political influence because they were willing in the nineteenth century to take the lead in a new kind of politics, a kind of politics in which there were new forces at work, and new faces evident. The politics of mid-Victorian Bucks were 'middle-class' for all that the leaders remained aristocratic.

Bucks politics were, of course, far from taking account of all that was important in national life. It used to be said that Palmerston's pugnacious foreign policy appealed to the 'middle-class' electorate. There is no evidence that Bucks electors had very strong feelings about it one way or the other. It is still often implied that legislation like the Ten Hour Act of 1847 was an aristocratic way of keeping the middle-classes in their places by playing the workers off against them. It would be difficult, to say the least, to fit this into a Bucks context. It is no part of the argument of this book that the explanation of all of Victorian politics must be sought in the constituencies. But it is probable that the explanation of a good deal that went on must be sought there. Historians have come to terms with the world of Jane Austen. They must now seek to understand the world of George Eliot. We have followed Bucks politics from before the former into and beyond the latter.

This book has been about continuity and change. The continuity has been more apparent than real, the change profound.

Notes

INTRODUCTION
(pages 8–14)

1 Roughly, historians from Thomas Babington Macaulay to George Macaulay Trevelyan, though it is easier to talk about 'Whig' history than to attribute it to any historian.

2 Clark, G. Kitson. *The Making of Victorian England* (New York, 1969), 214, 210, and 54

3 Moore, D. C. 'The Other Face of Reform' *Victorian Studies*, V (1961–62), 33–4. For plentiful evidence of the fragility of 'deference' even in 'oppressed' Ireland, see Michael Hurst, *Maria Edgeworth and the Public Scene* '1969': passim and especially pp 57–64 devoted to May 1831 in county Longford

4 Even John Vincent, who has been highly critical of some of the prevailing notions appears to accept this one. *Pollbooks: How Victorians Voted* (Cambridge, 1967), 2–3 and n

5 Gash, Norman. *Politics in the Age of Peel* (1953), 438–9, 193–201, and *passim*

6 Hanham, H. J. *Elections and Party Management: Politics in the Time of Disraeli and Gladstone* (1959), 45 and *passim*

7 Kitson Clark, 51

8 F. M. L. Thompson is an important exception. His study of the West Riding traces a complicated series of balances and alliances which I believe will be found to have been more characteristic of Victorian politics—and not only in urbanized counties—than the simplistic notions at present generally accepted. ('Whigs and Liberals in the West Riding, 1830–1860', *English Historical Review*, LXXIV 1959, 214–39.)

9 Aydelotte, W. O. 'The County Gentlemen and the Repeal of the Corn Laws', ibid, LXXXII 1967, 47–60

10 Hughenden Papers, B/I/C/135, the Rev W. Partridge to Mrs Disraeli, 18 Jun 1847

11 *Bucks Gazette*, 17 Jan 1835

12 Moore, 'The Other Face of Reform,' 8

13 See, for example, Gash, 185, and Hanham, 17

14 Gash, xvii

Chapter 1 BUCKINGHAMSHIRE SOCIETY AND POLITICS
BEFORE THE GREAT REFORM BILL
(pages 15–27)

1 Huntington Library, Stowe MSS, Elections, 'Bucks for Ever? Or, No Buck like a True Buck. A New Song.'
2 VCH Bucks, II, 107
3 Gibbs, R. *A History of Aylesbury with its Boroughs and Hundreds* (Aylesbury, 1885), 621
4 Baker, Margaret. 'Farming in Bucks in 1810', *Bucks Life* (Nov 1967), 24
5 Huntington Library, Stowe MSS, Samuel Bosanquet to the Marquis of Buckingham, 15 Aug 1816
6 *The Buckinghamshire, Bedfordshire, & Hertfordshire Chronicle,* 29 May, 23 Jul and 23 Sep 1826
7 VCH Bucks, II, 107
8 Ibid, 82
9 There are many definitions of the Vale, but this seems the most sensible one. See also the special issue on the Vale in *Bucks Life* (Aug 1970), 12
10 VCH Bucks, II, 83
11 Fowler, J. K. *Records of Old Times* (1898), 104
12 Lipscomb, George. *The History and Antiquities of the County of Buckingham* (1847), II, 31
13 BRO, 1835 Aylesbury pollbook
14 Baker, 'Farming in Bucks in 1810'
15 See the analysis of mid-nineteenth century farmers below 173ff
16 'A Freeholder', *Buckinghamshire Chronicle,* 11 Jan 1823
17 Hobsbawm, E. J. and Rudé, G. *Captain Swing* (1969), 43
18 G.E.C. *The Complete Peerage,* II (1912), 406n
19 BRO, Wilkes-Dell Corres, Wilkes to Dell, 21 Apr 1761
20 Spencer Bernard Papers, PFE 3/15(d)
21 See the correspondence between Acton Chaplin and Scrope Bernard in Dec 1790, ibid, OL2/ esp 25 and 28
22 Ibid, William Prickett to Scrope Bernard, 24 Aug 1797
23 VCH Bucks, II, 84
24 Lipscomb, II, 559
25 Huntington Library, Stowe MSS, George Denton to Richard Grenville, 20 Nov 1742
26 Ibid, Richard Grenville to George Grenville, ca 28 Apr 1748
27 Verney Papers, ? McNamara to ? Douglass, 11 Jun 1782
28 Huntington Library, Stowe MSS, Thomas Grenville to the Marquis of Buckingham, 8 Jul 1806
29 Quoted in Namier, Sir Lewis, and Brooke, John. *The House of Commons, 1754–90* (New York, 1964), I, 216
30 For Wycombe see Ashford, L. J. *The History of the Borough of Wycombe from its origins to 1880* (1960), chaps vi and vii

31 Oldfield, T. H. B. *The Representative History of Great Britain and Ireland* (1816), II, 86

32 Namier and Brooke, I, 217 err in thinking the Claytons sold to William Lee Antonie in 1787. See BRO, Lee Papers, D/LE 3/70, John Fiott to Sir William Lee, 30 Apr 1791

33 *Buckinghamshire Chronicle*, 10 Jun 1826

34 Namier and Brooke, I, 217

35 Ibid

36 *Bucks Gazette*, 31 Jul 1830

37 BRO, Shardeloes Papers, Ma/Dr/1, 'A Map of the Town of Agmondesham, 1742' shows the Drakes as possessing ninety-five out of two hundred and nine houses within the parliamentary borough

38 'Amicus', *Buckinghamshire Chronicle*, 1 May 1824

39 BRO, Shardeloes Papers, D/DR/12/46, Address from the electors of Amersham to their representatives in parliament, 12 Apr 1784

40 *Parliamentary History*, xxviii, 959

Chapter 2 PORTENTS OF CHANGE
(pages 28–42)

1 Thompson, 467

2 BRO, Wilkes-Dell Correspondence, Wilkes to Dell, 31 Jan [1757]

3 Ibid, Lee Papers, D/LE 2/98, Alexander Croke to Sir William Lee, 31 Mar 1768

4 Reproduced in Gibbs, R. *Buckinghamshire Local Occurrences* (Aylesbury, 1878–82), II, 155

5 Huntington Library, Stowe MSS, George Grenville to Earl Temple, 10 Sep 1769

6 BRO, Lee Papers, D/LE 2/84 and 12/53, Eyre Coote to Sir William Lee, 25 Feb 1768 and the Rev Robert Smith to the same, 4 Sep 1768

7 See, for example, Acton Chaplin's calculations, Spencer Bernard Papers, OL2/26

8 BRO, Lee Papers, D/LE 12/52, Sir William Lee to Sir W[illiam] S[tanhope], 17 Jan 1768

9 Ibid, 1/32, Sir Thomas Bernard to Sir William Lee, 21 Sep 1779; Huntington Library, Stowe MSS, Elections, newspaper clippings and addresses, Sep and Oct 1779

10 Rudé, 117–8

11 See Butterfield, H. *George III, Lord North, and the People* (1949), appendix A and Newman, Aubrey. *The Stanhopes of Chevening* (1969), 139

12 Christie, 169

13 Cannon, John. *The Fox-North Coalition* (Cambridge, 1969), 186

14 *Jackson's Oxford Journal*, 27 Mar 1784

15 Verney Papers, ? Webb to Earl Verney, nd

16 BRO, Lee Papers, D/LE 9/18, the Duke of Portland to Sir William Lee, 6 Jul 1784

17 Oxfordshire Record Office, Thame Papers, II/ii/5, Earl of Abingdon·
to Lord Wenman, 20 Apr 1784
18 BRO, Lee Papers, D/LE 11/47 and 9/12, Sir William Lee to Sir
John Borlase Warren, 21 Dec 1783; Lee to ? Lally, 21 Dec 1783;
the Duke of Portland to Lee, 27 Mar 1784
19 Ibid, 12/52, Sir William Lee to Sir W[illiam] S[tanhope], 17 Jan
1768 and other correspondence in the same collection
20 Fowler, *Records* 62–3
21 For all three addresses see *Jackson's Oxford Journal*, 27 Mar and
3 Apr 1784
22 Oxon RO, Thame Papers, II/ii/3, J. Bullock to Lord Wenman,
18 Apr 1784
23 Spencer Bernard Papers, PFE 6/9
24 BRO, D/LE 1/54, J. Bullock to Sir William Lee, 4 Apr 1784
25 BRO, 1784 pollbook. There is also a copy at the Institute
Historical Research.
26 Verney Papers, Webb to Earl Verney, nd
27 BRO, Morgan-Grenville Papers, AR 41/63, Lord Grenville to
Thomas Grenville, 6 Mar 1828
28 Ginter, Donald E. *Whig Organization in the General Election of* 1790
(Berkeley and Los Angeles, 1967)
29 BRO, Lee Papers, D/LE 9/14 and 9/15. On 18 April Sir William
Lee wrote to Portland stressing the need for funds and lamenting
the failure of efforts in the county to raise adequate sums; he later
endorsed the letter '1,800 subscription.' On 19 April Portland
replied to Lee's letter, hoping that he had relieved him from anxiety.
30 Documents describing the founding of the club are reproduced in
the *Bucks Gazette*, 8 Jul 1837
31 Verney, Lady (Margaret Maria). *Verney Letters of the Eighteenth
Century* (1930), II, 282
32 *Jackson's Oxford Journal*, 17 Oct 1789
33 BRO, D/LE 3/49A, Thomas Ewesly to Sir William Lee, 11 Jul 1795.
The Lee Papers contain the bulk of the material on the activities of
the Independent Club.
34 Bodleian Library, Dashwood Papers, F 1/11, G. A. H. Cavendish
to Sir John Dashwood King, 19 Nov 1809
35 *Bucks Gazette*, 8 Jul 1837
36 Ashford, 191
37 VCH Bucks, III, 121
38 Bodleian Library, Dashwood Papers, F 1/4, broadsheet
39 Ibid, F 1/5, the Marquis of Lansdowne to ?, 5 Mar 1784
40 BRO, Carrington Papers, D6, C. W. Raffety, 'Wycombe and Family
Notes', 5
41 Ashford, 193–5
42 *Bucks Gazette*, 7 May 1831
43 *Jackson's Oxford Journal*, 8 Feb 1794

Chapter 3   THE TRIUMPH OF 'INDEPENDENCE'
IN AYLESBURY, 1802–1818
(pages 43–58)

1   For the 1789 contest and the negotiations that followed it see the
Spencer Bernard Papers, OL 2
2   BRO, Robert Gibbs' scrapbook, newspaper clippings
3   County Museum, Aylesbury, *Report from the Select Committee on the
Aylesbury Election of* 1802, (1804), 181
4   Spencer Bernard Papers, PFE 3/27
5   Verney Papers, Sir Jonathan Lovett to Earl Verney, 5 Feb 1791
6   BRO, pollbooks for 1780 and 1802. In 1859, John Gibbs had the poll
for 1802 printed in the *Bucks Advertiser*. This was done from a
pollbook in his possession and is substantially correct, though he
fails to record thirty odd votes for a last-minute candidate. There is
also a manuscript poll in the Spencer Bernard Papers. William
Rutt's 1809 map of Aylesbury, in the collection at the Record Office,
is useful in giving some occupations as well as locating houses.
7   See for example Spencer Bernard Papers, William Prickett to
Scrope Bernard, 24 Aug 1797
8   Ibid, PFE 3/7a, William Rickford jr to Scrope Bernard, 2 Apr 1802
9   The details of these several business connexions will be found in the
Spencer Bernard Papers.
10 Ibid, PFE 3/15b, John Rawbone to Scrope Bernard, 18 Feb 1802
11 BRO, Close Smith Papers, AR 30/63, the Marquis of Buckingham
to Thomas Grenville, 25 Jan 1801
12 Lipscomb, II, 70. See also the Spencer Bernard and Close Smith
Papers for more on these transactions
13 Besides *Hansard*, Vols I and II, see Lipscomb, II, 24 for the bill
and its effects
14 *Jackson's Oxford Journal*, 16 May 1818
15 BRO, 1804 pollbook
16 BRO, Dayrell Papers, No 74, the Rev J. L. Dayrell to the Rev J.
Brewster, 18 Jul 1804
17 *Jackson's Oxford Journal*, 16 May 1807
18 Huntington Library, Stowe MSS, Elections, Chandos Temple,
address, 11 May 1807
19 BRO, Fremantle Papers, Earl Temple to W. H. Fremantle, 9 May
1807
20 Both addresses appear in *Jackson's Oxford Journal*, 16 May 1807
21 There is a manuscript pollbook for 1807 at the BRO
22 BRO, Fremantle Papers, Earl Temple to W. H. Fremantle, nd
23 Bodleian Library, John Johnson Collection, Thomas Hussey,
address, 6 Feb 1809
24 BRO, Spencer Bernard Papers, A 2/1(a), C.C. Cavendish, address,
15 Nov 1814
25 Oldfield (1816), III, 78
26 *Buckinghamshire Chronicle*, 10 June 1826

27 *Jackson's Oxford Journal*, 16 May–11 Jul 1818; and BRO, 1818 poll-book
28 *Jackson's Oxford Journal*, 11 Jul 1818
29 *Bucks Advertiser*, 30 Nov 1850
30 BRO, Fremantle Papers, the Marquis of Buckingham to W. H. Fremantle, 1 Jul 1818
31 Fowler, *Records*, 60–61
32 *Jackson's Oxford Journal*, 11 Jul 1818
33 BRO, Fremantle Papers, the Marquis of Buckingham to W. H. Fremantle, 2 Jul 1818

Chapter 4   THE COMING OF REFORM, 1820–1832
(pages 59–88)

1 *Hansard*, XXXII, 1209–11 and XXXIII, 25 and 927–29
2 BRO, Lee Papers, D/LE 1/17, Lord Nugent to Sir George Lee, 12 Nov 1821
3 Ibid, Morgan-Grenville Papers, AR 40/63, Thomas Grenville to the Duke of Buckingham, 22 Jan 1839
4 Letter cited n2
5 Huntington Library, Stowe MSS, Sir Henry Watkin Williams-Wynn to the Marquis of Buckingham, 11 Nov 1821
6 *Buckinghamshire Chronicle*, 30 Nov 1822 to 24 Jan 1823. See also the correspondence, BRO, Fremantle Papers, between the duke and Sir William Fremantle
7 *Buckinghamshire Chronicle*, 9 and 23 Apr 1825
8 BRO, Lee Papers, D/LE 1/35, Lord Carrington to Sir George Lee, 8 Aug 1826
9 Ibid, Dayrell Papers, 124, the Rev J. L. Dayrell to the Rev J. Brewster, 10 Apr 1820
10 Bodleian Library, Dashwood Papers, F1/17, the Rev Isaac King to Sir John Dashwood King, 12 Apr 1829
11 Huntington Library, Stowe MSS, Robert Plumer Ward to the Duke of Buckingham, 28 Sep 1824
12 *Buckinghamshire Chronicle*, 26 Feb 1825
13 *Bucks Gazette*, 15 Dec 1823
14 BRO, Morgan-Grenville Papers, AR 41/63, Lord Grenville to Thomas Grenville, 6 Mar 1828
15 Davis, 161
16 BRO, Durley, J. 'Brief Statement regarding the Growth of Methodism in the Aylesbury Circuit'
17 Letter cited n14
18 *Jackson's Oxford Journal*, 27 Feb 1790
19 Lipscomb, II, 67, citing the *Gentleman's Magazine*, xcix, p ii, 565
20 Whittaker, M. B. 'The Revival of Dissent, 1800–1835' (MLitt dissertation, Cambridge, 1958), Chap iv
21 Durley, cited n16

22 BRO, microfilm of 'The Register of Births, Baptisms, Burials &c, Hale Leys Chapel, Aylesbury, 1789–1837'. Lipscomb, II, 67–8 provides a useful background but is sometimes inaccurate.

23 BRO, QS/W/B/8, Returns of 'Places of Worship, not of the Church of England', 1829. The survey was carried out in accordance with a resolution of the House of Commons, and the clergyman in the parish made the return. Some clearly did not take their task too seriously, or consciously attempted to distort the evidence. The Rev Mr Morley, however, testified that he had derived his 'information from the best sources, *after strict* inquiry . . .' He thought his numbers were 'as correct as possible', and, since he was on the best of terms with the Aylesbury Dissenters, there is every reason to believe him.

24 It was, for example, common practice for Dissenters, and often Churchmen, to unite on the local level to raise funds for missionary activities and then to divide those funds between the several national missionary societies. Reports of annual meetings of these united bodies will be found in the local newspapers.

25 BRO, Robert Gibbs' scrapbook, reminiscences of John Gibbs for the *Aylesbury News* in December 1841

26 *The Buckinghamshire, Bedfordshire, & Hertfordshire Chronicle* was launched at the end of July 1821. The British Museum has copies from 1822.

27 Ibid, 2 Apr 1824 and 21 Jan 1826

28 Ibid, 1 Mar and 8 Mar 1828

29 Quoted in Spring, D. 'Lord Chandos and the Farmers, 1818–1846', *Huntington Library Quarterly*, Vol xxxiii, No 3 (May 1970), 258. Professor Spring's is a brief, but excellent, study of Chandos as a politician.

30 Huntington Library, Stowe MSS, W. H. Fremantle to the Duke of Buckingham, 18 Apr 1823

31 *Buckinghamshire Chronicle*, 30 Apr 1825

32 BRO, Dayrell Papers, No 135, the Rev J. L. Dayrell to the Rev J. Brewster, 5 Jul 1825

33 BRO, Morgan-Grenville Papers, AR 40/63, Lord Braybrooke to the (second) Duke of Buckingham, 18 Jan 1839

34 On several occasions Nugent offered to resign his seat for Aylesbury if his brother wished it. The last such occasion was in January 1822, when Nugent declared: 'If I am hereafter to hold the seat, I must consider it, (as he himself authorized me before in considering it,) as to be retained, as far as I can by my own personal interest with my constituents.' It would appear that Sir George Nugent and Sir John Dashwood King were acting as intermediaries between the two brothers. (Bodleian Library, Dashwood Papers, G/1/2/4, Lord Nugent, a memorandum, 31 Jan 1822.)

35 BRO, Fremantle Papers, Sir Thomas Fremantle to Sir W. H. Fremantle, 24 Aug 1822

36 *Buckinghamshire Chronicle,* 25 Jun 1824. Of another of Chandos' extravaganzas in 1825, the Rev Mr Dayrell wrote: 'this seems to savour something of an electioneering purpose' (letter cited above n32)

37 The duke later told Sir Thomas Fremantle, in explanation of his financial difficulties, that 'by overdoing the receiving of . . . company, much of these debts has been contracted.' He therefore would not 'receive the County as usual after the Buckm. assizes' (BRO, Fremantle Papers, 13 Jun 1832). At the beginning of 1829 W. H. Fremantle wrote to his nephew Sir Thomas: 'I think Lord Chandos quite right to assume all the power he can, & to exercise it for his own benefit, as long as his father tamely submits to it, as well as to spend the whole of the Duke's income' (Ibid, 20 Jan 1829)

38 Machin, G. I. T. *The Catholic Question in English Politics,* 1820 *to* 1830 (Oxford, 1964), 135–36

39 Letter cited n10

40 BRO, Fremantle Papers, Sir George Nugent to Sir Thomas Fremantle, 7 Feb and 9 Feb 1829

41 The account of the meeting is in the *Bucks Gazette,* 28 Feb 1829. According to Libscomb, II, 30 the *Gazette* was founded about 1812, and the *Buckinghamshire Chronicle* appears to have been founded as a Whig paper to oppose its views. But by 1829, when the *Chronicle* was in difficulties, the *Gazette* had become very whiggish. The British Museum collection of the *Gazette* commences in February 1829.

42 Northamptonshire Record Office, Temple (Stowe) Collection, F2. These annotated lists of the electors of the parliamentary borough of Buckingham for 1840–44 show no tenants of either Morgan or Dayrell; though the Dayrells of Lillingstone Dayrell were, of course, an old family.

43 BRO, Fremantle Papers, the Duke of Buckingham to Sir Thomas Fremantle, 9 May 1829

44 *Bucks Gazette,* 11 Apr 1829

45 A letter in ibid, 3 Jan 1829 quoted a letter from the duke to be shown to his tenants which was probably the letter sent to Parrott via Nugent: 'if any of my tenants or friends have, by mistaken notions, joined them (the Brunswickers), I wish them to withdraw themselves from, and by all means in their power to oppose, them . . .'

46 Huntington Library, Stowe MSS, Sir George Nugent to Lord Nugent, nd, and Sir George Nugent to the Duchess of Buckingham, 21 Feb 1829

47 The dinner is reported and discussed in the *Buckinghamshire Chronicle,* 25 Oct, 8 Nov, and 15 Nov 1828

48 All in inverted commas is from Moore's 'The Other Face of Reform'. Besides this article see also Moore's exchange with E. P. Hennock, 'The First Reform Act: A Discussion', *Victorian Studies,* Vol xiv, No 3 (March 1879), 321–337

49 Oldfield (1816), III, 85. The *Spectator* in 1831 put Dashwood King down as sitting on his own influence and Baring on the corporation's (quoted in *Bucks Gazette*, 19 Mar 1831)

50 *Bucks Gazette*, 27 Feb 1830. The requisition for the meeting appears in the 20 Feb issue

51 *Buckinghamshire Chronicle*, 10 Jun 1826

52 Huntington Library, Stowe MSS, Lord Nugent to George Canning, 4 May 1827

53 *Buckinghamshire Chronicle*, 2 Jun 1827

54 *Bucks Gazette*, 21 Feb and 28 Feb 1829 (the anti-Catholic requisition in the former, the reply by the friends of civil and religious liberty in the latter)

55 BRO, pollbook collection

56 BRO, Fremantle Papers, Sir W. H. Fremantle to Sir Thomas Fremantle, 'Easter', 29 Oct, and 8 Dec 1829

57 For the election see *Bucks Gazette*, 7 May and 14 May 1831. Nugent's remark is quoted in BRO, Lee Papers, D/LE 9/4, 'The Ghost of Hampden'

58 For Buckingham see my article 'Buckingham, 1832–1846: A Study of a "Pocket Borough" ', *Huntington Library Quarterly*, Vol xxxiv, No 2 (February 1971), 159–181; for Wycombe, Ashford's excellent account

59 *Buckinghamshire Chronicle* and *Bucks Gazette*, passim

60 Ibid, 19 Mar 1831

Chapter 5   PROSPECT AND RETROSPECT
(pages 89–105)

1 Hanham, vii

2 Ibid, 68

3 *Bucks Gazette*, 7 May 1831

4 *Hansard*, XXXIII, 927

5 Ibid, XXXII, 1210. Caird notes at mid-century that there does not appear to have been much capital expended on improvements by either landlords or tenants, as was evidenced by the rough farm buildings and the rudimentary drainage systems (*English Agriculture* [1851], 8). But the eminent suitability of the land to dairying and grazing made profitable farming possible without such expenditure

6 Spring, 'Lord Chandos'. As will be evident, my interpretation follows Professor Spring's, which my own research into the question only further substantiates

7 Priest, St John, *General View of the Agriculture of Buckinghamshire* (1810), 372; and Sheahan, J. J. *History and Topography of Buckinghamshire* (1862), 36

8 *Buckinghamshire Chronicle*, 24 Jun and 10 Jun 1826

9 *Bucks Gazette*, 25 Apr 1829

10 Moore, 'The Other Face of Reform', 12–13

11   Unless noted otherwise, the account of the election is drawn from the *Bucks Gazette*, 30 Apr to 21 May 1831, and from the 1831 county pollbook

12   Ibid, 30 Apr 1831

13   Ibid, 21 May 1831

14   Gash, N. *Reaction and Reconstruction in English Politics, 1832–1852* (Oxford, 1965), Chaps v and vi; Beales, D. E. D. 'Parliamentary Parties and the "Independent" member, 1810–1860', in Robson, R., ed., *Ideas and Institutions of Victorian Britain: Essays in honour of George Kitson Clark* (London, 1967), 1–19. See also Austin Mitchell's thorough study of the Whigs before 1830

15   Aydelotte, 'The Country Gentlemen and the Repeal of the Corn Laws'

16   Vincent, *Pollbooks*. For Moore, besides the article already discussed in some detail see 'Social Structure, Political Structure, and Public Opinion in Mid-Victorian England' in Robson, 20–57

17   Vincent, *The Formation of the Liberal Party, 1857–1868*

18   Gash, *Reaction and Reconstruction*, 66–67 and n3

19   *Bucks Gazette*, 22 Feb 1834

20   BRO, Fremantle Papers, the Rev David Aston to Sir Thomas Fremantle, nd Feb 1834

21   *Buckinghamshire Chronicle*, 8 Sept 1827

Chapter 6   CORN
(pages 106–126)

1   Seymour, Charles. *Electoral Reform in England and Wales: The Development and Operation of the Parliamentary Franchise, 1832–1855* (1915), 66. Reprinted 1970 with an introduction by Michael Hurst. Seymour remains the most useful guide to the electoral changes of the nineteenth century

2   Gash, *Politics in the Age of Peel*, Appendix B

3   BRO, 1832 Buckingham pollbook

4   Gash, *Politics in the Age of Peel*, 97

5   See Ashford, Chap x

6   Davis, 'Buckingham, 1832–1846'

7   BRO, three letters from Lord Nugent to Thomas Dell, 20 Sep 1832 to 2 Jan 1833; *Bucks Gazette*, 21 Jul 1832

8   Ibid, 15 Dec 1832

9   Ibid, 4 Aug 1832; Spencer Bernard Papers, A 2/8, Hanmer's *Address*. Though Nugent's views were not printed until 4 Aug and Hanmer's address was dated 20 Jul, it appears from both that Nugent had raised the issue first, perhaps in an off-the-cuff remark not previously reported

10   *Bucks Gazette*, 25 Aug 1832

11   Ibid, 11 Aug 1832

12   For the Tory handbills see the John Johnson Collection at the Bodleian

13 *Bucks Gazette*, 25 Aug 1832
14 Bodleian Library, Dashwood Papers, G 1/2/2, Lord Nugent to G. H. Dashwood, nd
15 *Bucks Gazette*, 22 Dec 1832
16 Ibid, 15 Dec 1832
17 Ibid, 10 Jan 1835
18 Ibid, 22 Dec 1832. The *Gazette* reported that the High Sheriff was much cheered by 'the Liberals' and criticised by 'the Tories'
19 The duke told Tom Grenville after the marquis' triumphant return in 1831 that 'the idea of standing another Tory of course naturally presented itself, but our friends were fearful (too much so in my opinion) of running against the old family pledge of noninterference with the second Member . . .' (BRO, Close Smith Papers, AR 30/63, 12 May 1831)
20 BRO, Fremantle Papers, Sir Thomas Fremantle to Arthur Charles Stone, 19 Dec 1832
21 Bodleian Library, John Johnson Collection, *Appeal to the good sense & good feeling of the Farmers of Bucks*
22 Ibid, John Newman to Sir Thomas Fremantle, 25 Dec 1832
23 *Bucks Gazette*, 26 Jan 1833
24 *Bucks Herald*, 26 Jan 1833
25 Ibid, 20 Apr 1833
26 Ibid, 19 Jan 1833
27 *Bucks Gazette*, 9 Nov 1833
28 Ibid, 20 Dec 1834
29 Ibid, 17 Jan 1834
30 Bodleian Library, Dashwood Papers, G 1/7/10, J. W. Millar to G. H. Dashwood, 4 Apr 1835
31 See my short piece on Lee, *Bucks Life*, Vol 3, No 5 (August 1968), 16–17
32 Bodleian Library, John Johnson Collection, *Dr Lee's Speech*, dated 17 Dec 1832
33 Ibid, *Dr Lee's Speech*, dated 1835
34 Ibid, *A Dissenter and Freeholder of Bucks*, dated 4 Dec 1834; *Bucks Gazette*, 17 Jan 1835
35 Ibid
36 *A Dissenter*, cited n34
37 *Bucks Gazette*, 17 Jan 1835
38 BRO, pollbook collection

Chapter 7 CATHOLICS
(pages 127–154)

1 Verney Papers, 'Letters from Sir Harry Verney to Henry Hearn, Esq. 1833–1891', Verney to Hearn, 14 Jun 1836
2 BRO, Fremantle Papers, Sir John Chetwode's Address in the form of a printed circular, dated 6 Apr 1837
3 *Bucks Gazette*, 28 Aug 1830

4   BRO, Fremantle Papers, Capt C. J. Grove to Sir Thomas Fremantle, 25 Mar 1834

5   Ibid, the Rev David Aston to Sir Thomas Fremantle, nd Feb 1834

6   Verney Papers, 'Letters', Sir Harry Verney to Thomas Hearn, 24 Sept 1833

7   Ibid, Lord Stanley to Sir Harry Verney, 25 Sep 1834

8   *Parliamentary Companion* (1837)

9   BRO, Fremantle Papers, *Meeting of Magistrates, Gentry, and Inhabitants of the Town of Buckingham* . . ., 8th of April [1835]

10 Verney Papers, 'Letters', Verney to Hearn, 14 Jun 1836

11 BRO, Fremantle Papers, Hearn, Thomas. *Friendly Address to the Electors of Buckingham and its Boundary Parishes* (Buckingham, 1837)

12 Ibid, Sir William Fremantle to Sir Thomas Fremantle, 30 Mar 1837

13 Davis, 'Buckingham, 1832–1846', 174–76

14 *Aylesbury News*, 29 Jul 1837

15 Ibid, 11 Nov 1837. The *News*, published by John Gibbs was proud of its Dissenting Radicalism

16 Ibid, 27 May and 3 Jun 1837

17 According to the calculations of W. H. Poole, who was in charge of registration for the Liberals in this period, the number of those eligible in 1835 was 1,372 as compared with 1,370 in 1837. Of course, the disqualification of Liberals and the qualification of Conservatives at the two intervening registrations could have altered the balance within the total. Neither was there a marked increase in the number of abstentions, 1,212 voting in 1835 as compared with 1,188 in 1837. (BRO, Tindal Papers, analysis by W. H. Poole, 4 Jan 1851)

18 *Bucks Herald*, 1 Jul 1837

19 Bodleian Library, Dashwood Papers, G 3/5/5, G. H. Dashwood to Mrs Dashwood, 21 Jan 1837

20 *Aylesbury News*, 18 Feb and 25 Feb 1837

21 Bodleian Library, Dashwood Papers, G 1/4/2, broadsheet signed by J. T. Leader and William Lowndes Stone, dated 13 Feb 1837

22 BRO, Fremantle Papers, printed requisition to Chandos, Young, and Harcourt, 1837

23 *Bucks Herald*, 5 Aug 1837

24 Ibid

25 *Bucks Gazette*, 13 Jun 1835

26 See ibid, 24 Jan 1835, *Aylesbury News*, 23 Feb 1839, and a letter from Sir Thomas Cotton Shepherd to Frederick Calvert, 1 Mar 1839 (Verney Papers)

27 *Aylesbury News*, 23 Sep 1837

28 BRO, Fremantle Papers, John Parrott to Sir Thomas Fremantle, 30 May 1839

29 See the correspondence between Grenville Pigott and Sir Thomas
    Fremantle in the late summer and autumn of 1841 (BRO, Fremantle
    Papers)
30 *Aylesbury News*, 26 Aug 1837
31 The account of the election is drawn from ibid, 20 and 27 July and
    3 Aug 1839
32 Ibid, 5 Oct 1839
33 Verney Papers, Frederick Calvert to Sir Harry Verney, 1 Jul 1841
34 *Bucks Gazette*, 12 and 19 Jun and 3 Jul 1841
35 *Bucks Herald*, 12 Jun 1841
36 For Verney's position see the letter cited in n33
37 BRO, Lee Papers, D/LE 1/22, Samuel Adcock (secretary of the
    Aylesbury Religious Freedom Association) to Dr Lee, 20 Apr 1840
38 The account of the election is drawn from the *Bucks Gazette*,
    3 Jul 1841
39 Bodleian Library, Dashwood Papers, G 3/5/11, G. H. Dashwood to
    Mrs Dashwood, 3 Jul 1837
40 *Aylesbury News*, 29 Jul 1837
41 Verney Papers, 'Letters', Sir Harry Verney to Thomas Hearn,
    8 Nov 1838; BRO, Fremantle Papers, T. P. Williams to Sir Thomas
    Fremantle, 25 Jan 1839
42 Bodleian Library, Dashwood Papers, G. H. Dashwood to Mrs
    Dashwood, nd 1 Jun, and 2 Jun 1841
43 The account of the election is based on the *Bucks Gazette*, 3 Jul 1841
44 Verney Papers, Sir Harry Verney's address, dated 12 Jun 1841
45 *Bucks Herald*, 26 Jun 1841
46 Gash, *Reaction and Reconstruction*, 210
47 BRO, Robert Gibbs' scrapbook, Lord Chandos to John Gibbs and
    John Hamilton, 15 Apr 1852; Philip Box to the same, 19 Apr 1852

Chapter 8   INFLUENCE, COERCION, AND PRINCIPLE:
PART I
(pages 155–172)

 1 Northamptonshire Record Office, Temple (Stowe) Collection, F2,
    Buckingham Electoral Lists, 1840–44. The lists, drawn up for
    the Buckingham Conservative Association, contain all the names on
    the register, their qualification and landlord, their political prefer-
    ences, whether or not they were Dissenters, and other comments
    thought useful.
 2 BRO, Fremantle Papers, Sir Thomas Fremantle's journal, 14 Jul
    1837
 3 Ibid, Sir John Chetwode to Sir Thomas Fremantle, nd Jun 1841
 4 Ibid, Henry Smith to Sir Thomas Fremantle, 11 May 1839
 5 Huntington Library, Stowe MSS, the Duke of Buckingham to
    J. C. Herries, nd
 6 Hughenden Papers, B/I/C/135, the Rev W. Partridge to Mrs Disraeli
 7 Ibid, B/I/C/150b, the Rev Edward Owen Sr to Humphrey Bull, nd

8 BRO, Fremantle Papers, Sir William Fremantle to Sir Thomas Fremantle, 20 Aug 1847
9 Ibid, AR 41/63, the Marquis of Chandos to Sir Robert Bateson Harvey, 8 Feb 1846; ibid, Lee Papers, D/LE 9/7, Henry Darvill to Dr Lee, 28 Nov 1857
10 Ibid, Tindal Papers, *A Lay of Aylesbury*, an election squib
11 Ibid, 'Harrison vs Bull, Brief for the Plaintiffs', Dec 1855, where the term is used
12 'Verbatim report of the proceedings before the Committee of the House of Commons on the Aylesbury Election Petitions', *Bucks Herald*, 6 Aug 1859
13 BRO, Tindal Papers, Frederick Calvert to Acton Tindal, 18 Jan 1851
14 Ibid, Humphrey Bull to Acton Tindal, answered 8 Dec 1850, and the article on Byles in the *DNB*
15 Report of the election committee, *Bucks Advertiser*, 5 Apr 1851 and correspondence between Calvert and Tindal at the BRO, especially 8 May 1851
16 *Bucks Advertiser*, 12 Apr 1851
17 BRO, Tindal Papers, Lord Carrington to Acton Tindal, 10 Mar 1852
18 *Bucks Advertiser*, 3 and 17 Apr 1852
19 BRO, Tindal Papers, *Meeting of the Liberal Electors of the Borough of Aylesbury held at Bell Inn on Monday evening the 12th of April* 1852
20 Ibid, correspondence in April between Tindal, Parkes, and Hayter
21 *Bucks Advertiser*, 1 May 1852
22 BRO, Tindal Papers, Lord Carrington to Acton Tindal, 18 Apr 1852
23 Ibid, Layard's printed address, 8 May 1852
24 *Bucks Advertiser*, 10 Jul 1852
25 BRO, Tindal Papers, *The Aylesbury Election Speeches of Mr Bethell and Mr Layard . . .*, *Jun* 17, 1852
26 Ibid, Edward Owen Jr to Acton Tindal, nd 1852
27 *Bucks Herald*, 27 Mar 1857
28 BRO, Tindal Papers, Acton Tindal to Henry Watson, 9 Apr 1859 and Sir William Hayter to Tindal, 10 Apr 1859; advertisement in *Bucks Herald*, 16 Apr 1859
29 Fowler, J. K. *Echoes of Old Country Life* (London, 1892), 31; *Bucks Herald*, 23 Apr 1859
30 BRO, Tindal Papers, Henry Darvill to Acton Tindal, 16 May 1859
31 *Bucks Herald*, 23 and 30 Apr 1859
32 Ibid, 30 Jul and 6 Aug 1859, proceedings of the election committee

Chapter 9 INFLUENCE, COERCION, AND PRINCIPLE: PART II
(pages 173–197)

1 Actually 479 names appear in both the 1847 and the 1859 pollbooks. Originally, however, I was unaware of the existence of the 1859 pollbook and based my calculations on 570 who appeared in both the

1847 and the 1857 pollbooks. Besides removing ninety-one names, the new pollbook caused only minor variations in the patterns already established, requiring the reclassification of only twelve individuals. I did not, therefore, feel it necessary to remove the ninety-one who had disappeared by 1859 from my calculations on the composition of parties, and on the six elections from 1847 to 1857. The 570 constitute a sample which ranges from a high of forty-seven per cent in 1852 to a low of forty-four per cent in 1848.

2 BRO, Tindal Papers, rough draft of Acton Tindal to C. C. Cavendish, 30 Dec 1852

3 See, for example, ibid, the Rev Oliver Bruce to Acton Tindal, 18 Apr 1859

4 Verney Papers, Abel Smith to Frederick Calvert, 23 Jun 1852

5 Actually Abel Smith had fourteen tenants represented in the sample; but six of them would not have been the sort to be influenced by their landlord—Gen Sir James Watson and one of his sons, two surgeons etc

6 *Bucks Advertiser*, 10 May 1851

7 BRO, Tindal Papers, Frederick Calvert to Acton Tindal, 22 Jul 1859

8 My test of party allegiance was both simple and empirical. In general, I required that an elector always vote for the candidates of his party. I did not, however, require plumpers when only one candidate of that party stood; and I also allowed strategic splitting in cases where there was a division within parties. These exceptions will become clear in the course of the analysis.

9 The pollbooks were the main source for occupations, though use was also made of several local directories, which naturally provide a great deal more detail than the pollbooks. The 'Bucks County Rate 1859: Extracts from Property Tax Assessments, 1857' too was most useful, especially in the case of farmers, who are sometimes not identified in the pollbooks. The ratebook, based on a survey done in 1857 and corrected for 1859, is also the source for wealth, as indicated by the annual value of property occupied, and for landlords. In the case of the landlords, it is, of course, possible that individuals might have had a different landlord before 1857; but it seems unlikely that there would have been many instances of this, as all the estates surveyed remained stable throughout the period. The sources on religious affiliation were microfilms of birth and baptismal records of Independent congregations in Aylesbury and Wendover and a Baptist congregation in Princes Risborough, and the nineteenth-century records of the Aylesbury Methodist Circuit. All of the material used is at the Bucks Record Office.

10 *Bucks Gazette*, 1 Sep 1832

11 See *Bucks Advertiser*, 6 Nov and 25 Dec 1847 for some of the debate on the question of accepting government grants

12 For Aylesbury's reaction to papal aggression see ibid, 18 Jan 1851;
    for Buckingham, 30 Nov 1850; for Wycombe, Marlow, Chesham,
    and Wendover, 7 Dec 1850
13 BRO, Tindal Papers, analysis done by W. H. Poole, 31 May 1851
14 *Bucks Herald*, 1 Apr 1848
15 BRO, Tindal Papers, Archibald White, memorandum, 20 May 1852
16 *Bucks Advertiser*, 28 Dec 1850
17 Ibid, 14 Dec 1850
18 Ibid, 21 Dec 1850
19 Ibid, 14 Dec 1850
20 *Aylesbury News*, 22 Apr 1837
21 Even the radicals would never have denied their Liberalism.
    Professor Gash suggests that there was a definitive split between
    Dissent and Liberalism from 1847 (*Reaction and Reconstruction*, 105).
    This may have been the case where Dissenters were rich and
    powerful enough to put up their own candidates, but not in areas
    like Bucks. As the editor of the *Bucks Advertiser* remarked in 1852:
    'Whiggism may be a sham, but Toryism is a terror' (3 Jul 1852).
22 Ibid, 28 Dec 1850
23 Evidence given before the Select Committee on the Aylesbury
    Election, 14 Jun 1851
24 Ibid, 12 and 19 Apr 1851
25 *Bucks Advertiser*, 19 Apr 1851
26 Ibid, 12 Apr 1851. Zachariah Phillips, a large Independent farmer
    who seconded Layard's nomination in 1852, said, when asked why
    he was not supporting protection that 'it was no use catching at
    shadows' (ibid, 10 Jul 1852)
27 Ibid, 17 Jul 1852
28 Ibid, 22 May 1852
29 An analysis by W. H. Poole (Tindal Papers, 15 Nov 1851) differs
    somewhat from figures quoted in the pollbooks and indicates that,
    so far as bad votes were concerned, the Conservatives did rather
    better than the Liberals, eliminating sixty-three who had voted for
    Bethell, while the Liberals were able to remove only fifty-two who
    had voted for Ferrand.
30 Ibid, Acton Tindal to Joseph Parkes, 24 Apr 1852
31 Ibid, copy Acton Tindal to J. James, 10 Mar 1853
32 *Bucks Herald*, 4 Apr 1857
33 BRO, newspaper clipping in Robert Gibbs' scrapbook
34 Tindal Papers, BRO. See particularly the correspondence between
    Acton Tindal and Lord Carrington, and Tindal and Henry Darvill in
    April and May
35 The sample for this election is the reduced one of 479 (36 per cent)
36 *Bucks Herald*, 26 Dec 1857
37 *Bucks Advertiser*, 15 Jul 1865

Chapter 10 THE SECOND REFORM ACT: AND ITS CONSEQUENCES
(pages 198–220)

1 Hanham xiv–xv
2 BRO, Tindal Papers, Lord Carrington to Acton Tindal, 14 Jul 1852
3 *Bucks Herald,* 12 Dec 1857 to 2 Jan 1858
4 Hughenden Papers, B/I/D/30, William Powell to Disraeli, 1 Dec 1857
5 Ibid, B/I/D/40, same to same, 3 Oct 1862
6 BRO, Carrington Papers, C 1 k, Lord Carrington to Charles Carrington, 15 Feb 1868, as well as correspondence in 1863
7 Hughenden Papers, B/I/D/68 a and b, Sir R. B. Harvey to ?, 16 Nov 1868, and William Powell to Montagu Corry, 16 Nov 1868
8 Quoted in Hanham, 15
9 Hughenden Papers, B/I/D/99a, William Powell to Disraeli, 1 Jan 1863 provides an example of Powell's loose use of the term. He says of the Borough of Wycombe, Chesham, and Wolverton that 'these places are under the influence of the Liberals.' He meant that they were Liberal strongholds
10 Ibid, B/I/D/72d, *Bucks County Election*
11 BRO, Fremantle Papers, rough draft Lord Cottesloe to Charles Fremantle, 11 Aug 1876
12 Ibid, Edward Baynes to Lord Cottesloe, 18 Aug 1876
13 *Bucks Advertiser,* 2 Sep 1876
14 Shannon, R. T. *Gladstone and the Bulgarian Agitation* 1876 (1963), 106–7
15 *Bucks Advertiser,* 2 Sep 1876
16 Ibid
17 Ibid, 9 Sep 1876
18 BRO, Fremantle Papers, the Dean of Ripon (William Fremantle) to Lord Cottesloe, 13 Sep 1876
19 Ibid, T. F. Fremantle to Lord Cottesloe, 5 Sep 1876
20 Hughenden Papers, B/I/D/80 and 78, T. T. Drake to Disraeli, 16 Sep 1876, and Powell's more detailed report to the same effect, 13 Sep 1876
21 Quoted in Hanham, 17
22 BRO, Fremantle Papers, copy T. T. Drake to Sir William Hart Dyke, 3 Dec 1876
23 Disraeli repeated these charges, which have found their way into Mr Blake's biography. There was, however, nothing to them, as correspondence in the Fremantle Papers makes clear
24 This was the figure Drake gave in launching a subscription. A bill in the Fremantle Papers gives a detailed breakdown for £6,200, indicating that almost £3,000 was spent on agency, £1,300 on transportation, and £1,100 on advertising. The subscription raised about £500, and Drake bullied Hart Dyke into finding £1,000
25 *Bucks Advertiser,* 3 Apr 1880

26 *Bucks Herald*, 2 Jan 1858
27 *Bucks Advertiser*, 31 Oct 1868
28 Bishopsgate Institute, the George Howell Collection, LB 4, Howell's address, dated 22 Oct 1868
29 *Bucks Advertiser*, 10 Oct and 21 Nov 1868
30 Bishopsgate Institute, Howell Collection, LB 4, N. M. de Rothschild to George Howell, 23 Nov 1868
31 *Bucks Advertiser*, 24 Oct 1868
32 Bishopsgate Institute, Howell Collection, LB 4, George Howell to John Porter, 2 Dec 1868
33 Ibid, George Howell to J. Bloxham, 26 Nov 1868
34 *Bucks Advertiser*, 31 Jan 1874
35 For this election see ibid, 13 Mar to 27 Mar 1880
36 BRO, R. Gibbs' scrapbook, newspaper clipping, 14 Dec 1880
37 *Bucks Advertiser*, 7 Feb 1874
38 Verney Papers, Sir Harry Verney to E. H. Verney, 19 Mar 1857; *Bucks Herald*, 4 Apr 1857
39 *Bucks Advertiser*, 7 May 1859
40 Bishopsgate Institute, Howell Collection, 'Election Reports', 'Buckingham Report as to September 6th 1868 to the Executive of the Reform League.'
41 *Bucks Advertiser*, 19 Sep 1868
42 *Buckingham Express*, February to April 1873
43 VHC Bucks, 110
44 *Bucks Advertiser*, 22 Mar 1862
45 Ibid, 3 Jul 1847
46 Ibid, 12 Jun to 10 Jul 1852; and Bodleian, Dashwood Papers
47 *Bucks Advertiser*, 8 Mar to 22 Mar 1862
48 BRO, Carrington, C 1 j, Lord Carrington to Charles Carrington, 19 Mar 1866
49 Ibid, C 1 k, same to same, 13 Jan 1868
50 *Bucks Advertiser*, 31 Jan and 7 Feb 1874
51 Ibid, 19 Sep 1868
52 *Bucks Gazette*, 10 Jan 1835 and 3 Jul 1841
53 Bucks County Museum, *Minutes of Proceedings and Evidence taken before the Committee on the Great Marlow Election*, 1842
54 *Bucks Advertiser*, 7 Aug 1847
55 Ibid, 10 Jul 1852
56 *Bucks Herald*, 7 May 1859
57 Ibid, 4 Apr 1857
58 *Bucks Advertiser*, 15 Aug to 21 Nov 1868
59 Ibid, 27 Mar 1880

CONCLUSION

1 Bishopsgate Institute, Howell Collection, Walter Morrison to George Howell, 12 Nov 1868
2 *Bucks Advertiser*, 15 Aug 1868 and 20 Mar 1880

3 BRO, Fremantle Papers, the Duke of Buckingham to the Hon
   Thomas Fremantle, 20 Dec 1885
4 Thompson, 237
5 *Bucks Advertiser*, 7 Nov 1868
6 Ibid and 14 Nov
7 Quoted in Gash, *Politics in the Age of Peel*, 94
8 Verney Papers, Sir Harry Verney to E. H. Verney, 18 Apr 1857

Bibliography

MANUSCRIPT COLLECTIONS
1 *In Libraries and Record Offices*

Bishopsgate Institute	The George Howell Collection
Bodleian Library	Dashwood papers
	John Johnson collection
British Library of Political and Economic Science	Correspondence of Henry Broadhurst
Buckingham Record Office (cited as BRO)	Addington scrapbooks etc
	Earl of Buckinghamshire papers
	Carrington papers
	Dayrell papers
	Fremantle papers
	Lee papers (Hartwell MSS)
	Papers of Captain the Hon H. Morgan-Grenville
	Papers of Captain the Hon R. W. Morgan-Grenville
	Pollbook collection
	Shardeloes papers
	Papers of the Hon Mrs T. Close Smith
	Tindal papers
	Wilkes-Dell correspondence
Huntington Library, San Marino, California	Stowe manuscripts
Northamptonshire Record Office	Temple (Stowe) collection

Oxfordshire Record Office   Thame papers
                                    Dillon papers

2 *Private Collections*

Hughenden Papers—Papers of Benjamin Disraeli, Earl of Beaconsfield, by courtesy of the National Trust

Spencer Bernard Papers—Papers of the Bernard family, by courtesy of Dr J. G. C. Spencer Bernard

Verney Papers—Papers of the Verney family, by courtesy of Sir Harry Verney, Bt, and Mr Ralph Verney

PERIODICALS AND NEWSPAPERS

The Aylesbury News and Bucks Advertiser
The Buckinghamshire, Bedfordshire, & Hertfordshire Chronicle (cited as *Buckinghamshire Chronicle*)
The Bucks Gazette
The Bucks Herald
Gentleman's Magazine
Jackson's Oxford Journal

CONTEMPORARY PRINTED WORKS AND PRINTED SOURCES

The Black Book: or Corruption Unmasked! (1820)
Broadhurst, Henry. *Henry Broadhurst, MP: The Story of His Life from a Stonemason's Bench to the Treasury Bench* (1901)
Buckingham, Duke of. *Memoirs of the Court and Cabinets of George III, the Regency, George IV, William IV and Victoria* (10 vols, 1855–61)
Burke, Edmund. *The Correspondence of* . . . , T. W. Copeland, gen ed, vols II & III (Cambridge, 1960–62)
Caird, Sir James. *English Agriculture* (1851)
Fowler, J. K. *Echoes of Old Country Life* (1895)
—— *Recollections of Old Country Life* (1895)
—— *Records of Old Times* (1898)
Gibbs, Robert. *Buckinghamshire Local Occurrences* 4 vols (Aylesbury 1878–82)
—— *A History of Aylesbury with its Boroughs and Hundreds* (Aylesbury, 1885)

The Grenville Papers, ed W. J. Smith 4 vols (1853)

Additional Grenville Papers, ed J. R. G. Tomlinson (Manchester, 1962)

Hansard's Parliamentary Debates

Lipscomb, George. *The History and Antiquities of the Country of Buckingham* 4 vols (1847)

Oldfield, T. H. B. *History of the Original Constitution of Parliament from the Time of the Britons to the present Day* (1797)

────── *The Representative History of Great Britain and Ireland* 6 vols (1816)

The Parliamentary History of England

Priest, the Rev St John. *General View of the Agriculture of Buckinghamshire* (1813)

Sheahan, James Joseph. *History and Topography of Bucks* (London, 1862)

Verney, Margaret Maria, Lady, ed *Verney Letters of the Eighteenth Century* (1930)

DIRECTORIES AND WORKS OF REFERENCE

Aylesbury Directory (1850)

Boase, Frederick. *Modern English Biography* 6 vols (Truro, 1892–1921)

Burke, John. *History of the Commoners of Great Britain and Ireland* (1836)

G.E.C. *The Complete Peerage*

Grant, James. *The Metropolitan and Weekly Press* (1872)

Judd, Gerrit P. *Members of Parliament, 1734–1832* (New Haven, 1955)

Musson and Craven's *Commercial Directory of the County of Buckingham* (Nottingham, 1853)

Parliamentary Companion

Pigot's Directory of Bucks (1830)

SECONDARY WORKS

Ashford, L. J. *The History of the Borough of High Wycombe: from its Origins to* 1880 (1960)

Blake, Robert. *Disraeli* (1966)

Butterfield, Herbert. *George III, Lord North, and the People, 1779–80* (1949)

Cannon, John. *The Fox-North Coalition* (Cambridge, 1969)

Chambers, J. D. and Mingay, G. E. *The Agricultural Revolution,* 1750–1880 (1966)

Christie, I. R. *Wilkes, Wyvill, and Reform* (1962)

Clark, G. Kitson. *The Making of Victorian England* (1965)

Cowling, Maurice. *Disraeli, Gladstone, and Revolution: the Passing of the Second Reform Bill* (Cambridge, 1967)

Davis, Richard W. *Dissent in Politics, 1780–1830: The Political Life of William Smith, MP* (1971)

Gash, Norman. *Politics in the Age of Peel* (1953)

―――― *Reaction and Reconstruction in English Politics, 1832–52* (Oxford, 1965)

Ginter, Donald E. *Whig Organization in the General Election of 1790* (Berkeley and Los Angeles, 1967)

Hanham, H. J. *Elections and Party Management in the Time of Disraeli and Gladstone* (1959)

Harrison, Royden. *Before the Socialists* (1965)

Hayes, B. D. 'Politics in Norfolk, 1750–1832' (PhD dissertation, Cambridge, 1957)

Hobsbawm, E. J. and Rudé, G. *Captain Swing* (1969)

Kemp, Betty. *Sir Francis Dashwood: An Eighteenth-Century Independent* (1967)

Lloyd, Trevor. *The General Election of 1880* (Oxford, 1967)

Machin, G. I. T. *The Catholic Question in English Politics, 1820 to 1830* (Oxford, 1964)

Mitchell, Austin. *The Whigs in Opposition, 1815–1830* (Oxford, 1967)

Morton, Frederick. *The Rothschilds* (London, 1962)

Namier, Sir Lewis and Brooke, John. *The House of Commons, 1754–90* (New York, 1964)

―――― Sir Lewis. *The Structure of Politics at the Accession of George III* (2nd ed, 1957)

Newman, Aubrey. *The Stanhopes of Chevening* (1970)

O'Leary, Cornelius. *The Elimination of Corrupt Practices in British Elections, 1868–1911* (Oxford, 1962)

Pelling, Henry. *Social Geography of British Elections, 1885–1910* (New York, 1967)

Plumb, J. H. *The Growth of Political Stability in England, 1675–1725* (1967)

Robbins, Caroline. *The Eighteenth-Century Commonwealthman* (New York, 1968)

Roberts, Michael. *The Whig Party*, 1807–1812 (New York, 1965)

Robson, R., ed *Ideas and Institutions of Victorian Britain: Essays in honour of George Kitson Clark* (1967)

Rudé, George. *Wilkes and Liberty* (Oxford, 1962)

Senior, Hereward. *Orangeism in Ireland and Britain*, 1795–1836 (1967)

Seymour, Charles. *Electoral Reform in England and Wales: The Development and Operation of the Parliamentary Franchise* (New Haven, 1915)

Shannon, R. T. *Gladstone and the Bulgarian Agitation*, 1876 (1963)

Speck, W. A. *Tory and Whig: The Struggle in the Constituencies*, 1710–1915 (1970)

Thompson, E. P. *The Making of the English Working Class* (1963)

Thompson, F. M. L. *English Landed Society in the Nineteenth Century* (1963)

Victoria History of the County of Buckingham

Vincent, John. *The Formation of the Liberal Party*, 1857–1868 (1966)

—— *Pollbooks: How Victorians Voted* (Cambridge, 1967)

Whittaker, M. B. 'The Revival of Dissent, 1800–1835' (MLitt dissertation, Cambridge, 1958)

ARTICLES

Aydelotte, William O. 'The Country Gentlemen and the Repeal of the Corn Laws,' *The English Historical Review*, vol LXXXII, no 322 (January 1967), 47–60

Baker, Margaret. 'Farming in Bucks in 1810,' *Bucks Life* (Nov. 1967)

Davis, Richard W. 'Buckingham, 1832–1846: A Study of a "Pocket Borough",' *The Huntington Library Quarterly*, vol XXXIV, no 2 (February 1971), 159–81

Hennock, E. P. and Moore, D. C. 'The First Reform Act: A Discussion,' *Victorian Studies*, vol XIV, no 3 (March 1971), 321–37

Machin, G. I. T. 'The Maynooth Grant, the Dissenters and Disestablishment,' *The English Historical Review*, vol LXXXII, no 322 (January 1967), 61–85

Moore, D. C. 'The Other Face of Reform,' *Victorian Studies*, vol
   V, no 1 (1961), 7–34
——— 'Concession or Cure: The Sociological Premises of the
First Reform Act,' *The Historical Journal*, vol IX (1966), 39–59
Richards, Peter. 'The Influence of Railways on the Growth of
   Wolverton, Buckinghamshire,' *Records of Bucks*, vol XVII
   (1961–64), 115–26
Spring, David. 'Lord Chandos and the Farmers, 1818–1846,' *The
   Huntington Library Quarterly*, vol XXXIII, no 3 (May 1970),
   257–81
Spring, David and Eileen, 'The Fall of the Grenvilles, 1844–1848,'
   The Huntington Library Quarterly, vol XIX, no 2 (February
   1956), 165–90
Thompson, F. M. L. 'The End of a Great Estate,' *Economic
   History Review*, 2nd Series, vol VIII (1955), 36–52
——— 'Whigs and Liberals in the West Riding, 1830–1860,' *The
   English Historical Review*, vol LXXIV (1959), 214–39

Acknowledgements

I am grateful to many people; more than I can mention by name. These are a few to whom my debt is greatest. J. H. Plumb first turned my mind to this kind of study. I should like to thank the librarians and staff of the Huntington Library, the British Museum at Colindale, and the Bodleian Library for their unfailing kindness. E. J. Davis and Hugh Hanley and the staff at the Bucks Record Office provided me not only with every aid and assistance known to their profession, but also with invaluable advice and criticism of the work itself. Lord Cottesloe and his family hastened the deposit of their family papers at the Record Office for my benefit. Dr J. G. C. Spencer Bernard allowed some of his papers to be brought there for my use. The publishers of the *Bucks Herald* did the same with newspapers from their collection. The Ralph Verneys made me welcome at Claydon House and Sir Harry Verney gave me much advice and assistance. The National Trust allowed me to consult the Disraeli Papers at Hughenden. The Rev Ralph Bates and Mr Edward Legg provided me with useful information and advice. Michael Hurst has been a good friend and stimulating critic. J. G. A. Pocock, W. N. Chambers, and R. K. Webb have read and criticized parts of the manuscript, David Spring a very large portion of it.

I should also like to thank those who have provided me with generous financial assistance, the National Endowment for the Humanities for a year in England, the American Philosophical Society, the Regents of the University of California, and Washington University for two summers there. The secretaries at the History Department have been even more kind and helpful than usual. My wife has assisted me with the research and the typing of the manuscript. Any faults in it are my own.

Washington University, St Louis, Missouri, 1971.   R. W. Davis

Index